Penguin Books

ETHICS

John Mackie was born in Sydney, Australia, in 1917 and graduated from Sydney University in 1938. Awarded the Wentworth Travelling Fellowship, he was at Oriel College, Oxford, from 1938 to 1940, graduating with a First in Greats. After serving in the army during the Second World War, he became a lecturer and then a senior lecturer in Moral and Political Philosophy at Sydney University (1946-54). He was Professor of Philosophy at Otago University, Dunedin, New Zealand (1955–9), at Sydney University (1959–63) and at the University of York, England (1963–7). From 1967 until his death in 1981 he was a Fellow of University College, Oxford, and became a Fellow of the British Academy in 1974.

Among his publications are *Truth, Probability, and Paradox* (1973), *The Cement of the Universe*, a study of causation (1974), *Problems From Locke* (1976), *Hume's Moral Theory* (1980) and *The Miracle of Theism* (1982).

J. L. Mackie

Ethics

Inventing Right and Wrong

Penguin Books

PENGUIN BOOKS

Published by the Penguin Group
Penguin Books Ltd, 27 Wrights Lane, London W8 5TZ, England
Penguin Books USA Inc., 375 Hudson Street, New York, New York 10014, USA
Penguin Books Australia Ltd, Ringwood, Victoria, Australia
Penguin Books Canada Ltd, 10 Alcorn Avenue, Toronto, Ontario, Canada M4V 3B2
Penguin Books (NZ) Ltd, 182–190 Wairau Road, Auckland 10, New Zealand

Penguin Books Ltd, Registered Offices: Harmondsworth, Middlesex, England

First published in Pelican Books 1977
Reprinted in Penguin Books 1990
10 9 8 7 6

Printed in England by Clays Ltd, St Ives plc
Set in Intertype Times

Contents

CONTENTS

Preface

A moral or ethical statement may assert that some particular action is right or wrong; or that actions of certain kinds are so; it may offer a distinction between good and bad characters or dispositions; or it may propound some broad principle from which many more detailed judgements of these sorts might be inferred – for example, that we ought always to aim at the greatest general happiness, or try to minimize the total suffering of all sentient beings, or devote ourselves wholly to the service of God, or that it is right and proper for everyone to look after himself. All such statements express first order ethical judgements of different degrees of generality. By contrast with all these, a second order statement would say what is going on when someone makes a first order statement, in particular, whether such a statement expresses a discovery or a decision, or it may make some point about how we think and reason about moral matters, or put forward a view about the meanings of various ethical terms.

I am concerned in this book with both first and second order topics, with both the content and the status of ethics. In our ordinary experience we first encounter first order statements about particular actions; in discussing these, we may go on to frame, or dispute, more general first order principles; and only after that are we likely to reflect on second order issues. But in putting forward my opinions in a fairly systematic way I have had to reverse this order, to try to settle what is going on in first order ethical discussion before making my own contribution to it. The natural order of exposition is the opposite of the natural order of acquaintance. Part I, therefore, is about the status of ethics; Part II is mainly about its content, though Chapter 5 is really transitional between the two. Part III deals, only briefly,

9

with what I call the frontiers of ethics, that is, with various ways in which psychology and metaphysics and theology and law and political theory bear upon ethics, or in which ethics bears upon one or other of these.

An unavoidable consequence of this order of treatment is that the driest and most difficult and abstract discussions come first: someone who has not read much philosophical ethics may find Chapter 1 hard going. My advice to such a reader is not, indeed, to skip Chapter 1 or the rest of Part I, but to be content with a fairly superficial first reading of it, to try to pick up the main ideas of Part I but not to worry about obscure details or difficult arguments. He may be able to make more of these if he comes back to them after seeing the use that I make in Parts II and III of the conclusions reached and defended in Part I.

I would like to thank Mrs E. Hinkes not only for typing the book but for retyping changed versions of several chapters. Among colleagues whose comments have helped me I would particularly like to thank Derek Parfit, who read the whole of the first version of Parts I and II and suggested a great many improvements and corrections.

References to works quoted and to authors whose opinions are mentioned in the text are given not in footnotes but (grouped chapter by chapter) at the end of the book. Very detailed references seem unnecessary, since I am nowhere mainly concerned to refute any individual writer. I believe that all those to whom I have referred, even those with whom I disagree most strongly, have contributed significantly to our understanding of ethics: where I have quoted their actual words, it is because they have presented views or arguments more clearly or more forcefully than I could put them myself.

I have drawn freely on the ideas both of contemporary writers and of such classical moral philosophers as Plato, Aristotle, Hobbes, Hume, Kant, and Sidgwick. But perhaps the truest teachers of moral philosophy are the outlaws and thieves who, as Locke says, keep faith and rules of justice with one another, but practise these as rules of convenience without which they cannot hold together, with no pretence of receiving them as innate laws of nature. I hope that the explanation of this paradox will become clear in the course of the book.

January 1976   J.L.M.

Part I : The Status of Ethics

Chapter 1   The Subjectivity of Values

1. Moral scepticism

There are no objective values. This is a bald statement of the
thesis of this chapter, but before arguing for it I shall try to
clarify and restrict it in ways that may meet some objections
and prevent some misunderstanding.

The statement of this thesis is liable to provoke one of three
very different reactions. Some will think it not merely false but
pernicious; they will see it as a threat to morality and to everything else that is worthwhile, and they will find the presenting of
such a thesis in what purports to be a book on ethics paradoxical or even outragecus. Others will regard it as a trivial
truth, almost too obvious to be worth mentioning, and certainly
too plain to be worth much argument. Others again will say that
it is meaningless or empty, that no real issue is raised by the
question whether values are or are not part of the fabric of the
world. But, precisely because there can be these three different
reactions, much more needs to be said.

The claim that values are not objective, are not part of the
fabric of the world, is meant to include not only moral goodness, which might be most naturally equated with moral value,
but also other things that could be more loosely called moral
values or disvalues – rightness and wrongness, duty, obligation,
an action's being rotten and contemptible, and so on. It also
includes non-moral values, notably aesthetic ones, beauty and
various kinds of artistic merit. I shall not discuss these explicitly, but clearly much the same considerations apply to
aesthetic and to moral values, and there would be at least some
initial implausibility in a view that gave the one a different
status from the other.

Since it is with moral values that I am primarily concerned, the view I am adopting may be called moral scepticism. But this name is likely to be misunderstood: 'moral scepticism' might also be used as a name for either of two first order views, or perhaps for an incoherent mixture of the two. A moral sceptic might be the sort of person who says 'All this talk of morality is tripe,' who rejects morality and will take no notice of it. Such a person may be literally rejecting all moral judgements; he is more likely to be making moral judgements of his own, expressing a positive moral condemnation of all that conventionally passes for morality; or he may be confusing these two logically incompatible views, and saying that he rejects all morality, while he is in fact rejecting only a particular morality that is current in the society in which he has grown up. But I am not at present concerned with the merits or faults of such a position. These are first order moral views, positive or negative: the person who adopts either of them is taking a certain practical, normative, stand. By contrast, what I am discussing is a second order view, a view about the status of moral values and the nature of moral valuing, about where and how they fit into the world. These first and second order views are not merely distinct but completely independent: one could be a second order moral sceptic without being a first order one, or again the other way round. A man could hold strong moral views, and indeed ones whose content was thoroughly conventional, while believing that they were simply attitudes and policies with regard to conduct that he and other people held. Conversely, a man could reject all established morality while believing it to be an objective truth that it was evil or corrupt.

With another sort of misunderstanding moral scepticism would seem not so much pernicious as absurd. How could anyone deny that there is a difference between a kind action and a cruel one, or that a coward and a brave man behave differently in the face of danger? Of course, this is undeniable; but it is not to the point. The kinds of behaviour to which moral values and disvalues are ascribed are indeed part of the furniture of the world, and so are the natural, descriptive, differences between them; but not, perhaps, their differences in value. It is a hard fact that cruel actions differ from kind ones, and hence that we can learn, as in fact we all do, to distinguish them fairly well in practice, and to use the words 'cruel' and 'kind' with fairly clear descriptive meanings; but is it an equally hard fact that actions which are cruel in such a descriptive sense are to be condemned? The present issue is with regard to the objectivity specifically of value, not with regard to the objectivity of those natural, factual, differences on the basis of which differing values are assigned.

2. Subjectivism

Another name often used, as an alternative to 'moral scepticism', for the view I am discussing is 'subjectivism'. But this too has more than one meaning. Moral subjectivism too could be a first order, normative, view, namely that everyone really ought to do whatever he thinks he should. This plainly is a (systematic) first order view; on examination it soon ceases to be plausible, but that is beside the point, for it is quite independent of the second order thesis at present under consideration. What is more confusing is that different second order views compete for the name 'subjectivism'. Several of these are doctrines about the meaning of moral terms and moral statements. What is often called moral subjectivism is the doctrine that, for example, 'This action is right' *means* 'I approve of this action', or more generally that moral judgements are equivalent to reports of the speaker's own feelings or attitudes. But the view I am now discussing is to be distinguished in two vital respects from any such doctrine as this. First, what I have called moral scepticism is a negative doctrine, not a positive one: it says what there isn't, not what there is. It says that there do not exist entities or relations of a certain kind, objective values or requirements, which many people have believed to exist. Of course, the moral sceptic cannot leave it at that. If his position is to be at all plausible, he must give some account of how other

17

people have fallen into what he regards as an error, and this account will have to include some positive suggestions about how values fail to be objective, about what has been mistaken for, or has led to false beliefs about, objective values. But this will be a development of his theory, not its core: its core is the negation. Secondly, what I have called moral scepticism is an ontological thesis, not a linguistic or conceptual one. It is not, like the other doctrine often called moral subjectivism, a view about the meanings of moral statements. Again, no doubt, if it is to be at all plausible, it will have to give some account of their meanings, and I shall say something about this in Section 7 of this chapter and again in Chapters 2, 3, and 4. But this too will be a development of the theory, not its core.

It is true that those who have accepted the moral subjectivism which is the doctrine that moral judgements are equivalent to reports of the speaker's own feelings or attitudes have usually presupposed what I am calling moral scepticism. It is because they have assumed that there are no objective values that they have looked elsewhere for an analysis of what moral statements might mean, and have settled upon subjective reports. Indeed, if all our moral statements were such subjective reports, it would follow that, at least so far as we are aware, there are no objective moral values. If we were aware of them, we would say something about them. In this sense this sort of subjectivism entails moral scepticism. But the converse entailment does not hold. The denial that there are objective values does not commit one to any particular view about what moral statements mean, and certainly not to the view that they are equivalent to subjective reports. No doubt if moral values are not objective they are in some very broad sense subjective, and for this reason I would accept 'moral subjectivism' as an alternative name to 'moral scepticism'. But subjectivism in this broad sense must be distinguished from the specific doctrine about meaning referred to above. Neither name is altogether satisfactory: we simply have to guard against the (different) misinterpretations which each may suggest.

3. The multiplicity of second order questions

The distinctions drawn in the last two sections rest not only on the well-known and generally recognized difference between first and second order questions, but also on the more controversial claim that there are several kinds of second order moral question. Those most often mentioned are questions about the meaning and use of ethical terms, or the analysis of ethical concepts. With these go questions about the logic of moral statements: there may be special patterns of moral argument, licensed, perhaps, by aspects of the meanings of moral terms – for example, it may be part of the meaning of moral statements that they are universalizable. But there are also ontological, as contrasted with linguistic or conceptual, questions about the nature and status of goodness or rightness or whatever it is that first order moral statements are distinctively about. These are questions of factual rather than conceptual analysis: the problem of what goodness is cannot be settled conclusively or exhaustively by finding out what the word 'good' means, or what it is conventionally used to say or to do.

Recent philosophy, biased as it has been towards various kinds of linguistic inquiry, has tended to doubt this, but the distinction between conceptual and factual analysis in ethics can be supported by analogies with other areas. The question of what perception is, what goes on when someone perceives something, is not adequately answered by finding out what words like 'see' and 'hear' mean, or what someone is doing in saying 'I perceive . . .', by analysing, however fully and accurately, any established concept of perception. There is a still closer analogy with colours. Robert Boyle and John Locke called colours 'secondary qualities', meaning that colours as they occur in material things consist simply in patterns of arrangement and movement of minute particles on the surfaces of objects, which make them, as we would now say, reflect light of some frequencies better than others, and so enable these objects to produce colour sensations in us, but that colours as we see them do not

19

literally belong to the surfaces of material things. Whether Boyle and Locke were right about this cannot be settled by finding out how we use colour words and what we mean in using them. Naïve realism about colours might be a correct analysis not only of our pre-scientific colour concepts but also of the conventional meanings of colour words, and even of the meanings with which scientifically sophisticated people use them when they are off their guard, and yet it might not be a correct account of the status of colours.

Error could well result, then, from a failure to distinguish factual from conceptual analysis with regard to colours, from taking an account of the meanings of statements as a full account of what there is. There is a similar and in practice even greater risk of error in moral philosophy. There is another reason, too, why it would be a mistake to concentrate second order ethical discussions on questions of meaning. The more work philosophers have done on meaning, both in ethics and elsewhere, the more complications have come to light. It is by now pretty plain that no simple account of the meanings of first order moral statements will be correct, will cover adequately even the standard, conventional, senses of the main moral terms; I think, none the less, that there is a relatively clear-cut issue about the objectivity of moral values which is in danger of being lost among the complications of meaning.

4. Is objectivity a real issue?

It has, however, been doubted whether there is a real issue here. I must concede that it is a rather old-fashioned one. I do not mean merely that it was raised by Hume, who argued that 'The vice entirely escapes you ... till you turn your reflexion into your own breast,' and before him by Hobbes, and long before that by some of the Greek sophists. I mean rather that it was discussed vigorously in the nineteen thirties and forties, but since then has received much less attention. This is not because it has been solved or because agreement has been reached: instead it seems to have been politely shelved.

But was there ever a genuine problem? R.M. Hare has said that he does not understand what is meant by 'the objectivity of values', and that he has not met anyone who does. We all know how to recognize the activity called 'saying, thinking it to be so, that some act is wrong', and he thinks that it is to this activity that the subjectivist and the objectivist are both alluding, though one calls it 'an attitude of disapproval' and the other 'a moral intuition': these are only different names for the same thing. It is true that if one person says that a certain act is wrong and another that it is not wrong the objectivist will say that they are contradicting one another; but this yields no significant discrimination between objectivism and subjectivism, because the subjectivist too will concede that the second person is negating what the first has said, and Hare sees no difference between contradicting and negating. Again, the objectivist will say that one of the two must be wrong; but Hare argues that to say that the judgement that a certain act is wrong is itself wrong is merely to negate that judgement, and the subjectivist too must negate one or other of the two judgements, so that still no clear difference between objectivism and subjectivism has emerged. He sums up his case thus: 'Think of one world into whose fabric values are objectively built; and think of another in which those values have been annihilated. And remember that in both worlds the people in them go on being concerned about the same things – there is no difference in the "subjective" concern which people have for things, only in their "objective" value. Now I ask, "What is the difference between the states of affairs in these two worlds?" Can any answer be given except "None whatever"?'

Now it is quite true that it is logically possible that the subjective concern, the activity of valuing or of thinking things wrong, should go on in just the same way whether there are objective values or not. But to say this is only to reiterate that there is a logical distinction between first and second order

21

ethics: first order judgements are not necessarily affected by the truth or falsity of a second order view. But it does not follow, and it is not true, that there is no difference whatever between these two worlds. In the one there is something that backs up and validates some of the subjective concern which people have for things, in the other there is not. Hare's argument is similar to the positivist claim that there is no difference between a phenomenalist or Berkeleian world in which there are only minds and their ideas and the commonsense realist one in which there are also material things, because it is logically possible that people should have the same experiences in both. If we reject the positivism that would make the dispute between realists and phenomenalists a pseudo-question, we can reject Hare's similarly supported dismissal of the issue of the objectivity of values.

In any case, Hare has minimized the difference between his two worlds by considering only the situation where people already have just such subjective concern; further differences come to light if we consider how subjective concern is acquired or changed. If there were something in the fabric of the world that validated certain kinds of concern, then it would be possible to acquire these merely by finding something out, by letting one's thinking be controlled by how things were. But in the world in which objective values have been annihilated the acquiring of some new subjective concern means the development of something new on the emotive side by the person who acquires it, something that eighteenth-century writers would put under the head of passion or sentiment.

The issue of the objectivity of values needs, however, to be distinguished from others with which it might be confused. To say that there are objective values would not be to say merely that there are some things which are valued by everyone, nor does it entail this. There could be agreement in valuing even if valuing is just something that people do, even if this activity is not further validated. Subjective agreement would give intersubjective values, but intersubjectivity is not objectivity. Nor is objectivity simply universalizability: someone might well be prepared to universalize his prescriptive judgements or approvals – that is, to prescribe and approve in just the same ways in all relevantly similar cases, even ones in which he was involved differently or not at all – and yet he could recognize that such prescribing and approving were his activities, nothing more. Of course if there were objective values they would presumably belong to *kinds* of things or actions or states of affairs, so that the judgements that reported them would be universalizable; but the converse does not hold.

A more subtle distinction needs to be made between objectivism and descriptivism. Descriptivism is again a doctrine about the meanings of ethical terms and statements, namely that their meanings are purely descriptive rather than even partly prescriptive or emotive or evaluative, or that it is not an essential feature of the conventional meaning of moral statements that they have some special illocutionary force, say of commending rather than asserting. It contrasts with the view that commendation is in principle distinguishable from description (however difficult they may be to separate in practice) and that moral statements have it as at least part of their meaning that they are commendatory and hence in some uses intrinsically action-guiding. But descriptive meaning neither entails nor is entailed by objectivity. Berkeley's subjective idealism about material objects would be quite compatible with the admission that material object statements have purely descriptive meaning. Conversely, the main tradition of European moral philosophy from Plato onwards has combined the view that moral values are objective with the recognition that moral judgements are partly prescriptive or directive or action-guiding. Values themselves have been seen as at once prescriptive and objective. In Plato's theory the Forms, and in particular the Form of the Good, are eternal, extra-mental, realities. They are a very central structural element in the fabric of the world. But it is held also that just knowing them or 'seeing' them will not merely tell men what to do but will ensure that they do it, overruling any contrary inclinations. The philosopher-kings in the *Republic* can, Plato thinks, be trusted with unchecked

23

power because their education will have given them knowledge of the Forms. Being acquainted with the Forms of the Good and Justice and Beauty and the rest they will, by this knowledge alone, without any further motivation, be impelled to pursue and promote these ideals. Similarly, Kant believes that pure reason can by itself be practical, though he does not pretend to be able to explain how it can be so. Again, Sidgwick argues that if there is to be a science of ethics – and he assumes that there can be, indeed he defines ethics as 'the science of conduct' – what ought to be 'must in another sense have objective existence: it must be an object of knowledge and as such the same for all minds'; but he says that the affirmations of this science 'are also precepts', and he speaks of happiness as 'an end *absolutely* prescribed by reason'. Since many philosophers have thus held that values are objectively prescriptive, it is clear that the ontological doctrine of objectivism must be distinguished from descriptivism, a theory about meaning.

But perhaps when Hare says that he does not understand what is meant by 'the objectivity of values' he means that he cannot understand how values could be objective, he cannot frame for himself any clear, detailed, picture of what it would be like for values to be part of the fabric of the world. This would be a much more plausible claim; as we have seen, even Kant hints at a similar difficulty. Indeed, even Plato warns us that it is only through difficult studies spread over many years that one can approach the knowledge of the Forms. The difficulty of seeing how values could be objective is a fairly strong reason for thinking that they are not so; this point will be taken up in Section 9 (pp. 38–42) but it is not a good reason for saying that this is not a real issue.

I believe that as well as being a real issue it is an important one. It clearly matters for general philosophy. It would make a radical difference to our metaphysics if we had to find room for objective values – perhaps something like Plato's Forms – somewhere in our picture of the world. It would similarly make a difference to our epistemology if it had to explain how such objective values are or can be known, and to our philosophical psychology if we had to allow such knowledge, or Kant's pure practical reason, to direct choices and actions. Less obviously, how this issue is settled will affect the possibility of certain kinds of moral argument. For example, Sidgwick considers a discussion between an egoist and a utilitarian, and points out that if the egoist claims that his happiness or pleasure is objectively desirable or good, the utilitarian can argue that the egoist's happiness 'cannot be more objectively desirable or more a good than the similar happiness of any other person: the mere fact ... that *he is he* can have nothing to do with its objective desirability or goodness'. In other words, if ethics is built on the concept of objective goodness, then egoism as a first order system or method of ethics can be refuted, whereas if it is assumed that goodness is only subjective it cannot. But Sidgwick correctly stresses what a number of other philosophers have missed, that this argument against egoism would require the objectivity specifically of goodness: the objectivity of what ought to be or of what it is rational to do would not be enough. If the egoist claimed that it was objectively rational, or obligatory upon him, to seek his own happiness, a similar argument about the irrelevance of the fact that he is he would lead only to the conclusion that it was objectively rational or obligatory for each other person to seek *his* own happiness, that is, to a universalized form of egoism, not to the refutation of egoism. And of course insisting on the universalizability of moral judgements, as opposed to the objectivity of goodness, would yield only the same result.

5. Standards of evaluation

One way of stating the thesis that there are no objective values is to say that value statements cannot be either true or false. But this formulation, too, lends itself to misinterpretation. For there are certain kinds of value statements which undoubtedly can be true or false, even if, in the sense I intend, there are no objective values. Evaluations of many sorts are commonly made in relation to agreed and assumed standards. The classing of wool, the grading of apples, the awarding of prizes at sheepdog trials, flower shows, skating and diving championships, and even the marking of examination papers are carried out in relation to standards of quality or merit which are peculiar to each particular subject-matter or type of contest, which may be explicitly laid down but which, even if they are nowhere explicitly stated, are fairly well understood and agreed by those who are recognized as judges or experts in each particular field. Given any sufficiently determinate standards, it will be an objective issue, a matter of truth and falsehood, how well any particular specimen measures up to those standards. Comparative judgements in particular will be capable of truth and falsehood: it will be a factual question whether this sheepdog has performed better than that one.

The subjectivist about values, then, is not denying that there can be objective evaluations relative to standards, and these are as possible in the aesthetic and moral fields as in any of those just mentioned. More than this, there is an objective distinction which applies in many such fields, and yet would itself be regarded as a peculiarly moral one: the distinction between justice and injustice. In one important sense of the word it is a paradigm case of injustice if a court declares someone to be guilty of an offence of which it knows him to be innocent. More generally, a finding is unjust if it is at variance with what the relevant law and the facts together require, and particularly if it is known by the court to be so. More generally still, any award of marks, prizes, or the like is unjust if it is at variance with the agreed standards for the contest in question: if one diver's performance in fact measures up better to the accepted standards for diving than another's, it will be unjust if the latter is awarded higher marks or the prize. In this way the justice or injustice of decisions relative to standards can be a thoroughly objective matter, though there may still be a subjective element in the interpretation or application of standards. But the statement that a certain decision is thus just or unjust will not be objectively prescriptive: in so far as it can be simply true it

26

leaves open the question whether there is any objective requirement to do what is just and to refrain from what is unjust, and equally leaves open the practical decision to act in either way.

Recognizing the objectivity of justice in relation to standards, and of evaluative judgements relative to standards, then, merely shifts the question of the objectivity of values back to the standards themselves. The subjectivist may try to make his point by insisting that there is no objective validity about the choice of standards. Yet he would clearly be wrong if he said that the choice of even the most basic standards in any field was completely arbitrary. The standards used in sheepdog trials clearly bear some relation to the work that sheepdogs are kept to do, the standards for grading apples bear some relation to what people generally want in or like about apples, and so on. On the other hand, standards are not as a rule strictly validated by such purposes. The appropriateness of standards is neither fully determinate nor totally indeterminate in relation to independently specifiable aims or desires. But however determinate it is, the objective appropriateness of standards in relation to aims or desires is no more of a threat to the denial of objective values than is the objectivity of evaluation relative to standards. In fact it is logically no different from the objectivity of goodness relative to desires. Something may be called good simply in so far as it satisfies or is such as to satisfy a certain desire; but the objectivity of such relations of satisfaction does not constitute in our sense an objective value.

6. Hypothetical and categorical imperatives

We may make this issue clearer by referring to Kant's distinction between hypothetical and categorical imperatives, though what he called imperatives are more naturally expressed as 'ought'-statements than in the imperative mood. 'If you want X, do Y' (or 'You ought to do Y') will be a hypothetical imperative if it is based on the supposed fact that Y is, in the circumstances, the only (or the best) available means to X, that is, on a causal relation between Y and X. The reason for doing Y lies in its causal connection with the desired end, X; the oughtness is contingent upon the desire. But 'You ought to do Y' will be a categorical imperative if you ought to do Y irrespective of any such desire for any end to which Y would contribute, if the oughtness is not thus contingent upon any desire. But this distinction needs to be handled with some care. An 'ought'-statement is not in this sense hypothetical merely because it incorporates a conditional clause. 'If you promised to do Y, you ought to do Y' is not a hypothetical imperative merely on account of the stated if-clause; what is meant may be either a hypothetical or a categorical imperative, depending upon the implied reason for keeping the supposed promise. If this rests upon some such further unstated conditional as 'If you want to be trusted another time', then it is a hypothetical imperative; if not, it is categorical. Even a desire of the agent's can figure in the antecedent of what, though conditional in grammatical form, is still in Kant's sense a categorical imperative. 'If you are strongly attracted sexually to young children you ought not to go in for school teaching' is not, in virtue of what it explicitly says, a hypothetical imperative: the avoidance of school teaching is not being offered as a means to the satisfaction of the desires in question. Of course, it could still be a hypothetical imperative, if the implied reason were a prudential one; but it could also be a categorical imperative, a moral requirement where the reason for the recommended action (strictly, avoidance) does not rest upon that action's being a means to the satisfaction of any desire that the agent is supposed to have. Not every conditional ought-statement or command, then, is a hypothetical imperative; equally, not every non-conditional one is a categorical imperative. An appropriate if-clause may be left unstated. Indeed, a simple command in the imperative mood, say a parade-ground order, which might seem most literally to qualify for the title of a categorical imperative, will hardly ever be one in the sense we need here. The implied reason for complying with such an order will almost always be some desire of the person addressed, perhaps simply the desire to keep out of trouble. If so, such an apparently categorical order will be in our sense a hypothetical imperative. Again, an imperative remains hypothetical even if we change the 'if' to 'since': the fact that the desire for X is actually present does not alter the fact that the reason for doing Y is contingent upon the desire for X by way of Y's being a means to X. In Kant's own treatment, while imperatives of skill relate to desires which an agent may or may not have, imperatives of prudence relate to the desire for happiness which, Kant assumes, everyone has. So construed, imperatives of prudence are no less hypothetical than imperatives of skill, no less contingent upon desires that the agent has at the time the imperatives are addressed to him. But if we think rather of a counsel of prudence as being related to the agent's future welfare, to the satisfaction of desires that he does not yet have – not even to a present desire that his future desires should be satisfied – then a counsel of prudence is a categorical imperative, different indeed from a moral one, but analogous to it.

A categorical imperative, then, would express a reason for acting which was unconditional in the sense of not being contingent upon any present desire of the agent to whose satisfaction the recommended action would contribute as a means – or more directly: 'You ought to dance', if the implied reason is just that you want to dance or like dancing, is still a hypothetical imperative. Now Kant himself held that moral judgements are categorical imperatives, or perhaps are all applications of one categorical imperative, and it can plausibly be maintained at least that many moral judgements contain a categorically imperative element. So far as ethics is concerned, my thesis that there are no objective values is specifically the denial that any such categorically imperative element is objectively valid. The objective values which I am denying would be action-directing absolutely, not contingently (in the way indicated) upon the agent's desires and inclinations.

Another way of trying to clarify this issue is to refer to moral reasoning or moral arguments. In practice, of course, such

THE STATUS OF ETHICS

reasoning is seldom fully explicit: but let us suppose that we could make explicit the reasoning that supports some evaluative conclusion, where this conclusion has some action-guiding force that is not contingent upon desires or purposes or chosen ends. Then what I am saying is that somewhere in the input to this argument – perhaps in one or more of the premisses, perhaps in some part of the form of the argument – there will be something which cannot be objectively validated – some premiss which is not capable of being simply true, or some form of argument which is not valid as a matter of general logic, whose authority or cogency is not objective, but is constituted by our choosing or deciding to think in a certain way.

7. The claim to objectivity

If I have succeeded in specifying precisely enough the moral values whose objectivity I am denying, my thesis may now seem to be trivially true. Of course, some will say, valuing, preferring, choosing, recommending, rejecting, condemning, and so on, are human activities, and there is no need to look for values that are prior to and logically independent of all such activities. There may be widespread agreement in valuing, and particular value-judgements are not in general arbitrary or isolated: they typically cohere with others, or can be criticized if they do not, reasons can be given for them, and so on: but if all that the subjectivist is maintaining is that desires, ends, purposes, and the like figure somewhere in the system of reasons, and that no ends or purposes are objective as opposed to being merely intersubjective, then this may be conceded without much fuss.

But I do not think that this should be conceded so easily. As I have said, the main tradition of European moral philosophy includes the contrary claim, that there are objective values of just the sort I have denied. I have referred already to Plato, Kant, and Sidgwick. Kant in particular holds that the categorical imperative is not only categorical and imperative but objectively so: though a rational being gives the moral law to

30

himself, the law that he thus makes is determinate and necessary. Aristotle begins the *Nicomachean Ethics* by saying that the good is that at which all things aim, and that ethics is part of a science which he calls 'politics', whose goal is not knowledge but practice; yet he does not doubt that there can be *knowledge* of what is the good for man, nor, once he has identified this as well-being or happiness, *eudaimonia*, that it can be known, rationally determined, in what happiness consists; and it is plain that he thinks that this happiness is intrinsically desirable, not good simply because it is desired. The rationalist Samuel Clarke holds that

these eternal and necessary differences of things make it *fit and reasonable* for creatures so to act ... even separate from the consideration of these rules being the *positive will* or *command of God*; and also antecedent to any respect or regard, expectation or apprehension, of any *particular private and personal advantage or disadvantage, reward or punishment*, either present or future ...

Even the sentimentalist Hutcheson defines moral goodness as 'some quality apprehended in actions, which procures approbation ...', while saying that the moral sense by which we perceive virtue and vice has been given to us (by the Author of nature) to direct our actions. Hume indeed was on the other side, but he is still a witness to the dominance of the objectivist tradition, since he claims that when we 'see that the distinction of vice and virtue is not founded merely on the relations of objects, nor is perceiv'd by reason', this 'wou'd subvert all the vulgar systems of morality'. And Richard Price insists that right and wrong are 'real characters of actions', not 'qualities of our minds', and are perceived by the understanding; he criticizes the notion of moral sense on the ground that it would make virtue an affair of taste, and moral right and wrong 'nothing in the objects themselves'; he rejects Hutcheson's view because (perhaps mistakenly) he sees it as collapsing into Hume's.

But this objectivism about values is not only a feature of the philosophical tradition. It has also a firm basis in ordinary thought, and even in the meanings of moral terms. No doubt it

31

was an extravagance for Moore to say that 'good' is the name of a non-natural quality, but it would not be so far wrong to say that in moral contexts it is used as if it were the name of a supposed non-natural quality, where the description 'non-natural' leaves room for the peculiar evaluative, pre-scriptive, intrinsically action-guiding aspects of this supposed quality. This point can be illustrated by reflection on the conflicts and swings of opinion in recent years between non-cognitivist and naturalist views about the central, basic, mean-ings of ethical terms. If we reject the view that it is the function of such terms to introduce objective values into discourse about conduct and choices of action, there seem to be two main alternative types of account. One (which has importantly different subdivisions) is that they conventionally express either attitudes which the speaker purports to adopt towards whatever it is that he characterizes morally, or prescriptions or recom-mendations, subject perhaps to the logical constraint of univer-salizability. Different views of this type share the central thesis that ethical terms have, at least partly and primarily, some sort of non-cognitive, non-descriptive, meaning. Views of the other type hold that they are descriptive in meaning, but descriptive of natural features, partly of such features as everyone, even the non-cognitivist, would recognize as distinguishing kind actions from cruel ones, courage from cowardice, politeness from rude-ness, and so on, and partly (though these two overlap) of re-lations between the actions and some human wants, satis-factions, and the like. I believe that views of both these types capture part of the truth. Each approach can account for the fact that moral judgements are action-guiding or practical. Yet each gains much of its plausibility from the felt inadequacy of the other. It is a very natural reaction to any non-cognitive analysis of ethical terms to protest that there is more to ethics than this, something more external to the maker of moral judgements, more authoritative over both him and those of or to whom he speaks, and this reaction is likely to persist even when full allowance has been made for the logical, formal, constraints of full-blooded prescriptivity and universalizability.

Ethics, we are inclined to believe, is more a matter of knowledge and less a matter of decision than any non-cognitive analysis allows. And of course naturalism satisfies this demand. It will not be a matter of choice or decision whether an action is cruel or unjust or imprudent or whether it is likely to produce more distress than pleasure. But in satisfying this demand, it introduces a converse deficiency. On a naturalist analysis, moral judgements can be practical, but their practicality is wholly relative to desires or possible satisfactions of the person or persons whose actions are to be guided; but moral judgements seem to say more than this. This view leaves out the categorical quality of moral requirements. In fact both naturalist and non-cognitive analyses leave out the apparent authority of ethics, the one by excluding the categorically imperative aspect, the other the claim to objective validity or truth. The ordinary user of moral language means to say something about whatever it is that he characterizes morally, for example a possible action, as it is in itself, or would be if it were realized, and not about, or even simply expressive of, his, or anyone else's, attitude or relation to it. But the something he wants to say is not purely descriptive, certainly not inert, but something that involves a call for action or for the refraining from action, and one that is absolute, not contingent upon any desire or preference or policy or choice, his own or anyone else's. Someone in a state of moral perplexity, wondering whether it would be wrong for him to engage, say, in research related to bacteriological warfare, wants to arrive at some judgement about this concrete case, his doing this work at this time in these actual circumstances; his relevant characteristics will be part of the subject of the judgement, but no relation between him and the proposed action will be part of the predicate. The question is not, for example, whether he really wants to do this work, whether it will satisfy or dissatisfy him, whether he will in the long run have a pro-attitude towards it, or even whether this is an action of a sort that he can happily and sincerely recommend in all relevantly similar cases. Nor is he even wondering just whether to recommend such action in all relevantly similar cases. He wants to know whether this course of action would be wrong in itself. Something like this is the everyday objectivist concept of which talk about non-natural qualities is a philosopher's reconstruction.

The prevalence of this tendency to objectify values – and not only moral ones – is confirmed by a pattern of thinking that we find in existentialists and those influenced by them. The denial of objective values can carry with it an extreme emotional reaction, a feeling that nothing matters at all, that life has lost its purpose. Of course this does not follow; the lack of objective values is not a good reason for abandoning subjective concern or for ceasing to want anything. But the abandonment of a belief in objective values can cause, at least temporarily, a decay of subjective concern and sense of purpose. That it does so is evidence that the people in whom this reaction occurs have been tending to objectify their concerns and purposes, have been giving them a fictitious external authority. A claim to objectivity has been so strongly associated with their subjective concerns and purposes that the collapse of the former seems to undermine the latter as well.

This view, that conceptual analysis would reveal a claim to objectivity, is sometimes dramatically confirmed by philosophers who are officially on the other side. Bertrand Russell, for example, says that 'ethical propositions should be expressed in the optative mood, not in the indicative'; he defends himself effectively against the charge of inconsistency in both holding ultimate ethical valuations to be subjective and expressing emphatic opinions on ethical questions. Yet at the end he admits:

Certainly there *seems* to be something more. Suppose, for example, that some one were to advocate the introduction of bullfighting in this country. In opposing the proposal, I should *feel*, not only that I was expressing my desires, but that my desires in the matter are *right*, whatever that may mean. As a matter of argument, I can, I think, show that I am not guilty of any logical inconsistency in holding to the above interpretation of ethics and at the same time expressing strong ethical preferences. But in feeling I am not satisfied.

But he concludes, reasonably enough, with the remark: 'I can only say that, while my own opinions as to ethics do not satisfy me, other people's satisfy me still less.'

I conclude, then, that ordinary moral judgements include a claim to objectivity, an assumption that there are objective values in just the sense in which I am concerned to deny this. And I do not think it is going too far to say that this assumption has been incorporated in the basic, conventional, meanings of moral terms. Any analysis of the meanings of moral terms which omits this claim to objective, intrinsic, prescriptivity is to that extent incomplete; and this is true of any non-cognitive analysis, any naturalist one, and any combination of the two.

If second order ethics were confined, then, to linguistic and conceptual analysis, it ought to conclude that moral values at least are objective: that they are so is part of what our ordinary moral statements mean: the traditional moral concepts of the ordinary man as well as of the main line of western philosophers are concepts of objective value. But it is precisely for this reason that linguistic and conceptual analysis is not enough. The claim to objectivity, however ingrained in our language and thought, is not self-validating. It can and should be questioned. But the denial of objective values will have to be put forward not as the result of an analytic approach, but as an 'error theory', a theory that although most people in making moral judgements implicitly claim, among other things, to be pointing to something objectively prescriptive, these claims are all false. It is this that makes the name 'moral scepticism' appropriate.

But since this is an error theory, since it goes against assumptions ingrained in our thought and built into some of the ways in which language is used, since it conflicts with what is sometimes called common sense, it needs very solid support. It is not something we can accept lightly or casually and then quietly pass on. If we are to adopt this view, we must argue explicitly for it. Traditionally it has been supported by arguments of two main kinds, which I shall call the argument from relativity and the argument from queerness, but these can, as I shall show, be supplemented in several ways.

8. The argument from relativity

The argument from relativity has as its premiss the well-known variation in moral codes from one society to another and from one period to another, and also the differences in moral beliefs between different groups and classes within a complex community. Such variation is in itself merely a truth of descriptive morality, a fact of anthropology which entails neither first order nor second order ethical views. Yet it may indirectly support second order subjectivism: radical differences between first order moral judgements make it difficult to treat those judgements as apprehensions of objective truths. But it is not the mere occurrence of disagreements that tells against the objectivity of values. Disagreement on questions in history or biology or cosmology does not show that there are no objective issues in these fields for investigators to disagree about. But such scientific disagreement results from speculative inferences or explanatory hypotheses based on inadequate evidence, and it is hardly plausible to interpret moral disagreement in the same way. Disagreement about moral codes seems to reflect people's adherence to and participation in different ways of life. The causal connection seems to be mainly that way round: it is that people approve of monogamy because they participate in a monogamous way of life rather than that they participate in a monogamous way of life because they approve of monogamy. Of course, the standards may be an idealization of the way of life from which they arise: the monogamy in which people participate may be less complete, less rigid, than that of which it leads them to approve. This is not to say that moral judgements are purely conventional. Of course there have been and are moral heretics and moral reformers, people who have turned against the established rules and practices of their own communities for moral reasons, and often for moral reasons that we would endorse. But this can usually be understood as the extension, in ways which, though new and unconventional, seemed to them to be required for consistency, of rules to which they already adhered as arising out of an existing way of life. In short, the argument from relativity has some force simply because the actual variations in the moral codes are more readily explained by the hypothesis that they reflect ways of life than by the hypothesis that they express perceptions, most of them seriously inadequate and badly distorted, of objective values.

But there is a well-known counter to this argument from relativity, namely to say that the items for which objective validity is in the first place to be claimed are not specific moral rules or codes but very general basic principles which are recognized at least implicitly to some extent in all society – such principles as provide the foundations of what Sidgwick has called different methods of ethics: the principle of universalizability, perhaps, or the rule that one ought to conform to the specific rules of any way of life in which one takes part, from which one profits, and on which one relies, or some utilitarian principle of doing what tends, or seems likely, to promote the general happiness. It is easy to show that such general principles, married with differing concrete circumstances, different existing social patterns or different preferences, will beget different specific moral rules; and there is some plausibility in the claim that the specific rules thus generated will vary from community to community or from group to group in close agreement with the actual variations in accepted codes.

The argument from relativity can be only partly countered in this way. To take this line the moral objectivist has to say that it is only in these principles that the objective moral character attaches immediately to its descriptively specified ground or subject: other moral judgements are objectively valid or true, but only derivatively and contingently – if things had been otherwise, quite different sorts of actions would have been right. And despite the prominence in recent philosophical ethics of universalization, utilitarian principles, and the like, these are very far from constituting the whole of what is actually affirmed as basic in ordinary moral thought. Much of this is concerned rather with what Hare calls 'ideals' or, less kindly, 'fanaticism'. That is, people judge that some things are good or right, and others are bad or wrong, not because – or at any rate not only because – they exemplify some general principle for which widespread implicit acceptance could be claimed, but because something about those things arouses certain responses immediately in them, though they would arouse radically and irresolvably different responses in others. 'Moral sense' or 'intuition' is an initially more plausible description of what supplies many of our basic moral judgements than 'reason'. With regard to all these starting points of moral thinking the argument from relativity remains in full force.

9. The argument from queerness

Even more important, however, and certainly more generally applicable, is the argument from queerness. This has two parts, one metaphysical, the other epistemological. If there were objective values, then they would be entities or qualities or relations of a very strange sort, utterly different from anything else in the universe. Correspondingly, if we were aware of them, it would have to be by some special faculty of moral perception or intuition, utterly different from our ordinary ways of knowing everything else. These points were recognized by Moore when he spoke of non-natural qualities, and by the intuitionists in their talk about a 'faculty of moral intuition'. Intuitionism has long been out of favour, and it is indeed easy to point out its implausibilities. What is not so often stressed, but is more important, is that the central thesis of intuitionism is one to which any objectivist view of values is in the end committed: intuitionism merely makes unpalatably plain what other forms of objectivism wrap up. Of course the suggestion that moral judgements are made or moral problems solved by just sitting down and having an ethical intuition is a travesty of actual moral thinking. But, however complex the real process, it will require (if it is to yield authoritatively prescriptive conclusions) some input of this distinctive sort, either premises or forms of argument or both. When we ask the awkward question, how we can

38

be aware of this authoritative prescriptivity, of the truth of these distinctively ethical premises or of the cogency of this distinctively ethical pattern of reasoning, none of our ordinary accounts of sensory perception or introspection or the framing and confirming of explanatory hypotheses or inference or logical construction or conceptual analysis, or any combination of these, will provide a satisfactory answer; 'a special sort of intuition' is a lame answer, but it is the one to which the clear-headed objectivist is compelled to resort.

Indeed, the best move for the moral objectivist is not to evade this issue, but to look for companions in guilt. For example, Richard Price argues that it is not moral knowledge alone that such an empiricism as those of Locke and Hume is unable to account for, but also our knowledge and even our ideas of essence, number, identity, diversity, solidity, inertia, substance, the necessary existence and infinite extension of time and space, necessity and possibility in general, power, and causation. If the understanding, which Price defines as the faculty within us that discerns truth, is also a source of new simple ideas of so many other sorts, may it not also be a power of immediately perceiving right and wrong, which yet are real characters of actions?

This is an important counter to the argument from queerness. The only adequate reply to it would be to show how, on empiricist foundations, we can construct an account of the ideas and beliefs and knowledge that we have of all these matters. I cannot even begin to do that here, though I have undertaken some parts of the task elsewhere. I can only state my belief that satisfactory accounts of most of these can be given in empirical terms. If some supposed metaphysical necessities or essences resist such treatment, then they too should be included, along with objective values, among the targets of the argument from queerness.

This queerness does not consist simply in the fact that ethical statements are 'unverifiable'. Although logical positivism with its verifiability theory of descriptive meaning gave an impetus to non-cognitive accounts of ethics, it is not only logical positivists but also empiricists of a much more liberal sort who should find objective values hard to accommodate. Indeed, I would not only reject the verifiability principle but also deny the conclusion commonly drawn from it, that moral judgements lack descriptive meaning. The assertion that there are objective values or intrinsically prescriptive entities or features of some kind, which ordinary moral judgements presuppose, is, I hold, not meaningless but false.

Plato's Forms give a dramatic picture of what objective values would have to be. The Form of the Good is such that knowledge of it provides the knower with both a direction and an overriding motive; something's being good both tells the person who knows this to pursue it and makes him pursue it. An objective good would be sought by anyone who was acquainted with it, not because of any contingent fact that this person, or every person, is so constituted that he desires this end, but just because the end has to-be-pursuedness somehow built into it. Similarly, if there were objective principles of right and wrong, any wrong (possible) course of action would have not-to-be-doneness somehow built into it. Or we should have something like Clarke's necessary relations of fitness between situations and actions, so that a situation would have a demand for such-and-such an action somehow built into it.

The need for an argument of this sort can be brought out by reflection on Hume's argument that 'reason' – in which at this stage he includes all sorts of knowing as well as reasoning – can never be an 'influencing motive of the will'. Someone might object that Hume has argued unfairly from the lack of influencing power (not contingent upon desires) in ordinary objects of knowledge and ordinary reasoning, and might maintain that values differ from natural objects precisely in their power, when known, automatically to influence the will. To this Hume could, and would need to, reply that this objection involves the postulating of value-entities or value-features of quite a different order from anything else with which we are acquainted, and of a corresponding faculty with which to detect them. That is, he would have to supplement his explicit argument with what I have called the argument from queerness.

Another way of bringing out this queerness is to ask, about anything that is supposed to have some objective moral quality, how this is linked with its natural features. What is the connection between the natural fact that an action is a piece of deliberate cruelty – say, causing pain just for fun – and the moral fact that it is wrong? It cannot be an entailment, a logical or semantic necessity. Yet it is not merely that the two features occur together. The wrongness must somehow be 'consequential' or 'supervenient'; it is wrong because it is a piece of deliberate cruelty. But just what *in the world* is signified by this 'because'? And how do we know the relation that it signifies, if this is something more than such actions being socially condemned, and condemned by us too, perhaps through our having absorbed attitudes from our social environment? It is not even sufficient to postulate a faculty which 'sees' the wrongness: something must be postulated which can see at once the natural features that constitute the cruelty, and the wrongness, and the mysterious consequential link between the two. Alternatively, the intuition required might be the perception that wrongness is a higher order property belonging to certain natural properties; but what is this belonging of properties to other properties, and how can we discern it? How much simpler and more comprehensible the situation would be if we could replace the moral quality with some sort of subjective response which could be causally related to the detection of the natural features on which the supposed quality is said to be consequential.

It may be thought that the argument from queerness is given an unfair start if we thus relate it to what are admittedly among the wilder products of philosophical fancy – Platonic Forms, non-natural qualities, self-evident relations of fitness, faculties of intuition, and the like. Is it equally forceful if applied to the terms in which everyday moral judgements are more likely to be expressed – though still, as has been argued in Section 7, with a claim to objectivity – 'you must do this', 'you can't do that', 'obligation', 'unjust', 'rotten', 'disgraceful', 'mean', or talk about good reasons for or against possible actions? Admittedly not; but that is because the objective prescriptivity, the element a claim for whose authoritativeness is embedded in ordinary moral thought and language, is not yet isolated in these forms of speech, but is presented along with relations to desires and feelings, reasoning about the means to desired ends, interpersonal demands, the injustice which consists in the violation of what are in the context the accepted standards of merit, the psychological constituents of meanness, and so on. There is nothing queer about any of these, and under cover of them the claim for moral authority may pass unnoticed. But if I am right in arguing that it is ordinarily there, and is therefore very likely to be incorporated almost automatically in philosophical accounts of ethics which systematize our ordinary thought even in such apparently innocent terms as these, it needs to be examined, and for this purpose it needs to be isolated and exposed as it is by the less cautious philosophical reconstructions.

10. Patterns of objectification

Considerations of these kinds suggest that it is in the end less paradoxical to reject than to retain the common-sense belief in the objectivity of moral values, provided that we can explain how this belief, if it is false, has become established and is so resistant to criticisms. This proviso is not difficult to satisfy.

On a subjectivist view, the supposedly objective values will be based in fact upon attitudes which the person has who takes himself to be recognizing and responding to those values. If we admit what Hume calls the mind's 'propensity to spread itself on external objects', we can understand the supposed objectivity of moral qualities as arising from what we can call the projection or objectification of moral attitudes. This would be analogous to what is called the 'pathetic fallacy', the tendency to read our feelings into their objects. If a fungus, say, fills us with disgust, we may be inclined to ascribe to the fungus itself a non-natural quality of foulness. But in moral contexts there is more than this propensity at work. Moral attitudes themselves are at least partly social in origin: socially established – and socially necessary – patterns of behaviour put pressure on individuals, and each individual tends to internalize these pressures and to join in requiring these patterns of behaviour of himself and of others. The attitudes that are objectified into moral values have indeed an external source, though not the one assigned to them by the belief in their absolute authority. Moreover, there are motives that would support objectification. We need morality to regulate interpersonal relations, to control some of the ways in which people behave towards one another, often in opposition to contrary inclinations. We therefore want our moral judgements to be authoritative for other agents as well as for ourselves: objective validity would give them the authority required. Aesthetic values are logically in the same position as moral ones; much the same metaphysical and epistemological considerations apply to them. But aesthetic values are less strongly objectified than moral ones; their subjective status, and an 'error theory' with regard to such claims to objectivity as are incorporated in aesthetic judgements, will be more readily accepted, just because the motives for their objectification are less compelling.

But it would be misleading to think of the objectification of moral values as primarily the projection of feelings, as in the pathetic fallacy. More important are wants and demands. As Hobbes says, 'whatsoever is the object of any man's Appetite or Desire, that is it, which he for his part calleth *Good*'; and certainly both the adjective 'good' and the noun 'goods' are used in non-moral contexts of things because they are such as to satisfy desires. We get the notion of something's being objectively good, or having intrinsic value, by reversing the direction of dependence here, by making the desire depend upon the goodness, instead of the goodness on the desire. And this is aided by the fact that the desired thing will indeed have features that make it desired, that enable it to arouse a desire or that make it such as to satisfy some desire that is already there. It is fairly easy to confuse the way in which a thing's desirability is indeed objective with its having in our sense objective value. The fact that the word 'good' serves as one of our main moral terms is a trace of this pattern of objectification.

Similarly related uses of words are covered by the distinction between hypothetical and categorical imperatives. The statement that someone 'ought to' or, more strongly, 'must' do such-and-such may be backed up explicitly or implicitly by reference to what he wants or to what his purposes and objects are. Again, there may be a reference to the purposes of someone else, perhaps the speaker: 'You must do this' – 'Why?' – 'Because I want such-and-such'. The moral categorical imperative which could be expressed in the same words can be seen as resulting from the suppression of the conditional clause in a hypothetical imperative without its being replaced by any such reference to the speaker's wants. The action in question is still required in something like the way in which it would be if it were appropriately related to a want, but it is no longer admitted that there is any contingent want upon which its being required depends. Again this move can be understood when we remember that at least our central and basic moral judgements represent social demands, where the source of the demand is indeterminate and diffuse. Whose demands or wants are in question, the agent's, or the speaker's, or those of an indefinite multitude of other people? All of these in a way, but there are advantages in not specifying them precisely. The speaker is expressing demands which he makes as a member of a community, which he has developed in and by participation in a joint way of life; also, what is required of this particular agent would be required of any other in a relevantly similar situation; but the agent too is expected to have internalized the relevant demands, to act as if the ends for which the action is required were his own. By suppressing any explicit reference to demands and making the imperatives categorical we facilitate conceptual moves from one such demand relation to another. The moral uses of such words as 'must' and 'ought' and 'should', all of which are used also to express hypothetical imperatives, are traces of this pattern of objectification.

It may be objected that this explanation links normative ethics too closely with descriptive morality, with the mores or

THE SUBJECTIVITY OF VALUES

socially enforced patterns of behaviour that anthropologists record. But it can hardly be denied that moral thinking starts from the enforcement of social codes. Of course it is not confined to that. But even when moral judgements are detached from the mores of any actual society they are liable to be framed with reference to an ideal community of moral agents, such as Kant's kingdom of ends, which but for the need to give God a special place in it would have been better called a commonwealth of ends.

Another way of explaining the objectification of moral values is to say that ethics is a system of law from which the legislator has been removed. This might have been derived either from the positive law of a state or from a supposed system of divine law. There can be no doubt that some features of modern European moral concepts are traceable to the theological ethics of Christianity. The stress on quasi-imperative notions, on what ought to be done or on what is wrong in a sense that is close to that of 'forbidden', are surely relics of divine commands. Admittedly, the central ethical concepts for Plato and Aristotle also are in a broad sense prescriptive or intrinsically action-guiding, but in concentrating rather on 'good' than on 'ought' they show that their moral thought is an objectification of the desired and the satisfying rather than of the commanded. Elizabeth Anscombe has argued that modern, non-Aristotelian, concepts of *moral* obligation, *moral* duty, of what is *morally* right and wrong, and of the *moral* sense of 'ought' are survivals outside the framework of thought that made them really intelligible, namely the belief in divine law. She infers that 'ought' has 'become a word of mere mesmeric force', with only a 'delusive appearance of content', and that we would do better to discard such terms and concepts altogether, and go back to Aristotelian ones.

There is much to be said for this view. But while we can explain some distinctive features of modern moral philosophy in this way, it would be a mistake to see the whole problem of the claim to objective prescriptivity as merely local and unnecessary, as a post-operative complication of a society from

45

which a dominant system of theistic belief has recently been rather hastily excised. As Cudworth and Clarke and Price, for example, show, even those who still admit divine commands, or the positive law of God, may believe moral values to have an independent objective but still action-guiding authority. Responding to Plato's *Euthyphro* dilemma, they believe that God commands what he commands because it is in itself good or right, not that it is good or right merely because and in that he commands it. Otherwise God himself could not be called good. Price asks, 'What can be more preposterous, than to make the Deity nothing but will; and to exalt this on the ruins of all his attributes?' The apparent objectivity of moral value is a widespread phenomenon which has more than one source: the persistence of a belief in something like divine law when the belief in the divine legislator has faded out is only one factor among others. There are several different patterns of objectification, all of which have left characteristic traces in our actual moral concepts and moral language.

11. The general goal of human life

The argument of the preceding sections is meant to apply quite generally to moral thought, but the terms in which it has been stated are largely those of the Kantian and post-Kantian tradition of English moral philosophy. To those who are more familiar with another tradition, which runs through Aristotle and Aquinas, it may seem wide of the mark. For them, the fundamental notion is that of the good for man, or the general end or goal of human life, or perhaps of a set of basic goods or primary human purposes. Moral reasoning consists partly in achieving a more adequate understanding of this basic goal (or set of goals), partly in working out the best way of pursuing and realizing it. But this approach is open to two radically different interpretations. According to one, to say that something is the good for man or the general goal of human life is just to say that this is what men in fact pursue or will find ultimately satisfying, or perhaps that it is something which, if postulated as an implicit goal, enables us to make sense of actual human strivings and to detect a coherent pattern in what would otherwise seem to be a chaotic jumble of conflicting purposes. According to the other interpretation, to say that something is the good for man or the general goal of human life is to say that this is man's proper end, that this is what he ought to be striving after, whether he in fact is or not. On the first interpretation we have a descriptive statement, on the second a normative or evaluative or prescriptive one. But this approach tends to combine the two interpretations, or to slide from one to the other, and to borrow support for what are in effect claims of the second sort from the plausibility of statements of the first sort.

I have no quarrel with this notion interpreted in the first way. I would only insert a warning that there may well be more diversity even of fundamental purposes, more variation in what different human beings will find ultimately satisfying, than the terminology of '*the* good for man' would suggest. Nor indeed, have I any quarrel with the second, prescriptive, interpretation, provided that it is recognized as subjectively prescriptive, that the speaker is here putting forward his own demands or proposals, or those of some movement that he represents, though no doubt linking these demands or proposals with what he takes to be already in the first, descriptive, sense fundamental human goals. In fact, I shall myself make use of the notion of the good for man, interpreted in both these ways, when I try in Chapter 8 to sketch a positive moral system. But if it is claimed that something is objectively the right or proper goal of human life, then this is tantamount to the assertion of something that is objectively categorically imperative, and comes fairly within the scope of our previous arguments. Indeed, the running together of what I have here called the two interpretations is yet another pattern of objectification: a claim to objective prescriptivity is constructed by combining the normative element in the second interpretation with the objectivity allowed by the first, by the statement that such and such are fundamentally pursued or ultimately satisfying human goals. The argument from rela-

47

tivity still applies: the radical diversity of the goals that men actually pursue and find satisfying makes it implausible to construe such pursuits as resulting from an imperfect grasp of a unitary true good. So too does the argument from queerness; we can still ask what this objectively prescriptive rightness of the true goal can be, and how this is linked on the one hand with the descriptive features of this goal and on the other with the fact that it is *to some extent* an actual goal of human striving.

To meet these difficulties, the objectivist may have recourse to the purpose of God: the true purpose of human life is fixed by what God intended (or, intends) men to do and to be. Actual human strivings and satisfactions have some relation to this true end because God made men for this end and made them such as to pursue it – but only *some* relation, because of the inevitable imperfection of created beings.

I concede that if the requisite theological doctrine could be defended, a kind of objective ethical prescriptivity could be thus introduced. Since I think that theism cannot be defended, I do not regard this as any threat to my argument. But I shall take up the question of relations between morality and religion again in Chapter 10. Those who wish to keep theism as a live option can read the arguments of the intervening chapters hypothetically, as a discussion of what we can make of morality without recourse to God, and hence of what we can say about morality if, in the end, we dispense with religious belief.

12. Conclusion

I have maintained that there is a real issue about the status of values, including moral values. Moral scepticism, the denial of objective moral values, is not to be confused with any one of several first order normative views, or with any linguistic or conceptual analysis. Indeed, ordinary moral judgements involve a claim to objectivity which both non-cognitive and naturalist analyses fail to capture. Moral scepticism must, therefore, take the form of an error theory, admitting that a belief in objective values is built into ordinary moral thought and language, but holding that this ingrained belief is false. As such, it needs arguments to support it against 'common sense'. But solid arguments can be found. The considerations that favour moral scepticism are: first, the relativity or variability of some important starting points of moral thinking and their apparent dependence on actual ways of life; secondly, the metaphysical peculiarity of the supposed objective values, in that they would have to be intrinsically action-guiding and motivating; thirdly, the problem of how such values could be consequential or supervenient upon natural features; fourthly, the corresponding epistemological difficulty of accounting for our knowledge of value entities or features and of their links with the features on which they would be consequential; fifthly, the possibility of explaining, in terms of several different patterns of objectification, traces of which remain in moral language and moral concepts, how even if there were no such objective values people not only might have come to suppose that there are but also might persist firmly in that belief. These five points sum up the case for moral scepticism; but of almost equal importance are the preliminary removal of misunderstandings that often prevent this thesis from being considered fairly and explicitly, and the isolation of those items about which the moral sceptic is sceptical from many associated qualities and relations whose objective status is not in dispute.

But what if we can establish this negative conclusion, that there are no objective values? How does it help us to say anything positively about ethics? Does it not at one stroke rule out all normative ethics, laying it down that all affirmative first order judgements are false, since they include, by virtue of the very meanings of their terms, unwarranted claims to objectivity? I shall take up these questions in Chapter 5; but first I want to amplify and reinforce the conclusion of this chapter by some investigations of the meanings and logical connections of moral terms.

Chapter 2   The Meaning of 'Good'

1. The general meaning of 'good'

Philosophers have often thought that they could find out more about moral goodness if they could decide what 'good' means when used as a moral term. The arguments of Chapter 1 cast doubt on this; but they will themselves be clarified and reinforced by a better understanding of the meaning of this word.

G.E. Moore thought that there were just three possibilities: that 'good' (in its ethical sense) 'denotes' something simple and indefinable (that is, that it stands for some simple property or characteristic that things or actions may have); that it denotes something complex; and that it denotes no property either simple or complex, so that it means nothing at all, and there is no such subject as ethics. Rejecting the second and third possibilities, he settled for the first, and argued that this simple indefinable something must be a non-natural quality. Some of his successors agreed with him in rejecting the second possibility but were sceptical also about the first, and escaped the third by pointing out that a word can mean something without standing for any property. They concluded that 'good' in ethics has a primarily non-descriptive, non-cognitive, meaning, though its meaning is perhaps also partly and secondarily descriptive, but variably descriptive, pointing to different features in different contexts. But others have suggested that Moore did not consider a wide enough range of ways in which 'good' may 'denote something complex', and that even its primary ethical meaning may be descriptive after all.

Moore had two main reasons for doubting this. First, he thought that those who tried to define 'good' and give it a descriptive meaning confused the question of what sorts of things are good with the question of what goodness itself is: the former can no doubt be answered in descriptive, natural, terms; but only an answer to the latter would constitute a definition or analysis of 'good'. Secondly, he relied on what has been called the 'open question' argument. Take some proposed analysis of 'good', say 'conducive to pleasure': we can surely understand the view of someone who says 'I admit that such-and-such is conducive to pleasure, but is it good?' The same move holds if we substitute for 'conducive to pleasure' any other proposed definition, say 'more evolved' or 'socially approved' or 'in tune with the universe' or 'in accordance with God's will'; it is still an open question whether what is so described is good, or at least we can understand the view of someone who holds that it is still open. But if the proposed definition had been a correct account of the meaning of 'good', this question could not still be open.

These arguments have been very influential, and they are indeed forceful. We could add to the first that even the qualities that in some sense make something good have to be distinguished from goodness itself. An action may be good because it is generous, but its goodness is not identical with its generousness; this is different from a figure's being square because it has four straight sides equal in length and each of its angles a right angle, where we can hardly distinguish the squareness from the features that together make the figure square.

These arguments, however, apply particularly to moral goodness, and it is only with regard to moral (and perhaps also aesthetic) goodness that Moore's conclusion is at all plausible. Though it is with this that we are mainly concerned, it would be most implausible to give to the word 'good' in moral uses a sense quite unconnected with its sense or senses in other contexts. There cannot be two or more words 'good', mere homonyms of one another, like 'bank' (of a river) and 'bank' (a financial institution); for 'good' in English has counterparts in many other languages that have much the same range of moral and non-moral uses. We must hope to find either a single general meaning that the word has in both moral and non-moral contexts, or at least a core meaning of which its other senses are outgrowths.

Peter Geach has argued that the key to the difficulties about the meaning of 'good' is that it is what he calls a (logically) attributive adjective. Just as 'x is a big flea' is not equivalent to 'x is big and x is a flea' or 'x is a forged banknote' to 'x is forged and x is a banknote', so 'x is a good A' – whatever an A may be – is not equivalent to 'x is good and x is an A', whereas 'x is a red book', is equivalent to 'x is red and x is a book', 'red' being a (logically) predicative adjective, not an attributive one. Attributive adjectives, we may say, are operators on predicates; they construct new descriptions in systematic ways out of the meanings of the nouns to which they are attached. A forged A is something that is not an A but has been made so as to pass for one, a big A is (roughly) an A that is bigger than most As, and so on. The crucial experiment that distinguishes attributive from predicative adjectives is this: if 'C' is predicative, then if x is both an A and a B, then if x is a CA it must also be a CB; but if 'C' is attributive, and x is both an A and a B, x can be a CA but not a CB. Thus 'big' is attributive because something that is both a flea and an animal may be a big flea but not a big animal. By this test 'good' is attributive, since a man who is both a tennis player and a conversationalist may be a good tennis player but not a good conversationalist.

An attributive adjective is not on that account ambiguous or vague or indeterminate or variable in meaning, though the criteria for its correct application will vary as it leans on different nouns. The size requirements for a big flea are different from those for a big elephant, but 'big' has exactly the same meaning in both cases. Given any class or collection of objects that have size, we pick out the subset of the big ones among them in exactly the same way. But it is not only with attributive adjectives that the same meaning can yield varying applications. Something similar happens with 'egocentric' or 'indexical' terms. 'I' is used of any number of different persons, but it is not therefore ambiguous: it is used with just the same meaning in every case, namely by each person of himself; and 'here', 'now', 'this', and so on work in similar ways.

There is no doubt that 'good' is often attributive in this sense, and it remains so even when it is not in a grammatically attributive position, and even when the noun on which it leans is not explicitly mentioned. ('Billie Jean King is very good' will mean that she is a good tennis player if it occurs in the context of talk about tennis or if it is primarily as a tennis player that the speaker and hearer are interested in Billie Jean King.) But we have still to discover just how 'good' is attributive, just what operation upon predicates it performs; and then we face the controversial question whether it is always attributive in this way.

There is an important class of nouns which R.M. Hare has called 'functional words', such as 'knife' and 'hygrometer'; to explain fully the meaning of any such word, we have to say what the thing it refers to is for, what it is used to do or is supposed to do. Where 'A' is a functional noun, as soon as we know what an A is supposed to do we can infer what the criteria are for a good A. There is indeed a risk of circularity if we say that since a knife is for cutting, a good knife is one which cuts, or rather can cut, well. What, it may be objected, does 'well' mean? Have we made any progress if we have merely shifted the problem from the meaning(s) of 'good' to the meaning(s) of 'well'? But this circularity can be avoided: we can put what counts as cutting well into what a knife is supposed to do. A carving knife, for example, is supposed to cut smoothly, to enable one to slice meat thinly, and to keep on doing this, not to become blunt or break or wear out too quickly. Once we have said fully enough what an A is supposed to do, a good A will simply be an A which is such as to be able to do that.

We can apply this account to what are functional nouns only in a broad sense. A rock-climber is not for anything, yet there is something which, as a rock-climber, he is supposed to do – roughly, to scale safely cliffs that are hard to scale – and a good rock-climber is one who does, or perhaps who is able to do, that. Wherever 'good' is used in association with a functional noun, it says that the thing has such characteristics as enable it to perform that function.

However, there is another word which means exactly this: 'efficient'. And while where '*A*' is a functional noun, something is a good *A* if and only if it is an efficient *A*, there are other contexts in which 'good' cannot be replaced by 'efficient', and yet it is implausible to say that 'good' *means* the same as 'efficient' in contexts of one sort and something different elsewhere. Can we find any general meaning which 'good' has in all contexts, and which will explain why it coincides with 'efficient' in association with functional nouns?

Hare suggests that both where it precedes a functional noun and where it precedes a non-functional one, say 'sunset', 'good' means (roughly) 'having the characteristic qualities (whatever they are) which are commendable in the kind of object in question'. Commendation, he holds, is the thread that ties the various uses of 'good' together. Where there is a functional noun about, commendable qualities are those that enable the thing to perform its function; but what is commendable in sunsets is determined, presumably, by the preferences of those who like looking at them. But what is it to commend something? Putting together two dictionary definitions, Hare infers that to commend is to mention as being good. But if so, to define 'good' in terms of what is commendable, though not wrong, will be circular and unilluminating.

To break out of this circle, we might suggest that to commend something is to show (or purport to show) favour or support for it. But commonly when one commends something one also describes it: someone may commend a curry in saying that it is hot or a wine in saying that it is unassuming. On this view, to commend something is to say that it satisfies certain requirements, while at the same time indicating that one endorses those requirements. But what if one does not commend the curry as hot, or explicitly as anything in particular? Can one not just commend it by saying that it is good? Surely one can. It is this possibility that is suggested when the dictionary calls 'good' 'the most general adjective of commendation'. One is then saying that the thing satisfies certain requirements which one does not explicitly specify, but at the same time indicating that one endorses those requirements whatever they are, expressing rather than stating one's support for them. Commendation of either of these sorts is egocentric in that it is done essentially from the speaker's point of view.

We can break out of the circle in this way, but a definition of 'good' in terms of egocentric commendation would be too narrow. The functional uses already mentioned fall outside it: while I am in some sense commending someone or something in calling him or it a good rock-climber or a good carving knife I need not even pretend to be endorsing the requirements in question. I may be a convinced vegetarian and think it perverse to go up mountains the hard way. Again one may say, 'That is a good sunset, but the beauties of nature leave me cold.' Philosophers who take egocentric commendation as the core meaning of 'good' have called this an 'inverted commas use', as if one were saying not that the sunset is good, but that it is such as some other people call good; but in fact no inverted commas are required or implied. Besides, we have the phrases 'good for' and 'good from the point of view of'. The weather may be good for potatoes or for potato-growers, though not for haymakers or holidaymakers. No doubt one can stretch the notion of egocentric commendation to cover all these uses, by saying that appropriate conditional, perhaps counterfactually conditional, clauses are to be assumed. The carving knife is one such as I would favour if I wanted to slice meat; the sunset is one such as I would favour if I were one for the beauties of nature; the weather is such as I would favour if I were a potato-grower – or, more dubiously, if I were a potato. But this is stretching the account, and it is gratuitous. What is common to all these cases is that in each there is, somewhere in the picture, some set of requirements or wants or interests, and the thing that is called good is being said to be such as to satisfy those requirements or wants or interests. We can then offer a general definition of 'good': *such as to satisfy requirements (etc.) of the kind in ques-*

tion. We need, I think, 'such as to satisfy' rather than 'satisfies', for two reasons. First, a good carving knife is still a good one if it is never used, and never even needed. It could still, perhaps, be said to satisfy 'requirements', but these are themselves only abstract requirements, abstracted from any concrete relations of requiring. There need not be any full-blooded requirings, let alone interests or wants, to be satisfied: it is enough that the thing should be such that it would satisfy wants, interests, requirings of the sort indicated if any were brought to bear upon it. Secondly, it seems to me that in calling something good, we are saying something about how it is in itself; we are referring immediately to its qualities, its intrinsic features, rather than directly to any relation that it has to anything else, as we would be if we said that it satisfied, say, some interest. There is indeed a curious interplay between qualities and relations here. In calling this a good carving knife I am not quite ascribing to it the intrinsic features, sharpness and so on, that make it good in this respect, that is, that enable it to carve meat well, to do what a meat carver wants it to do; nor am I quite saying that it meets the needs of any actual meat carver, or even that it would meet those of a potential meat carver; rather I am saying something between these two, namely that it has certain characteristics, but these characteristics are themselves introduced obliquely and unexplicitly by some vague reference to the meat carver's demands.

'Requirements (etc.) of the kind in question' is vague: deliberately so. This general definition covers different uses of the word 'good' – not, I should say, different senses – because it leaves open just how the requirements in question are specified or indicated; it leaves room for interests to be fed in in different ways in different sorts of case. Where there is a functional noun about, one which has, as part of its meaning, what the thing is supposed to do, the kind of requirement in question will be that the thing should do just that: if it is a functional noun in the narrow sense that covers 'hygrometer' but not 'rock-climber', the interests in question will be those of someone who uses the thing to do what it is meant to do. If one calls a sunset good, the interests in question are probably those of typical people who like to look at sunsets. If in speaking just of some occurrence or event, perhaps the outcome of a political crisis or industrial conflict or the settlement of some private difficulty, I say 'That's good' (as I certainly can), I may be looking at the episode from my own point of view. The interests in question may be mine – or ours: that is, those of some group to which I belong or with which I identify myself. The interests in question may be introduced egocentrically. I may be engaging in what I have called egocentric commendation, as I may be also in speaking of a good sunset. Contrary to what Geach claims, 'good' is not always attributive in the sense of needing some determinate noun to lean upon. We often say 'That was a good thing' meaning 'a good thing to happen', which can be paraphrased as 'a welcome occurrence', leaving to whom it is welcome undecided. But if I say that something is good for potato-growers, then of course the interests of the kind in question are potato-growing interests; if I say that it is good for potatoes, then I am suggesting that the potatoes themselves have what we can regard, perhaps by analogy with human beings, as their wants or needs, and it is these that the weather, or whatever it is, is being said to be such as to satisfy.

There are, then, several typical ways in which the vagueness of 'requirements (etc.) of the kind in question' can be removed, in which the context can supply an indication of what kinds of requirements are in question; and there may be more. There certainly are uses that combine functional with egocentric elements. 'Car' is a functional noun; there are some fairly determinate things that a car is supposed to do. But there is also plenty of room for differing individual preferences about cars. So your idea of a good car may not coincide with mine, though they will have to have some features in common.

Some further examples will illustrate the contrast between functional and other kinds of commendation. A 'good measure', if 'good' leant upon the functional noun 'measure', would be an accurate one; but 'He gave me good measure' means that he gave me something in excess of the amount stated, it commends the measure from the customer's point of view, not for its accuracy but for a favourable inaccuracy. 'Bad' seems to be more persistently attributive than 'good'. It is evil communications that corrupt what St Paul meant by good manners, that is, morals or character; bad communications corrupt good manners only in the modern sense, for in 'bad communications' the functional noun would dominate. We need 'evil' to indicate that the communications are not inefficient, but bad from some other point of view.

> Said Nebuchadnezzar as he munched his food,
> 'It may be wholesome but it isn't good.'

But Nebuchadnezzar would have had to admit that, functionally speaking, it was good food; what he was withholding was an egocentric commendation.

I want to guard, however, against an interpretation that would make the proposed definition even more vague. By 'requirements' I do not mean simply 'criteria' or even 'standards of evaluation'. To bring in standards of evaluation here would make the analysis too circular to be illuminating, and to refer merely to criteria would leave out something essential. We might call someone a paradigmatic bore; he would then be such as to satisfy the criteria in question – namely, those for bores – but 'a good bore' is hardly comprehensible. 'Good', I think, always imports some reference to something like interests or wants, and I intend 'requirements' to be read in this sense, not so colourlessly as to be almost equivalent to 'criteria'.

It might be objected that there are uses where nothing like interests is involved, where something is being called merely good of its kind, where 'good' is tantamount to 'paradigmatic'. We can certainly understand in this way 'a good ammonite' or 'a good solar corona'. But surely there are interests in question here; these are good specimens for someone who wants to know, or to show others, what an ammonite or a corona is like, and perhaps to keep the one in a museum and to photograph and record the other for similar subsequent use; and 'a good bore' becomes marginally comprehensible if we think of someone going round collecting bores as others collect celebrities. 'A good hiding' is sometimes offered as an example in this connection; but here there is undoubtedly a reference to desires or interests, with some intended vagueness about whose interests they are.

2. 'Good' in moral contexts

If something along these lines is a correct account of the general meaning of 'good', it does little to restrict the possible ethical uses of the word. (There is not, of course, just one ethical use. 'Good' can be predicated in moral contexts of a wide range of kinds of subject – results, states of affairs, people, characters or character-traits, actions, choices, ways of life. In more technical philosophical writing we find Kant's 'good will', Aristotle's 'the good for man', Plato's 'the Good' or 'the Form of the Good'.) Given that even in moral contexts 'good' still has its general meaning, that it still characterizes something as being such as to satisfy requirements or interests or wants of the kind in question, it is still undecided whether such requirements (etc.) are fed in from the point of view of the speaker, or of (some?/all?) other people, whether the reference is somehow to all the interests of everyone, or whether the interests in question are, as in functional or attributive uses, somehow determined by the noun to which the adjective 'good' is explicitly or implicitly attached. But though the general meaning leaves all these possibilities open, there is a further possibility which it also leaves open and which, I think, ethical uses are particularly likely to exemplify. Someone who uses the concept of objective moral value will suppose that there are requirements which simply are there, in the nature of things, without being the requirements of any person or body of persons, even God. To be morally good will then be to be such as to satisfy these intrinsic requirements. It is this notion that Sidgwick almost captures when he equates 'objectively a good' with 'good from the point of view of the universe'. When Kant characterizes the intrinsic goodness of the good will by contrasting its 'dignity' or 'worthiness' (*Würde*) with 'price' (*Preis*) he is making not only this point but also two others. A price, which is goodness relative to some subjective demand, will also, he thinks, be relative in that the price of one thing can be compared with and equated with, or exceeded by, the price of others; but dignity is absolute in two senses that contrast with these: it is an incomparable value as well as an intrinsic one. But also we find here what I called in Chapter 1 the reversal of the direction of dependence: what has dignity does not merely answer to requirements, even universal ones. The requirements in question are also intrinsic to what has dignity, the good will itself. The making of the law which determines all (other?) moral value stands above requirements: it is the requiring. Yet as good it is, I think, also seen as answering requirements; so perhaps we should say that it is seen as the source of the requirements which it also is such as to satisfy. These are difficult notions and perhaps cannot be made fully coherent, yet I think that Kant is struggling to bring out something that is latent in ordinary moral thought, not merely constructing a philosophical fantasy.

In the light of all this we can better understand the force of Moore's open question argument. This trades, we may say, on the indeterminacy of the notion, built into the meaning of the word 'good', which I have tried to indicate by means of the phrase 'requirements of the kind in question'. Sometimes these requirements may relate, say, to *A*'s pleasure. But if we ask 'Though *x* is conducive to *A*'s pleasure, is it good?' we indicate, just by asking this question, that we are bringing some other requirements into view. Similarly with 'I agree that *x* is in accordance with God's purpose, but is it good?' The requirements with reference to which we ask '. . . is it good?' will not be those which *x* has already been admitted to be such as to satisfy. Hare has suggested that Moore's argument rests on a secure foundation which Moore himself did not see clearly: if goodness were equated with any set of defining characteristics, we could not commend something for having those characteristics. True; but while this commending which remains open to us may be what I have called egocentric commendation, it need not be so: it can be with reference to various other requirements, so long as they are also other than ones whose satisfaction has been included in the characteristics for which the thing is to be commended. The open question argument can indeed be turned against a definition of 'good' in terms of egocentric commendation: while sincerely commending something from my own point of view, I can still make sense of the further question whether it is really good. A definition of 'good' in terms of commending that can resist the argument will have to contain the same sort of flexibility that is indicated, in our definition, by 'requirements (etc.) of the kind in question'.

It might seem that objective value alone would resist the open question argument: the point of view of the universe would incorporate all requirements, so that about what was good from this point of view we could no longer question whether it was such as to satisfy requirements of any sort. But this is a vain hope. Nothing can satisfy all requirements, interests, wants, and the like at once; there cannot be an all-inclusive point of view. The apparently comforting dictum that partial evil is universal good prompts the less comforting reflection that universal good may nonetheless be partial evil.

Moore was wrong, then, in thinking that 'good', even in moral contexts, is indefinable, or stands for an unanalysable quality. Does a definition of our sort also re-establish 'good' as a word of purely descriptive meaning? Egocentric commendation should, perhaps, be called not purely descriptive, since an essential element in it is the speaker's implicit endorsing of the requirements – whether these are made explicit or not – which the thing commended is being said to be such as to satisfy. But it is partly descriptive in that it claims both that the thing has the intrinsic characteristics, whatever they are, that enable it to satisfy these requirements, whatever they are, and (hence) that it bears this relation to those requirements. Other things that we can call commendation in a broad sense are purely descriptive: for example uses of 'good' in association with functional nouns. The use of 'good' to refer to a supposed objective moral value is trickier. On the one hand it refers to the alleged hard facts that these intrinsic requirements are there and that this thing is such as to satisfy them; on the other hand just because this is intrinsically required, 'good from the point of view of the universe', the statement that it is so is also prescriptive – but not subjectively prescriptive; it does not have the egocentricity that is at least implicit in the most obvious examples of not purely descriptive terms. Thus although 'good' can be defined, the definition involves an indeterminacy which has the consequence that calling something good either may, or may not, be purely descriptive. But our definition does entail that there is a certain descriptive constraint on' uses of 'good'; to be called good a thing must be such as to have some satisfying relation to something like interests. But 'something like interests', or their possible objects, cannot be logically restricted in turn.

These elements of descriptive meaning are very far, however, from entailing that 'good' ever means the specific features that make something good. It would be a mistake to take these even as part of its meaning, to say, for example, that, when applied to a carving knife, 'good' even partly means 'sharp'. There is no need to say that 'good' changes its meaning at all as its application shifts from carving knives to cushions, any more than 'big' changes its meaning as its application shifts from fleas to elephants, or 'I' or 'here' as it is used by different speakers. 'Big' never *means* 'more than a millimetre long', and 'here' never *means* 'near John Mackie': these are never even parts of their meaning, though they are features that can be inferred from their meanings in certain of their applications.

But a more important matter is this. What in Chapter 1 was called 'moral scepticism' or 'subjectivism', the denial of objective moral values, has often been associated with non-cognitive, non-descriptive, views of the meanings of ethical terms (though as I have argued it does not entail any such view). Consequently it might appear that if 'good' could be shown to have a descriptive meaning after all, objective values would also be rehabilitated. But it should be clear that such elements of descriptive meaning as are revealed by our account have no such tendency.

It is true that the general meaning of 'good' leaves it open that the word may be used in moral contexts with reference to supposed intrinsic requirements; but it equally leaves it open that 'good' in moral contexts may be used for egocentric commendation. The general meaning of the word is neutral as between these rival views. But further, even if I am right in thinking that the main ethical use does refer to supposed intrinsic requirements, this does not entail that there are objective values, but only that moral thought traditionally and conventionally – and, I have suggested, very naturally and comprehensibly – includes a claim to objectivity. I have noted a descriptive constraint on the use of 'good', that to be good something must be related to something like interests; but even if there were much tighter constraints than this nothing would follow about objective values. There are words like 'brave' which have fairly definite descriptive meanings but also a conventional illocutionary force of egocentric commendation: one can hardly call a person or an action brave without oneself thereby endorsing the favourable evaluation of such a character or of such actions. But it does not follow that courage has objective value; only that the favourable estimation of it is so well established that it has been absorbed into the ordinary conventions of language.

I conclude that we can give an account of the meaning of 'good' which relates its ethical uses to those in other contexts, and which brings together aspects that have been emphasized in opposing philosophical theories. But the outcome of this investigation of meaning is largely negative. The general meaning of 'good' does not in itself determine how the word is to be used in ethics, and neither this general meaning nor any special ethical meaning will yield answers to substantive moral questions.

Chapter 3   Obligations and Reasons

1. 'Is' and 'ought'

Writers on morality, Hume noted, often move imperceptibly from statements joined by 'is' to ones joined by 'ought' and 'ought not'. These, he protests, express some new relation, make some new sort of claim, which needs to be explained: 'a reason should be given, for what seems altogether inconceivable, how this new relation can be a deduction from others which are entirely different from it.' This protest has since hardened into a dictum, sometimes called Hume's Law, that one cannot derive an 'ought' from an 'is'. Along with Moore's naturalistic fallacy and open question argument, this is one of the best-known ways of drawing a sharp distinction between moral facts and all others, or between all facts on the one hand and values on the other, between description and evaluation. But those who query such distinctions often challenge Hume's Law.

It is curious that so much interest has been concentrated on the word 'ought', which is a relatively weak modal auxiliary. Anyone who really means business uses 'must' or 'shall' rather than 'ought' (or 'should') in his moral pronouncements. The Ten Commandments are not given in English in the form 'You ought not to have any other gods before me . . . You ought not to kill . . .' and we should get a rather different message if they were. But since much of what holds for 'ought' holds also for 'must', it will do no harm to follow the usual practice of discussing the problem mainly in terms of 'ought', but to note if 'must' differs in any significant way.

'Ought' and 'must' and 'shall' and 'should' are constantly used in non-moral as well as moral contexts, and as with 'good' it is not likely that their moral uses are completely cut off from the others. So we may start by glancing at some of these. One might say to a beginner in chess, 'You must not move your rook diagonally.' It would be even more natural to say 'You can't' here, for though he physically can so move it, just as he can throw it across the room, he cannot thereby make a move in a game of chess. Similarly if someone tries to move (in what would otherwise be the correct way) a rook which is pinned against his king by an enemy bishop, one might say that he must not, or can't, do that. If someone is thinking of moving a rook which is similarly pinned against his own queen, so that the move, though valid, would result in the loss of the queen without adequate compensation, and probably therefore in the loss of the game, one might still say 'You can't' (or 'You must not', or 'You ought not to') move that rook.' 'Can't' or 'must not' may be used because it is not the right sort of move for that piece, or because, though the right sort of move, it is not allowable in the circumstances, or because, though allowable, it would be disastrous. In the third case, though hardly in the others, 'ought not' could be used instead; and one might also say 'ought not' if one thought that the proposed move, though not plainly disastrous, was unwise.

In such examples, there is no difficulty about a transition from 'is' to 'ought'. The rules of the game, together with the actual positions of the pieces, and perhaps what it is likely that his opponent will do, coupled with the general aim of winning, are sufficient to determine that the player must not do this, or ought not to do that. Here there is no 'new relation', but just the old ones that could be stated in 'is'-linked premisses, of being contrary to the rules of chess, likely to lead to the loss of the queen, and so on. (We shall consider in Section 2 how 'must' and 'ought' come to express such relations.)

There is no more difficulty about hypothetically imperative 'ought'-statements in other contexts. If someone wants to get to London by twelve o'clock, and the only available means of transport that will get him there is the ten-twenty train, and catching this train will not conflict with any equally strong desires or purposes that he has, then he ought to, indeed must, catch the ten-twenty. If smoking has the effects it is alleged to have, then if a heavy smoker wants to live long and be healthy, and doesn't get much enjoyment from smoking, and, if he gave it up, would not feel it much of a loss and would not switch to other indulgences, such as overeating, which were likely to be even worse for his prospects of long life and health, then he ought to give up smoking. When we put in enough factual conditions about the agent's desires and about causal, including psychologically causal, relations, the 'ought' conclusion follows. But no 'new relation' is involved. 'Ought', as we shall see, says that the agent has a reason for doing something, but his desires along with these causal relations constitute the reason.

But a moral 'ought', it may be said, does introduce a new relation, and cannot therefore be derived from an 'is'. Admittedly a moral 'ought' conclusion may follow from a statement whose explicit connective is an 'is': Doing X is wrong, therefore you ought not to do X. This inference is valid, if any coherent and corresponding senses are given to 'wrong' and 'ought'; but anyone who is defending Hume's Law will brush this sort of example aside as irrelevant, saying that there is an 'ought' concealed within the predicate 'wrong', so that 'Doing X is wrong' is not an 'is'-statement in the intended sense.

A more serious challenge to Hume's Law is made by John Searle, who discusses the following argument in five steps:

(1) Jones uttered the words 'I hereby promise to pay you, Smith, five dollars.'

(2) Jones promised to pay Smith five dollars.

(3) Jones placed himself under (undertook) an obligation to pay Smith five dollars.

(4) Jones is under an obligation to pay Smith five dollars.

(5) Jones ought to pay Smith five dollars.

Searle concedes that this is not watertight as it stands: (2) would not in all circumstances follow from (1), or (4) from (3), or (5) from (4). But it is easy in principle to insert unquestionably factual premisses from the conjunction of which with (1) (2) will follow. It is not so easy to supplement (3) and (4) with factual premises which will exclude competing claims and extenuating circumstances which might otherwise undermine the conclusion. But, as Searle says, it is not these that have been seen as the problem for a derivation of 'ought' from 'is'. The view that this problem is insoluble will be sufficiently refuted by the derivation even of the weakened conclusion 'Other things being equal, Jones ought to pay Smith five dollars'; let us read (5) as saying this.

With these stipulations, the argument goes through for some sense of (5); but for what sense (or senses)? Searle suggests that the gap between description and evaluation, the sharp distinction that has made it seem impossible to derive 'ought' from 'is', is bridged by the recognition of a peculiar class of facts, institutional facts as opposed to brute facts. It can be a matter of institutional, though not of brute, fact that one undertakes and then has certain obligations.

However, this explanation runs together two different ways of speaking. We can describe an institution as it were from the outside: there is an institution or social practice of promising, somewhat as there is a practice of playing chess. This institution has as a part the making of certain demands on those who participate in it; we may say, roughly, that the promising institution demands that promises be kept, much as chess requires that moves of only certain sorts be made. But as an alternative to describing any such institution and its demands from the outside, we can speak as it were within the institution; we can say simply 'You must not move that rook (because this would leave your king in check)' or 'Jones ought to pay Smith five dollars (because he promised to do so)'.

It is true that these same words could serve as an elliptical expression of a statement of the former sort, as shorthand for, say, 'The promising institution demands (in these circumstances) that Jones pay Smith five dollars.' But though the same words could do either job, these are two radically different jobs.

But in which sense is (5) to be taken? If it is taken (elliptically) as describing the institution from the outside, then the argument goes through as a matter of general logic, with purely factual supplementary premises about the circumstances and the character of the institution. But the facts about the institution asserted in some of the premises and in the conclusion are as brute facts as any other. Institutional facts may be more complicated than some others, but they are no less hard and purely factual than, say, palaeontological facts. Alternatively, if (5) is taken as spoken within the institution, (4) will have to be taken in the same way, and then there is a vital transition concealed within (3). What follows from (2) – taking this as factual, as said from outside the institution – is that Jones tried or purported to place himself under an obligation, but it is only by invoking (not merely reporting) the rules of the institution that one can infer that he did place himself under an obligation, so that he is now under one. The argument is valid not by general logic but by a special logic by which one reasons within the promising institution.

If we take (5) in the first way, then, it cannot reasonably be resisted by anyone who accepts (1) and the hard facts about the circumstances and about the institution. But since (5), thus interpreted, is itself a matter of brute fact, in no way evaluative or prescriptive, no-one needs to reject this inference in order to maintain Hume's Law. If we take (5) in the second way, then it is evaluative and prescriptive, but it is derived from (1) and the other unstated, factual premises only by a special logic, only by an appeal to and endorsement of the rules of the promising institution, and no-one who is concerned for the spirit rather than the letter of Hume's Law needs to be worried by a derivation of this sort. It can be dangerously misleading to speak of institutional facts if we then run these two interpretations together, and apply simultaneously to (5) comments which properly belong separately to the two interpretations – in particular, if we suppose that (5), with the evaluative and prescriptive force that it has when we speak within the institution, can be established, given (1) and a few more hard facts, including ones about the institution seen from outside, irresistibly by general logic alone.

For example, Searle claims that ' "promise" is an evaluative word since . . . the notion of promising is logically tied to the evaluative notion of obligation, but since it also is purely "descriptive" (because it is a matter of objective fact whether or not someone has made a promise) . . . the whole distinction [between "evaluative" and "descriptive"] needs to be re-examined.' He thinks there are two non-coincident distinctions, one between evaluation and description as two kinds of illocutionary acts among many others, and one between what can and what cannot be objectively decided as true or false. But the truth of the matter is that someone who promises purports to put himself under an obligation by implementing the constitutive rules of a certain institution. That is how 'Jones promised . . .', as used from outside the institution, is at once purely descriptive (and objectively decidable) and 'logically tied to the evaluative notion of obligation'; it refers to a purported evaluative item, but is not itself evaluative.

The key point may be made clearer if we note two senses in which (5) is not established by Searle's argument. One is that in which (5) would assert what I have called an objective value, in which it would say that Jones's paying of five dollars to Smith is now intrinsically required – not just required by the institution of promising, but, given the facts that there is such an institution and that Jones has tangled with it, required simply by the nature of things. The other is that in which anyone who accepts (5) thereby himself endorses or subscribes to the relevant prescription. It is very obvious that (5) in the first of these two senses does not follow from (1) in conjunction with any other hard facts about the circumstances and the institution; this would be, in Hume's words, a new relation, and it would be inconceivable that it should be deduced from those others that are entirely different from it. What we are to say about the second sense is less clear. I can surely refrain from endorsing the promising institution; I can decline to speak within it. No doubt this would be eccentric, unconventional, it might well make people distrust or dislike me, but it is not logically ruled out. But what if I am Jones? Is this move open to him? Can he consistently refrain from endorsing the institution of promising? Has he not committed himself to the observance of this institution just by doing what premiss (1) reports in the appropriate circumstances? In the same way someone who undertakes to play chess cannot consistently evade the conclusion 'You must not move that rook' by declining to endorse the rules of chess.

This objection mixes up three distinct points. First, there is the hypothetical imperative: if you want to play chess you had better obey the rules of the game – not merely analytically, because if you don't obey the rules it won't be chess, but because if you want to play even anything like chess you need someone to play with, no-one will play with you unless you abide by some rules, and it will be easier to follow the established rules than to invent and consistently observe new ones. Similarly, if Jones wants to retain, for any length of time, the benefits of the institution of promising, he had better stick to its rules. Secondly, if Jones makes a sincere promise, he is at least at that time endorsing the institution, and so is prepared to speak within the institution and to subscribe to a future tense version of (5); if asked at the time he makes the promise, he will say with equal sincerity that he will be obliged to pay when the time comes. But, thirdly, it may be argued that by making the promise at one time he has committed himself to the promising institution in such a way that it will be not merely a change of mind but wrong for him to refuse to endorse it when the time comes for payment. This third claim is different from the other two. The alleged commitment is, in effect, a promise: the claim is that Jones has as it were promised to go on endorsing the promising institution. But then this attempt to validate the obligation of a promise is circular: we have to assume that Jones ought to fulfil his commitment to the promising institution before we can establish, in this way, his obligation to keep his promise to Smith. It is only this third, viciously circular, form of the objection which appears to show even that Jones himself cannot refuse to endorse the institution and hence to assert (5), speaking within it, when the time comes for payment. It is neither here nor there that he previously implicitly asserted a future tense version of (5) if and when he made a sincere promise, and that he may be well advised to keep the promise if he wants to go on using and benefiting from the institution. This objection seems formidable mainly because the harmlessly correct first and second points are liable to be confused with the third, unsound because circular, argument. True, Jones cannot 'consistently' decline to accept (5) as spoken within the institution; but only in that he will have changed his mind: there is no logical inconsistency here.

There are other institutions, with associated speech acts, that have the same logical form as promising. Children use the word 'Bags' as part of a well-defined institution. Whoever first says 'Bags I the chocolate cake' thereby purports to acquire an exclusive right to the chocolate cake. So we can construct an argument like Searle's, leading from 'John first said "Bags . . ." ' by way of 'John bagged . . .' to 'John has a right to . . .' But here it is even more obviously an open question whether we are to endorse the institution or not.

Searle's argument has been much discussed, and he has replied to such objections as I have stated here. Bagging differs from promising in that it purports to secure a right whereas promising purports to give a right to someone else. But this does not affect the cogency of the inference form, on which Searle originally relied. Nor can it matter that promising is a better-established institution than bagging, and is built into the ordinary language, not only into juvenile slang. But Searle's main reply to his critics is a protest against the 'anthropological attitude', that is, against the use of the distinction on which I have relied between speaking outside and speaking within the institution. He argues that if we rely on such a distinction here, we must, for consistency, do so with regard to all parts of language, and this would undermine the validity of arguments on all topics, not just his. But this is not so. Words like 'promise' and 'bags', as used within their respective institutions, have a peculiar logical feature not shared by most parts of language. The performance of a certain speech act in appropriate circumstances is, in virtue of one part of the meaning of the words,

71

sufficient to validate the statement 'Jones promised . . .' or 'John bagged . . .'. But also, in virtue of another part of their meaning, such a statement entails 'Jones ought to . . .' or 'John has a right to . . .' The very meanings of these words thus embody synthetic claims, in fact justifications of transitions from 'is' to 'ought'. For this reason the adopting of such fragments of language is not a neutral matter, as is the use of most parts of language, such as figure in most arguments: to use the word 'promise' or 'bags' with its full within-the-institution meaning is already to endorse the institution in a substantial way, to adopt and support certain distinctive patterns of behaviour and to condemn others.

Other arguments have been suggested as ways of bridging the gap between 'is' and 'ought', but I have concentrated on Searle's because it is representative of the whole class. Such arguments, therefore, constitute no threat to any sensible interpretation of Hume's Law, or indeed to any point that Hume himself was making. Nevertheless, the popular formulation of the law is misleading. From sets of 'is'-statements which are purely factual, which conceal no value terms, we can derive not only hypothetically imperative 'ought'-statements but also moral ones. Admittedly we do so only by speaking within some institution, but this can itself be part of ordinary language. Such derivations can be linguistically orthodox: the forms of reasoning that go with the central moral institutions have been built into ordinary language, and in merely using parts of that language in a standard way we are implicitly accepting certain substantive rules of behaviour. To bring out what does not go through we have to isolate the key aspects of possible senses of 'ought', either the alleged objective intrinsic requirement or the speaker's own endorsement of an institution and its demands. These do not normally occur in isolation, and views which single out any one of them as *the* meaning of moral terms are implausible and indeed incorrect analyses of ordinary moral language. These aspects commonly occur in close combination with factual (including institutionally factual) elements. We learn the concept of 'ought' along with the concept of a promise, the concepts of meanness and generosity, courage and cowardice, and the like. Meanness is not only a certain kind of spirit but also one to be discouraged, not only a certain kind of behaviour but also one not to be practised. Such concepts, and the words that express them, bridge the gap between description and prescription. The distinction between the factual and the evaluative is not something with which we are presented, but something that has to be achieved by analysis.

But to concede in this way that 'ought' can be derived from 'is' by virtue of forms of reasoning embedded in ordinary language, in the established concepts and the standard meanings of certain words, makes no inroads upon the moral scepticism formulated in Chapter 1. It yields no way of demonstrating that objective values, intrinsic prescriptions, practical necessities and the like are part of the nature of things, no way of constraining assent or adherence to moral views. And this is the central meta-ethical question, the objectivity or subjectivity of values and requirements, not the analysis of moral concepts or of moral language.

2. The meaning of 'ought'

Language and meaning, then, are not our main concern. But the argument of the last section may be reinforced by a more accurate study of the meanings of the key terms. I have spoken loosely of different senses in which 'ought'-statements and remarks about obligation can be taken; but (as with 'good' in Chapter 2) we might hope to find a single meaning for 'ought' in both moral and non-moral uses, with perhaps some inbuilt indeterminacy that invites resolution, but that can be resolved in various ways. We must take account not only of moral and prudential and hypothetically imperative 'oughts' but also of such statements as 'This ought to do the trick', 'They ought to be across the border by now', and 'It ought to have dissolved; I wonder why it didn't', which we can perhaps call epistemic. A first attempt at a general equivalent of 'a ought to G', might be

73

'There is a reason for a's G-ing.' (In many cases the not quite equivalent, and stronger, 'There is a reason against a's not G-ing' would seem to be a little nearer the mark, but the simpler formula, without the negations, may be accurate enough for our purposes.) We could then say that different uses (not different senses) of 'ought' introduce different kinds of reason. The epistemic 'ought'-statements refer to what are or were reasons for expecting such-and-such an outcome. We can also draw some illumination here from etymology. 'Ought' is a past tense of 'owe', but used as a present: if a ought to G, then a somehow owes that he/she/it should G. But what is it for Jones, say, to owe Smith five dollars? Is it as if five dollars in Jones's pocket or bank account were trying to fly across into Smith's? Rather, since Jones's pocket and bank account may both be empty, it is as if there were an invisible hook reaching out from Smith and fishing for the money in Jones's pocket. Or an immaterial suction-pipe. The owing is itself something like a demand for payment. Similarly if a ought to G, there is something about the situation that sets up an expectation or presumption of a's G-ing. A similar metaphor is buried in the term 'obligation'. If a is obliged to G, it is as it were tied down to G-ing: an obligation is an invisible cord. If something is offered without obligation, there are no strings attached. 'a is bound to G' is, like an 'ought'-statement, indeterminate between epistemic and moral uses. It also has purely legal uses, which 'ought', it seems, does not. This may be because 'is bound' is stronger than 'ought'; like 'must', it brooks no denial, whereas 'ought' is more pusillanimous. We cannot say 'It was bound to dissolve; I wonder why it didn't'. Nor is 'bound to' used in hypothetical imperatives, though 'obliged' is. I can be obliged to catch the ten twenty if I want to be in London by twelve, but I cannot be thus bound to catch it. The reason for this cannot be that 'bound to' is too strong; there can be strong hypothetical imperatives, and 'must' can be used to state them: 'You must catch the ten twenty if you want to be in London by twelve.' Perhaps 'bound to' is excluded because it would too strongly suggest an epistemic reading: it is if I start early enough from home that I shall be bound to catch the ten twenty. But otherwise 'ought' is like 'bound to', but weaker: if a ought to G, it is only half bound to G.

If something like this is the general meaning of 'ought', we can understand how it can be used in epistemic contexts as well as in hypothetically imperative and moral ones. There are not radical changes of meaning between these different uses, only different ways in which the notion of something's being half bound, or of there being a reason, can be filled out and substantiated. Leaving aside the epistemic uses, we can see how even where what ought to do something is a human agent there are several possible sorts of reasons, several ways of being half bound. One sort is the hypothetically imperative, where some want or purpose or ideal that the agent has requires the action for its fulfilment, given the concrete state of affairs and the relevant causal relations. The hypothetical imperative 'If you want X you ought to do Y,' does not mean exactly 'Doing Y is, in the circumstances, causally necessary for achieving X,' though it will hold if and only if this causal relation does; rather it looks at this causal relation from the point of view of a (possible) desire for X. The consequent of the conditional is not fully detachable; even if you do want X, the judgement that you ought to do Y still implicitly incorporates that want as what creates the reason for doing Y, the agent's being weakly tied to the doing of Y, which the 'ought'-statement asserts. Another way in which an agent can be half bound is that some institution may demand something of him or tend to restrict his choices of action in certain respects. If Jones literally owes Smith five dollars, some established system of commercial (or other similar) practice demands that he pay at some time. But, as I have stressed, this sort of requirement can itself be looked at in either of two ways, either neutrally, from the outside, or from the point of view of the institution itself or of someone who endorses it and joins in expressing its demands. 'Ought' can then express, in part, the demands of the speaker; his attitude can help to constitute the reason for the proposed action. But a third person 'ought', where the speaker is not himself the agent, seems never to refer only to the speaker's demands. 'Must', indeed, sometimes does. 'You must do this' – 'Why?' – 'Because I say so'; but not 'You ought to do this' – 'Why?' – 'Because I say so.' 'Ought' is never purely egocentric; it always points to a reason of some kind other than the speaker's attitude, though it can in part indicate that the speaker gives that reason his backing. Again etymology is surprisingly relevant here: 'must', unlike 'ought', is descended from a verb whose primary use was to give or withhold permission.

But as I suggested in Section 1, as well as hypothetically imperative and institutional and partly egocentric reasons and requirements, there are commonly believed to be intrinsic requirements, the situation itself or the nature of things is seen as demanding some action (or refraining from action); an agent is felt to be half bound to do something, and yet not by his own desires or by any specifiable institution or by the speaker's attitude, or at any rate not only by these; some intrinsic requirement backs up, say, an institutional one. When 'ought' refers to reasons or semi-bindings of this supposed sort, it is thought to be a peculiarly moral 'ought'. But on our view this moral 'ought' does not have an essentially different meaning or sense from other 'oughts': we have still the same basic meaning but a (partly) different way of resolving its indeterminacy. Besides, 'ought' seldom, if ever, in ordinary use, refers to such supposed intrinsic requirements alone; it typically refers also to reasons or requirements of at least one of the other sorts, the intrinsic requirements being seen as backing them up.

'Must', as we have seen, is stronger than 'ought', but otherwise works similarly. It, too, contains an indeterminacy which can be resolved in several ways. The general meaning of 'a must G' is something like 'a is not permitted not to G'; but there can be causal, epistemic, institutional, legal, hypothetically imperative, egocentric, and supposedly objective, intrinsic, non-permissions. 'Must' and 'is bound to' cover much the same ground, but as a result of metaphorical extensions in opposite directions. In 'is bound to' what is literally a physical tying down is extended metaphorically to human demands and the like; in 'must' what is literally the human performance of withholding permission is extended metaphorically to causal relations, epistemic guarantees, and supposed intrinsic moral necessities.

3. Varieties of reason

It was suggested that a rough general equivalent of '*a* ought to *G*' would be 'There is a reason for *a*'s G-ing.' Confining ourselves to human agents and their choices of action, we might then hope to determine what people ought to do by seeing what can count as reasons for action. There seem to be several kinds. Most obviously, we would say that there is a reason for *a*'s G-ing, or that *a* has a reason to *G*, if *G*-ing would lead to the fulfilment of some desire or purpose or ideal that *a* now has, and *a* knows this. But what if *G*-ing would lead to such fulfilment but *a* does not know this, and again if *a* wrongly believes that *G*-ing will lead to such fulfilment when it will not? Does *a* have a reason for *G*-ing – and hence, ought *a* to *G* – in either or both of these cases? In each of these cases the statement that *a* has a reason, and ought to *G*, is a thoroughly intelligible implementation of the general meanings of the terms, and, suitably understood, is correct; there is no need to choose between them, or to dispute whether *a* really ought to *G* or to *H*, if, say, *G*-ing will in fact lead to the fulfilment of his desires, but he does not know this, and wrongly believes that *H*-ing will do so. This issue could be raised if we supposed that there were intrinsic requirements: does the nature of things, in these circumstances, demand that *a* should *G* or that he should *H*? But if we dispense with such a supposition, there seems to be no real issue: in one way *a* ought to *G*, in another he ought to *H*, and that's that. It is, of course, idle to dispute what general instruction we might give to *a*: when he comes to implement them, 'Do what you believe will satisfy your desires' and 'Do what will really satisfy your desires' will guide *a* to exactly the same choice.

Someone can have a reason, then, for doing what will lead or is likely to lead or even is wrongly believed by him to be likely to lead to the satisfaction, perhaps in the remote future, of some desire (etc.) that he now has. But what if he will have (and knows that he will have) some desire or purpose at some future date, and something that he can do now is likely to lead to its fulfilment; does this constitute a reason for his now doing this? Can we say that he now has a (prudential) reason for an action which will tend to satisfy not any desire which he now has, not even a present desire that his future desires should be fulfilled, but only a desire which he knows he will have later? We can indeed say that he has such a reason, and that (other things being equal) he ought to act in the way that is likely to lead to the fulfilment of the still future desire. But in saying this we are leaning on our concept of the identity of a person through time and the associated expectation that a human being will behave as a fairly coherent purposive unit over time, that his purposes at different times will agree with one another fairly well. Human beings are more likely to flourish if they show such purposive coherence over time, so that it is not surprising that we have this useful cluster of concepts and expectations. Still, we should note that these peculiarly prudential reasons are sharply distinguishable from reasons which rest upon an agent's present desires. Our established concept of personal identity through time is here functioning analogously to an institution like promising, introducing a requirement for attention to the future well-being of what will be the same human being as the agent in question.

Do the desires and especially the sufferings of other people, if known to me, constitute a reason for me to do something, if I can, or to try to do something to satisfy those desires or to relieve those sufferings? It would be natural to say that they constitute some reason; how strong a reason, how easily over-ruled by other considerations, may be a matter of dispute. It would generally be thought that there would be a stronger reason if the other people were closely related to me by family ties, friendship, and so on. But the important thing is that if we recognize this as a further class of reasons, independent of any desire that I now have to help these other people, we are again bringing in the requirements of something like an institution: an established way of thinking, a moral tradition, demands that I show some concern for the well-being of others, or at least of some others, and this demand may have been written into ordinary language among rules about what can or cannot or must count as a reason. A faint suggestion of semi-identity between persons is also sometimes pressed into service here: 'No man is an island.' Provoked, perhaps, by Hume's deliberately paradoxical remark that it is not contrary to reason to prefer the destruction of the whole world to the scratching of my finger, we may well say, 'Surely if someone is writhing in agony before your eyes, or starving on your doorstep, this is in itself, quite apart from your feelings, a reason for you to do something about it if you can; if you don't admit that, you just don't know what a reason is, you can't be using the word "reason" with its ordinary meaning, you can't have the full concept of a reason.' But if we say this, we are again speaking within the institution. There would be no great difficulty in constructing an argument parallel to Searle's, starting, say, with the premiss 'Smith is starving on Jones's doorstep' and ending with 'Jones ought to give Smith some food.' But the logic of the situation would be similar, though admittedly the institution of helping others is less thoroughly built into ordinary language than that of promising, and starving is not a speech act. There may well be dispute about how near, in some sense, others must be to me for their needs to count as a reason for me to do something about them, and how strong a reason it will then be. Similarly there may be and indeed is dispute about the conceptual limits of (moral) reasoning in general. But all such disputes are idle. However one of them is settled, the conclusion that is firmly established will be only of the form: This institution requires such and such an action. If we move to a prescriptive interpretation, we shall be speaking within the institution. But nothing logically commits us to doing so, and certainly nothing compels us to reinterpret the requirements of an institution, however well established, however thoroughly enshrined in our ordinary ways of thinking and speaking, as objective, intrinsic, requirements of the nature of things.

4. Institutions

We have perhaps been speaking too casually about institutions and their requirements, about endorsing one or other of these, and about speaking within an institution; it may be thought that some further account of these is called for. However, the realities for which these terms are intended to stand are thoroughly familiar, and there should be no obscurity as long as it is understood that this cluster of terms is being used very widely, that 'institution' is meant to cover such diverse items as games like chess, the social practices that centre round the making of promises, and the thought and behaviour that supports or is supported by the notion of the identity of persons through time. Our talk about institutions is intended to bring out and make use of analogies between these superficially diverse items.

Any institution is constituted by many people behaving in fairly regular ways, with relations between them which transmit and encourage and perhaps enforce those ways of behaving. An institution will have rules or principles of action, or both, which the participants in the institution will formulate fairly explicitly, allow to guide their own actions, and infringements of which they will discourage and condemn. They will use concepts closely associated with these rules and principles which cannot be fully explained without reference to these rules and principles; and the rules and principles in turn will usually be formulated partly in terms of those concepts. An institution can be fairly adequately described in an abstract, formal, way simply by stating and explaining the rules and principles and concepts – the game of chess, for example, could be fully described in this way. But the concrete reality is more than this: it is chess-playing as a persisting social practice, not merely the abstract game. The abstract game exists only as an aspect, or rather as several aspects, of the concrete, traditionally maintained, social practice – partly in the (fairly) regular features of the sequences of moves actually made by chess-players, partly as the content of rules and principles which they have in mind and put forward. When I speak of the requirements of an institution, I am referring not only to the normative content of the abstract rules and principles, but to various things actually being demanded, condemned, enforced or encouraged. These requirements, then, are constituted by human thought, behaviour, feelings, and attitudes. To speak within an institution is to use its characteristic concepts, to assert or appeal to or implicitly invoke its rules and principles, in fact to speak in those distinctive ways by speaking and thinking in which the participants help to constitute the institution.

An institution, as I am using the word, does not need to be instituted. It need not be such an artificial creation as the game of chess. Promising may well be a universal human practice, to be found in all societies; it is certainly one that could grow very naturally out of the ordinary conditions of human life. But that does not alter its logical status, or the logical status of conclusions that can be established only within and by invoking that institution.

A promise, and the apparent obligation to keep a promise, are created not merely by a speaker's statement of intention in conjunction with the desire of the person to whom the promise is made that it should be fulfilled, or even by these together with the hearer's reliance on the statement and the speaker's expectation that the hearer will, and intention that he should, so rely. What creates the institution of promising is all these being embedded in and reinforced by general social expectations, approvals, disapprovals, and demands: promising, in contrast with the stating of an intention, can be done only where there is such a complex of attitudes.

It is not hard to understand how and why such attitudes, and hence the institution of promising, can have developed from statements of intention related to another person's wants; but this will become still clearer when (in Chapter 5) we follow

Hume in attending to the social function which this practice fulfils. But however natural and automatic this development is, what it constitutes is, logically speaking, an institution. To assert the obligation to keep a promise is to invoke or endorse this system of attitudes.

Not all 'oughts', let alone all reasons for action, are institutional, but many are. And it is not surprising that widespread, socially diffused, and not obviously artificial institutions – including personal identity plus prudence, as well as promising, both of these in contrast with, say, chess – should have helped to produce the notions of what is intrinsically fitting or required by the nature of things. These notions, which in turn contribute significantly to our ordinary concepts of good reasons and of moral obligation, embody very natural errors; but errors none the less.

Chapter 4 Universalization

1. The first stage of universalization: the irrelevance of numerical differences

Moral judgements are universalizable. Anyone who says, meaning it, that a certain action (or person, or state of affairs, etc.) is morally right or wrong, good or bad, ought or ought not to be done (or imitated, or pursued, etc.) is thereby committed to taking the same view about any other relevantly similar action (etc.). This principle, in some sense, is beyond dispute. But there is room for discussion about how it is to be interpreted, about its own status, and about what then follows about the content and the status of morality. Does this principle impose some sort of rational constraint on moral judgement, choices of action, or defensible patterns of behaviour?

For the interpretation of this principle, the key phrase is 'relevantly similar'. Though the identity of indiscernibles is not a necessary truth, in practice no two cases will ever be exactly alike; even if they were, they would still be numerically different just because they are two. Universalizability would be trivial and useless, therefore, if we could not rule out many of the inevitable differences as irrelevant.

In the first place, we want to rule out as irrelevant mere numerical as opposed to generic difference, the difference between one individual and another simply as such. It may be that what is wrong for you is right for me; but if it is, this can only be because there is some qualitative difference, some difference of kind, between you and me or between your situation and mine which can be held to be, in the actual context, morally relevant. What is wrong for you cannot be right for me merely because I am I and you are you, or because I am John Mackie and you are, say, Richard Roe.

Can we say that to be universalizable in this sense moral judgements must not contain proper names or indexical terms like 'I' and 'here'? This would not be accurate. A judgement may be universalizable, indeed already universalized, if it contains proper names used as variables: 'If John Doe has contracted with Richard Roe ... then John Doe ought to ...' Words like 'I' and 'you' can be harmlessly used as variables in much the same way: 'What's right for you is right for me.' A judgement containing a proper name or indexical term used not as a variable but as a constant (as the name of an actual person, or referring to the present speaker) will not yet be universalized; but it is universalizable if its proponent is willing to replace such singular terms with some general descriptions of persons, their relations, situations, and so on, and hence to assert the corresponding singular judgement with respect to any other individual case which satisfies that general description.

This kind of universalizability rules out one variety of egoism. It would also rule out a sort of inverted egoism adopted by some ascetics: 'I cannot allow myself such indulgences, but I do not condemn them in others.' But this kind of universalizability does not rule out the variety of egoism which says that everyone should seek (exclusively, or primarily) his own happiness. Similarly it rules out the kind of patriotism which demands that the interests of some one country should be supreme, or which says that it is right to serve, say, Ireland by methods which would be wrong if used to serve, say, France – unless, of course, this can be justified by pointing to sufficient relevant qualitative differences between Ireland and France, or between the situations in which they are placed – but it does not rule out the kind of patriotism which says that it is right for everyone to promote the interests of his own country, nor indeed the inverted patriotism which requires that everyone should love every country but his own. And in general this kind of universalizability does not rule out any variety of what has been called self-referential altruism – such maxims as 'Everyone should look after the welfare of his own children' (or 'his own relatives', or 'his friends', or 'those who have helped him', and so on).

Maxims which pass this test, but which are subject to no other constraints, can count as the products of a first stage of universalization. Let us consider the suggestion that any such maxim is a moral judgement, and that any coherent system of such maxims is a morality. On this view there are no other *a priori* limits to what differences can count as morally relevant. Of course every specific maxim will have implicit in it decisions about what generic differences are and are not morally relevant in whatever the particular context may be; but these decisions are not themselves determined or controlled by this first stage of universalization. Whatever differences of kind between persons and situations any particular moral thinker sincerely takes to be relevant are so for him. 'Sincerely takes to be relevant' is, however, intended to exclude the use of generic features as a mere cover for numerical differences, a device for surreptitiously reintroducing the essential reference to individuals which this first stage of universalization is meant to exclude. If an Italian patriot propounds the maxim that the interests of all boot-shaped countries should be specially favoured, we shall not accept this as universalized if it is a mere dodge for not using the proper name 'Italy'. But if he sincerely thinks that being boot-shaped is in itself a ground of merit – and patriots often refer with enthusiasm to almost equally trivial geographical and climatic features – and he is prepared to demand similar favours for, say, a reunited Korea, then his maxim passes this test.

The suggestion is that any sincerely universalized or universalizable prescription, which its proponent is ready to apply equally to himself and to others, and to go on applying in interpersonal situations when the roles are reversed, is a moral judgement. On this view there are only formal, but no material, constraints on what can count as moral. The form, universal prescriptivity, is determined by the logic of moral terms, but the content is entirely a matter for decision by the person – or of

85

course it may be a group of persons – who makes the moral judgements or subscribes to and adopts the moral system.

I do not believe that such a purely formal account would provide a correct analysis of what we ordinarily mean by 'morality' or 'moral judgement'. On the other hand, we can quickly dispose of one popular objection to this view. It is sometimes thought that if we say that any genuinely universalizable prescription can be moral, we thereby commit ourselves to endorsing all the maxims that would pass this test, or at least put ourselves in a position where we cannot condemn any of them, but must remain neutral between them all. But this appears to follow only if we confuse the use of 'moral' as a descriptive term, to mark off this whole kind of thinking, with its use to mean 'morally good' or 'morally right' or 'morally acceptable'. These are quite different. It is possible to recognize something as a morality, and to record this in a second order descriptive statement, and yet without any inconsistency to disagree radically with it and to condemn it in one's own first order judgements.

It has been argued (by Hare) that it is because moral terms like 'good' have both prescriptive and descriptive meaning that moral judgements are universalizable. But this is misleading. As I have argued in Chapter 2, the descriptions that one can infer from some application of the term 'good' – functional, egocentric, or whatever it may be – are no part of the meaning of 'good'. Even if we waived this point and, noting the description which could be inferred from the use of, say, 'a good man' by a group of speakers with some clearly defined moral views – for instance, puritans – called this the descriptive meaning of 'good' in this context for this group, even then it would be more correct to say that it is because the moral judgements of these speakers are universalizable, because they give moral commendation to men in some consistent way, that 'good' has for them this descriptive meaning, than to say that 'good' must have descriptive as well as prescriptive meaning, and that that is why the judgements are universalizable.

What is more, the kind of universalizability we are discussing, with its denial of moral relevance to proper names and purely numerical differences, would not be ensured by a combination of prescriptive and descriptive meaning, since the latter might itself involve reference to individuals as such. 'Francophile' is a word with a clear descriptive meaning; but if some group of speakers used 'good' of men in such a way that it could be said – waiving the above-mentioned objection – to have 'Francophile' as part of its descriptive meaning (in the way in which as used by puritans it might be said to have 'sober' as part of its descriptive meaning), then this group's judgements about men being good would not be universalizable in the sense with which we are now concerned: they would contain an essential, uneliminable, reference to the individual nation, France. The same would be true of the moral judgements of any group which included in its descriptive meaning of moral terms (in the sense indicated) some relation to the historical individual Jesus of Nazareth.

There is an associated but more important question: is the thesis of universalizability itself a logical thesis (as Hare also maintains) or a substantive moral principle? For the reasons just given, we cannot infer that it is a logical thesis from the suggestion that it is a consequence of the joint possession by moral terms of descriptive and prescriptive meaning. But it could be argued that this first kind of universalizability is a logical requirement for the distinctively moral use of 'good', 'ought', and similar words, that it is part of their logic that moral statements can be backed up by reasons in which proper names and indexical terms, as constants, play no essential part. Even this is dubious, since we can understand as moral the view of the ascetic that something that he does not condemn in others would be wrong for him, even though he does not claim that there is any relevant qualitative difference between himself and others. This view is more readily recognizable as moral than the corresponding form of egoism: morality, it seems, forbids one to demand more from others than from oneself, but not vice versa. If so, even this first kind of universalizability is not strictly speaking a logical requirement. However, this will be discussed again in Chapter 7. For the present we can say that even if the logical thesis for this first kind of universalizability is correct, it is so as part of a special logic of moral uses of these words: it is obviously not a part of general logic, nor is it even a consequence of the general meanings of words like 'good' and 'ought'. And if so, then it will be a substantive practical thesis that one should, in the thinking that guides one's choices of action, make a vital use of terms and concepts that have this special logic. This practical thesis is, no doubt, neutral as between all 'moralities', that is, as between all the action-guiding systems that are allowed, by this meaning of 'moral' and 'morality', to count as moralities. But it is not neutral as between all these 'moralities' on the one hand and other action-guiding systems on the other, for example one that includes a proper-name patriotism or a proper-name religion, or the extreme egoism that demands that everyone else should give way to me.

This substantive practical thesis is well formulated by Hobbes: 'That a man ... be contented with so much liberty against other men, as he would allow other men against himself.' Hobbes equates this with the Golden Rule of the New Testament, which he gives in the form 'Whatsoever you require that others should do to you, that do ye to them,' and with what he calls 'the law of all men', '*Quod tibi fieri non vis, alteri ne feceris*' – that is, 'Do not do to another what you don't want done to you.' But these are progressively less accurate formulations than the first. The principle that we need to isolate here is that of the universalizability of requirements by which the conduct of various agents is controlled, with purely numerical differences and proper-name constants being treated as irrelevant.

Hence, even if the universalizability (in this sense) of moral judgements is a logical thesis, the principle that actions are to be guided by judgements which pass this test, which conform to this special logic, is a substantive practical principle. It is a demand for a certain sort of fairness.

This is, however, only a limited sort of fairness, and still leaves plenty of room for unfairness of other kinds. Two of these are particularly important.

First, since only purely numerical differences have been declared irrelevant, and no generic, qualitative, differences have been ruled irrelevant in principle, our so far merely formal constraints allow a moral system to discriminate between people for reasons that we would in practice judge to be unfair, either generally or in some particular context. It is unfair in almost all circumstances to discriminate between people on grounds of colour; it is unfair to discriminate in the provision of educational opportunities on grounds of sex; it is unfair to discriminate in the allocation of council houses on grounds of religious affiliation; but none of these is excluded by our first stage of universalizability.

This kind of unfairness is, of course, most likely to result when people adopt universally prescriptive principles which differentially favour all those who are in some respect like themselves. The favoured likenesses need not be these obvious ones of race, colour, sex, and religion, but may be in kinds of strength or skill. The man who knows himself to be strong and therefore able to compete successfully may be inclined to endorse moral rules that allow tough competition. One who is a good swordsman and an accurate shot may think that the institution of duelling is a good way of safeguarding dignity and reputation, whereas one who has more skill with words than with weapons may think that this task should be assigned to courts of law.

The second kind of unfairness is highlighted by Bernard Shaw's comment on the Golden Rule: 'Do not do unto others as you would have that they should do unto you. Their tastes may not be the same.' In framing moral judgements that exclude all proper-name and indexical constants, we can still take account of our own distinctive preferences and values and ideals. The teetotaller may be happy to prescribe universally that no-one should drink wine or beer, the philistine that old houses should never be allowed to prevent the construction of motorways or divert their course, the sturdy individualist that social

89

services should be kept to a minimum. We may see little or no moral force in the protection of freedoms whose exercise we would not enjoy, and we may be more ready to regard as vices ways of behaving in which we do not want – or at any rate do not consciously want – to engage. But bias of such sorts as these may well be regarded as unfair.

Unfairnesses of both these kinds escape what I have called the first stage of universalization. But it may seem that they could be checked by further stages of the same procedure, by suitably extended interpretations of the principles of universalizability, that is, of the logical thesis and of the substantive practical thesis that can be associated with it.

2. The second stage of universalization: putting oneself in the other person's place

One such extension is this. To decide whether some maxim that you are inclined to assert is really universalizable, imagine yourself in the other man's place and ask whether you can then accept it as a directive guiding the behaviour of others towards you. Having a large income, no dependants, and an iron constitution, you are inclined to judge that everyone should pay in full, from his own pocket, for any medical attention he requires; but imagine that you are on a modest weekly wage and have developed a chronic kidney complaint, or have a child with a hole in the heart: do you still endorse the proposed rule?

In this second stage of universalization, we look for prescriptive maxims that we are prepared not only to apply to all persons (groups of persons, nations, and so on) alike as things are, but also to go on applying no matter how individuals change their mental and physical qualities and resources and social status. And we must allow not only for changes which may, as a matter of practical, causal, possibility come about, starting from where we are, but also for differences of condition and inversions of role that could not possibly occur, and which it may take a considerable effort even to imagine.

This extended procedure seems to be a powerful weapon against the residual unfairness that the first stage failed to check. But it might be argued that it is two-edged. Can we not challenge someone who thinks that there ought to be an efficient national health service by getting him to imagine that he has an iron constitution, no dependants, a large income, and besides no way of dodging the taxation that would be needed to pay for the health service? Would this show (if he then wavers) that the judgement he now makes in favour of such a service is not really a moral one, not fully universalizable, but merely a reflection of his own contingent special interests? If so, would any maxims at all survive so severe a test?

However, this difficulty can be met. Suppose that we do not merely test and reject proposed maxims, but rather go out and look for maxims that will stand up to this second sort of universalization. Let us think of ourselves as committed, for instance, to finding some principles which will bear upon the provision of medical services and which we could endorse whether we were hard up or wealthy, fit or ailing. (We need not ask here why we should be so committed. There is indeed a good reason, which will be brought out in Chapter 5. But at present we are concerned only with the character and implications of different kinds of universalization.) This might compel us to move to more general principles, to find ones which would bear upon many other analogous things as well as upon the provision of medical services. The man who has less need of a health service may well have more need of a police force; these are two different ways in which public resources may be deployed to give individuals some measure of protection against the risk of harm. By thinking along these lines we may be able to formulate a principle which would justify some public provision of both sorts of protection, and probably others as well, which we can imaginatively but honestly endorse from different points of view.

This second stage of universalization copes well with the first of the two sorts of unfairness noted at the end of Section 1. Differences can be fairly regarded as relevant if they look relevant from whichever side you consider them. I admit that principles which are fair in this respect may not be easy to find; indeed I see no guarantee that they can be found at all. But neither is there any *a priori* proof that they cannot be found, and if they can be found they will plainly be fairer than judgements that stand up to the first stage of universalization but not to the second.

The question about the status of the principle of universalizability itself can still be answered as before. It would be a logical thesis that moral terms have meanings such that judgements employing them are universalizable in this second way as well as the first; but it would be a substantive practical principle that actions are to be guided by maxims which pass this test. It is, indeed, even more doubtful this time whether the logical thesis is true: I shall discuss this after examining a possible third stage of universalization. In any case the logical thesis has little bearing on the substantive practical principle: we could adopt, or reject, the latter whether the former was true or false.

In this second stage of universalization, one imagines oneself in the other person's place, but still with one's own present tastes, preferences, ideals, and values. The judgements that result will not, then, take unfair account of one's own special abilities or resources or social position, or of one's interests in so far as they are determined by these. But they may still take unfair account of one's distinctive tastes, ideals, and so on. This second stage does not yet cope with the second kind of unfairness mentioned at the end of Section 1. To exclude this, a third stage of universalization is required.

3. The third stage of universalization: taking account of different tastes and rival ideals

Obviously, the third stage that is called for involves putting oneself even more thoroughly into the other person's place, so that one takes on his desires, tastes, preferences, ideals, and values as well as his other qualities and abilities and external situation. But then it hardly makes sense to talk of putting *one-self* in his place; hardly any of oneself is retained. Rather, what one is trying to do is to look at things both from one's own and from the other person's point of view at once, and to discover action-guiding principles (of course in first stage universalized or universalizable form) which one can accept from both points of view. Or rather, since there is not just one other person but indefinitely many, from all actual points of view, a point of view being now defined not just by the mental and physical qualities someone has and the situation in which he is placed, but also by his tastes, ideals, and so on.

But now, even more than at the second stage, it is doubtful whether any principles will pass so severe a test. Of course there are some basic desires that almost everyone has, but besides these there are radically divergent preferences and values, and it is from these that obstinate moral disagreements arise.

We must lower our sights a little, and look not for principles which can be wholeheartedly endorsed from every point of view, but for ones which represent an acceptable compromise between the different actual points of view. We shall see later that there are reasons why we need a compromise, and hence why something that does not fully satisfy one's initial demands may be acceptable.

In this third stage we are taking some account of all actual desires, tastes, preferences, ideals, and values, including ones which are radically different from and hostile to our own, and consequently taking some account of all the actual interests that anyone has, including those that arise from his having preferences and values that we do not share. If we press this to the point of trying to take not just some account but equal account of all actual interests, we shall be adopting the equivalent of some kind of utilitarian view. Some kind, because there are indeterminacies within utilitarianism, which may be mirrored in the present approach. How are we to weigh or measure the interests of which we are proposing to take equal account? What do we do about the interests of future generations – or, since present choices may variably determine what people there will be in the future, how do we weigh the interests of merely possible people? Such questions will be considered further, but not resolved, in Chapter 6, when we examine utilitarianism as a first order moral system. What matters for the present is just that such indeterminacies will be reflected in the universalization that corresponds to utilitarianism, so that even with the third stage included it will not yield completely definite answers to practical questions.

What I am calling this third stage is discussed by Hare in relation to a debate between a liberal and Nazis of two kinds. Hare's liberal is the man who goes in for this third stage of universalization: he respects the ideals of others and gives some weight to them, though it is not clear whether he could be said to give equal weight to all ideals. The thorough-going Nazi, the hard-core fanatic, is the man who will sincerely prescribe that he himself and his family should be exterminated if it turns out that they are Jews by descent. He is prepared to follow the second as well as the first stage of universalization, but not the third: his attachment to the Aryan ideal is so strong and inflexible that he will give no weight to interests which are incompatible with that ideal, and which would be valued in the light of other ideals which he neither shares nor respects. The ordinary run of Nazis, as distinct from these fanatics, are merely thoughtless and insensitive: they have failed to carry out the second stage of universalization, for example, to consider seriously what it would be like if they themselves were Jews; but, if they did this, their adherence to Nazism would be undermined.

The position of Hare's liberal reveals one of the above-mentioned indeterminacies. Can the liberal, if he is to give equal weight to all ideals, have any ideals of his own other than this liberal one itself – the second order ideal of weighting all first order ideals equally? If he has some first order ideals, we must distinguish him in his role as a participant in this first order conflict from him in his role as a third stage universalizer, giving equal weight to all actually-held ideals, and looking upon himself *qua* participant as one among many. The man as a whole, in both these roles together, does not give equal weight to all actually-held ideals; but he does still take some account of them all and does not, like the fanatic, rule out of consideration ideals other than his own and the interests associated with them.

The basic idea in John Rawls's theory of 'justice as fairness' is another way of achieving much the same as is achieved by our second and third stages of universalization: we can ask what principles for regulating the practices of a society and for judging complaints against them we, as rational egoists, would choose for a society of which we were to be members, if the choice had to be made in ignorance of our individual mental and physical qualities and of the particular place we would occupy in the society, and also of our values and tastes and ideals – in other words, if we had to commit ourselves in advance, from behind a 'veil of ignorance', to principles which would then be applied however our actual situation turned out. But the two approaches are not quite equivalent. Suppose that one of a pair of alternative sets of principles was likely to make most members of the society much happier than they would otherwise be, but at the price of making a few very unhappy, but not because either party deserved in any way this differential prosperity. As rational egoists, choosing from behind the veil of ignorance, we might well choose this set of principles: the odds would be in favour of our being among the happy majority and while there would be some risk of undeserved misery, it might be a risk that it was reasonable to take. But this set of principles would not be one that we could endorse, even as an acceptable compromise, no matter what our actual condition was. Indeed, we would not call them fair – though of course it could be argued that if someone took such a gamble, and lost, he could fairly be held to his bargain: it would not then be fair for him to complain of the unfairness. Principles which it is egoistically rational to choose even from behind the equalizing veil of ignorance need not be intrinsically fair in their operation. The notion of choosing principles from behind a veil of ignorance, picturesque and striking though it is, is therefore a less adequate guarantee of fairness than that of

95

seeking a compromise which is acceptable as such from every point of view. Rawls, in fact, tries to avoid this consequence of his approach and to make it yield rather the results of the third stage of universalization; but whether he can do so is open to dispute. A similar criticism can be made of any utilitarianism which takes only a quantitative account of interests or of happiness, and so allows the happiness of some to outweigh the undeserved misery of others.

With regard to each of the three stages of universalization we can distinguish a logical thesis from a substantive practical thesis. But the logical thesis for this third stage would be plainly false. Hare himself says that we are not *constrained*, under penalty of being said not to be thinking morally or evaluatively, to give equal weight to all ideals, or even to respect ideals that we do not share. Universalizability of this third sort is no part of the meaning of moral terms or of the special logic of moral thought. The logical thesis for the second stage is more controversial. On the one hand popular versions of this second stage of universalization are among the generally used and generally influential forms of moral argument: 'How would you like it if you were a Jew?' 'Would you take the same view if you were not so disgustingly healthy?' 'It's all very well for you to say that, but . . .' On the other hand it does not seem that moral terms are being misused if they are employed in judgements which are adhered to only because such challenges are brushed aside. Perhaps we should say that this second stage is a traditionally recognized and persuasive pattern of moral reasoning, but not one which has yet been clearly incorporated in the meanings of moral terms. Nevertheless, this second sort of universalizability is linked with the fact, stressed in Chapter 1, that moral judgements commonly include a claim to objectivity. The claim that some difference is objectively morally relevant in a certain context is not easy to reconcile with the admission that, while it appears relevant from one interested point of view, it does not appear relevant from the point of view of someone whose situation and qualities are different. By contrast, the claim to objectivity has no tendency to support the third stage of universalization. Quite the reverse. It is all too easy to believe that the objective validity of one's own ideals provides an overwhelmingly strong reason for taking no account at all of ideals that conflict with them, or of interests associated with the holding of such rival ideals.

It is, therefore, misleading to say, as Hare does, that 'it is characteristic of moral thought in general to accord equal weight to the interests of all persons'. At most, only the first stage of universalization could be said to be characteristic of moral thought in general, and it does not have this consequence. Even if we concede that the second stage too is characteristic of moral thought in general, this gives equal weight not to the actual interests of all persons, determined as they are by the various tastes, ideals, and so on that these persons in fact have, but only to the interests that they would have if they shared the tastes, ideals, and so on of the particular moral thinker in question. Even the third stage only approximates to the giving of equal weight to all real interests; but it is plainly not characteristic of moral thought in general.

4. Subjective elements in universalization

There are, then, different kinds or stages of universalization. In each of them a moral judgement is taken to carry with it a similar view about any relevantly similar case. But the first stage rules out as irrelevant only the numerical difference between one individual and another; the second stage rules out generic differences which one is tempted to regard as morally relevant only because of one's particular mental or physical qualities or condition, one's social status or resources; the third stage rules out differences which answer to particular tastes, preferences, values, and ideals. It is at most the first stage, the ruling out of purely numerical differences as morally irrelevant, that is built into the meaning of moral language: the corresponding logical thesis about the second stage is more controversial, while that about the third stage would be plainly false. On the other hand, it is only if we accept all three stages that we are committed to a 'liberal' view or to any approximation to utilitarianism. And at every stage what I have called the substantive practical principle is distinct from and independent of the corresponding logical thesis, whether the latter would be true or false.

Suppose that a logical thesis is true, say that of our first stage. Then one cannot express, in moral judgements in which the key terms are used with their full standard moral force, prescriptions or guides to action, bearing both upon oneself and upon others, which do not display a willingness to 'be contented with so much liberty against other men, as he would allow other men against himself'. Thinking in standard moral terms, seriously prescriptive and genuinely universalizable in this first way, carries such a willingness with it. But the (supposed) truth of this logical thesis does not compel anyone to think this way, even under penalty of illogicality. For one can with complete consistency refrain from using moral language at all, or again one can use moral terms with only part and not the whole of their standard moral force. The fact that the word 'atom', as used in nineteenth-century physics, had as part of its meaning 'indivisible particle of matter' did not in itself, even in the nineteenth century, compel anyone to believe that there are indivisible material particles. One could either refrain from using the term 'atom' in affirmative statements or, as physicists have subsequently done, use the term with other parts of its meaning only, dropping the requirement of indivisibility. A logical or semantic truth is no real constraint on belief; nor, analogously, can one be any real constraint upon action or prescription or evaluation or choice of policy.

We can apply here the notion, used in Chapter 3, of speaking within an institution. We may take morality itself, or the moral use of language, as the institution in question. Speaking within it, one logically cannot (on our supposition) endorse a prescription that would resist first stage universalization. But this does not give universalizable maxims any intrinsic, objective, superiority to non-universalizable ones. The institution of morality itself is not thus given any intrinsic authority, nor is the principle that we should use only universalizable maxims to guide conduct thus enabled to command rational assent. Bringing out the universalizability requirement within the institution of morality is analogous to Searle's deriving of an 'ought' from an 'is' within the institution of promising, and is no more authoritatively prescriptive than that.

It is sometimes suggested that it belongs to the meaning of moral judgements that they are final, overriding guides to choices of action; if it also is part of their meaning that they are universalizable at least in our first way, these two together seem to make it logically incumbent on anyone to use universalizable maxims as overriding guides to conduct. But if this holds at all, it holds only within the institution of morality. No-one is thereby constrained to adhere to that institution or to let it control his practical thinking. Such double definition is too easy a way of apparently settling substantive questions in any field whatever. It is a basic principle of general logic that you cannot get something for nothing, and this cannot be overruled or evaded by any special logic of morality.

The truth of one of our logical theses, then, does not in any way compel acceptance of the corresponding substantive practical principle. But equally if the logical thesis for some stage of universalization is false, as that of the third stage seems to be, someone may still coherently let his conduct be guided (only) by maxims which are universalizable in this way. Whatever the truth-value of the logical thesis, an independent decision for or against the corresponding substantive practical principle is still required. It is not only that the singular prescriptions which enter into an argument in terms of universalization represent decisions: the same is true of the general, formal, practical principle by whose application they are universalized or extended to relevantly similar cases.

The universalizability of moral judgements, then, does not impose any rational constraint on choices of action or defensible patterns of behaviour. And it would be little more than a verbal point that an action-guiding system of thought which

99

violates first stage universalizability, at least, cannot count as a morality, that if 'ought' and similar words are used in such a system, it will not be in a fully moral sense. Universalizability, then, poses no threat, not even a threat of limitation, to the moral scepticism or subjectivism advanced in Chapter 1.

This may be seen more clearly if we look at an example of the reasoning by which moral judgements are checked or controlled at each stage of universalization and note the various points at which subjective elements enter, at which there is an appeal to something that has the logical status of a decision.

Driving along a little-frequented road you pass another car with its wheels stuck in the ditch: the driver waves, apparently asking you either to help him yourself or to take a message to summon help. It is a nuisance, but you think you ought to stop. You have done a quick bit of first stage universalization, and have decided that you cannot endorse the maxim that no-one has a duty to stop and help someone else in circumstances like these. (Of course you might have reached this conclusion in some quite different way, but we are concerned with it only as a possible product of this sort of universalization.) One plainly subjective factor in your reasoning is your unwillingness to subscribe to the singular prescription 'Drive on' in the possible case when you are in the ditch and someone else is passing. If you were too proud ever to ask for help or were sure that you would never be such a fool as to get stuck you would not have reasoned in this way: the maxim that no-one is required to stop and help in these circumstances is one that you could then prescribe universally. But another subjective element is your resort to first stage universalization itself, your readiness to let your view about what you are to do be tested in this way. Even if this is implicit in your even asking yourself what you *ought* to do, it is a decision none the less. It is not the logic of 'ought' alone that is operating here, but your acceptance of the corresponding substantive practical principle. You are, as Hare has stressed, logically free to opt out of the moral language game; it is, then, logically speaking, a decision if you opt into it, even if, historically speaking, you have grown up in it and have never thought of thinking otherwise.

But suppose that this first stage of universalization fails to check you. Confident that you will never be such a fool as to get stuck in a ditch you are happy to endorse the maxim that anyone who passes someone who is stuck may drive on. But then you progress to the second stage: you put yourself in the other man's gumboots. If, *per impossibile*, you were ever stuck you would feel that you ought to be helped. Trying to find a universalizable maxim, relevant to this situation, to which you could subscribe without relying on your well-above-average common sense and practical skill, you find that it has to be not 'Drive on' but 'Stop and help'. At this stage your moral conclusion no longer rests on any desire that *you* should at some time be helped: that question does not arise. So far as desires that are contingent upon your actual qualities and expectable situations are concerned, you could endorse the universalized maxim that one may drive on. But your acceptance of the opposite conclusion still rests on some more basic preferences, which you would have even if you were more of a fool than you are but which you still have now. These constitute one subjective element in the reasoning towards the second stage conclusion; but another subjective element is your adopting of second stage universalization itself (as well as the first stage). Though this is a traditionally influential and widely accepted style of moral reasoning, it is, logically speaking, by a decision that you adopt the substantive practical principle of letting it control your actions.

But this second stage could still fail to check you. You are too proud ever to seek help in such a difficulty; you think it so degrading that you hope that even if, overcome by a momentary weakness, you yourself were to ask someone for help, he would ignore your appeal; and you feel that the kind of man who would ask for help is too contemptible to deserve consideration.

But, perhaps, you progress to the third stage. You reflect that not everyone shares your ideal of self-reliance. There are people

101

who don't mind being dependent on others, who actually subscribe to the servile principles of mutual aid. No doubt the man whose car is in the ditch and who is now appealing to you is one of these. You don't agree with his system of values, but you are willing to respect it, and to give some weight to interests which can arise only on his value-assumptions, not on yours. Trying to frame maxims which can be endorsed from all points of view, or which represent a compromise between radically different points of view, which would commend themselves to an impartially sympathetic spectator, you decide that after all you ought to stop and help. You believe in self-reliance, but you are not a hard-core fanatic about it. Your moral conclusion, thus arrived at, now owes much less to any of your subjective preferences. But as they have dropped out of the picture they have been replaced by another subjective element, your endorsement of the substantive practical principle of third stage universalization. This is not indeed any more subjective than your previous endorsement of the first and second stages, but it is more obviously subjective in that it is not incorporated, as they may be, into the meanings of moral terms or the traditionally accepted patterns of moral reasoning. It is not only logically possible to opt out of this third variety of moral language game; it is quite common and conventional for people with strong moral convictions to remain outside it, and it may well require a conscious decision to opt into it. Yet the logical status of the three substantive practical principles is the same.

Part II : The Content of Ethics

Chapter 5   The Object of Morality

1. Consequences of moral scepticism

I have argued in Chapter 1 that there are no objective values, and in Chapters 2, 3, and 4 that no substantive moral conclusions or serious constraints on moral views can be derived from either the meanings of moral terms or the logic of moral discourse. What tasks then remain for moral philosophy? One could study the moral views and beliefs of our own society or others, perhaps through time, taking as one's subject what is summed up in Westermarck's title, *The Origin and Development of the Moral Ideas*. But this perhaps belongs rather to anthropology or sociology. More congenial to philosophers and more amenable to philosophical methods would be the attempt systematically to describe our own moral consciousness or some part of it, such as our 'sense of justice', to find some set of principles which were themselves fairly acceptable to us and with which, along with their practical consequences and applications, our 'intuitive' (but really subjective) detailed moral judgements would be in 'reflective equilibrium'. That is, we might start both with some *prima facie* acceptable general principles, and with the mass of *prima facie* acceptable detailed moral judgements, and where they do not fully agree adjust either or both until the most satisfactory coherent compromise is reached. It is this that John Rawls calls 'a theory of justice' (in the book with that title). This is a legitimate kind of inquiry, but it must not be confused with the superficially similar but in purpose fundamentally different attempt of thinkers like Sidgwick to advance by way of our various 'intuitions' to an objective moral truth, a science of conduct. 'Our sense of justice,' whether it is just yours and mine, or that of some much larger group, has no authority over those who dissent from its recommendations or even over us if we are inclined to change our minds. But if there is no objective moral truth to be discovered, is there nothing left to do but to describe our sense of justice?

At least we can look at the matter in another way. Morality is not to be discovered but to be made: we have to decide what moral views to adopt, what moral stands to take. No doubt the conclusions we reach will reflect and reveal our sense of justice, our moral consciousness – that is, our moral consciousness as it is at the end of the discussion, not necessarily as it was at the beginning. But that is not the object of the exercise: the object is rather to decide what to do, what to support and what to condemn, what principles of conduct to accept and foster as guiding or controlling our own choices and perhaps those of other people as well.

However, even if we are looking at morality in this way, there is a distinction to be drawn. A morality in the broad sense would be a general, all-inclusive theory of conduct: the morality to which someone subscribed would be whatever body of principles he allowed ultimately to guide or determine his choices of action. In the narrow sense, a morality is a system of a particular sort of constraints on conduct – ones whose central task is to protect the interests of persons other than the agent and which present themselves to an agent as checks on his natural inclinations or spontaneous tendencies to act. In this narrow sense, moral considerations would be considerations from some limited range, and would not necessarily include everything that a man allowed to determine what he did. In this second sense, someone could say quite deliberately, 'I admit that morality requires that I should do such-and-such, but I don't intend to: for me other considerations here overrule the moral ones.' And he need not be putting 'morality' here into either visible or invisible inverted commas. It may well be his morality of which he is speaking, the moral constraints that he himself in general accepts and endorses as such. But because in this narrow sense moral considerations are only some considerations among others which he also endorses, not an inclusive system which incorporates and, where necessary, weighs against one another all the reasons that this man accepts as reasons for or against doing anything, it is possible that in some particular situation moral considerations should be overruled. But no-one could, in his choices of action, deliberately overrule what was his morality in the broad sense, though he might diverge from it through 'weakness of will'.

There is no point in discussing whether the broad or the narrow sense of 'morality' is the more correct. Both are used, and both have important roots and connections in our thought. But it is essential not to confuse them, not to think that what we recognize as (in the narrow sense) peculiarly moral considerations are (jumping to the broad sense) necessarily finally authoritative with regard to our actions. We should not suppose that any general system of principles of choice which we can on reflection accept must be constructed wholly of materials that we would call moral in the narrow sense.

However, I am certain that something of the kind I have so far indicated (only roughly) as morality in the narrow sense will be an important part of any reflectively acceptable morality in the broad sense. I want therefore to look at it more closely, to see what gives it its point and indeed accounts for the tendency it has to usurp both the name and the function of a general theory of conduct.

2. A device for counteracting limited sympathies

It is of morality in the narrow sense that G.J. Warnock is think-ing when he argues that we shall understand it better if we ask what it is for, what is the object of morality. Morality is a species of evaluation, a kind of appraisal of human conduct; this must, he suggests, have some distinctive point, there must be something that is supposed to bring about. Warnock explains this in terms of certain general and persistent features of the human predicament, which is 'inherently such that things are liable to go very badly' – badly in the natural, non-moral

THE CONTENT OF ETHICS

sense that human wants, needs, and interests are likely to be frustrated in large measure. Among the factors which contribute to make things go badly in the natural course of events are various limitations – limited resources, limited information, limited intelligence, limited rationality, but above all limited sympathies. Men sometimes display active malevolence to one another, but even apart from that they are almost always concerned more with their selfish ends than with helping one another. The function of morality is primarily to counteract this limitation of men's sympathies. We can decide what the content of morality must be by inquiring how this can best be done.

This is a useful approach, which has been stressed by a number of thinkers. There is a colourful version of it in Plato's dialogue *Protagoras,* where the sophist Protagoras incorporates it in an admittedly mythical account of the creation and early history of the human race. At their creation men were, as compared with the other animals, rather meagrely equipped. They had less in the way of claws and strength and speed and fur or scales, and so on, to enable them to find food and to protect them from enemies and the elements. To make up for this, they were given the various mechanical arts and the use of fire, so that they could make houses and clothes and tools and weapons and grow food for themselves. But even so they were in a pretty bad way, because when they lived scattered about in small groups they were no match for the wild beasts, and when they came together they ill-treated one another, because they lacked 'the political art'. Finally Zeus took pity on them and sent Hermes to give men *aidōs* (which we can perhaps translate as 'a moral sense') and *dikē* (law and justice) to be the ordering principles of cities and the bonds of friendship. Detached from its mythological framework, Protagoras's thesis is plain: a moral sense, law, and justice are needed to enable men to live together in communities large enough to compete successfully with the wild beasts.

Hobbes paints a similar picture, except that the beasts are forgotten and the danger is now the harm that men can do to

108

one another. Competition and mutual distrust make the natural state of man a war of all against all. But Hobbes is far more explicit than Protagoras about the solution. Fear of death and the desire both to preserve themselves and, by industry, to acquire the means to a decent life and to be secure in their possession of them give men a reason to seek peace. But no-one can stop fighting against others unless they will at the same time stop fighting against him; so what is needed for peace is an agreement to limit competitive claims. But even if such an agreement is made, no-one has a sufficient motive to abide by it unless he has some assurance that the other parties to it will do so too. Hence the only kind of agreement that will achieve this purpose of establishing peace (and thereby making life more secure and more comfortable) is one which sets up a mechanism for enforcing that agreement itself. This, Hobbes thinks, must be a political sovereign, a man (or body of men) that is not as such a party to the agreement but whom (or which) all the parties agree with one another that they will obey. The moral principles that Hobbes offers as the necessary solution to the problem of natural competition and distrust are stated as a series of 'laws of nature': to seek peace if there is hope of attaining it; to accept mutual limitation of competitive claims; to keep agreements; to show gratitude in return for benefits; to accommodate oneself to others; to pardon past offences of those who repent and give assurance of not repeating their offences; to refrain from backward-looking, retributive, punishment; and eight further 'laws' of the same general sort. But these alone are not sufficient. The essential device is a form of agreement which provides for its own enforcement. Each of the parties has a motive for supporting the authority who will himself have the job of punishing breaches of the agreement (and will himself have a motive for doing so). Consequently each party will have a double reason for fulfilling his side of the bargain: the fear of punishment for breaking it, and the expectation of benefits from keeping it, because the fulfilment by the other parties of their sides of the bargain is fairly well assured by the same motives. Though Hobbes speaks of men in the state of nature coming together and, by such a social contract, setting up a civil society and a sovereign power, we can regard this original historical contract as being no less mythical than the intervention of Zeus and Hermes in Protagoras's story, and yet accept or at least consider seriously all that is essential in Hobbes's account. It could be maintained that such a pattern of contract is implicit in human societies, and necessarily so, that the decay of the relations and motivations to which Hobbes draws attention would be liable to lead to unrestrained conflicts and radical insecurity of life.

Hume is another in this tradition: 'It is,' he says, 'only from the selfishness and confined generosity of man, along with the scanty provision nature has made for his wants, that justice derives its origin.' Justice (by which he means particularly respect for property and for rules governing its possession and transfer, honesty, and the keeping of promises) is an artifical virtue; it is not something of which we would have any natural, instinctive, tendency to approve, but a device which is beneficial because of certain contingent features of the human condition. If men had been overwhelmingly benevolent, if each had aimed only at the happiness of all, if everyone had loved his neighbour as himself, there would have been no need for the rules that constitute justice. Nor would there have been any need for them if nature had supplied abundantly, and without any effort on our part, all that we could want, if food and warmth had been as inexhaustibly available as, until recently, air and water seemed to be. The making and keeping of promises and bargains is a device that makes possible mutually beneficial cooperation between people whose motives are mainly selfish, where the contributions of the different parties need to be made at different times. 'Your corn is ripe today; mine will be so tomorrow. It is profitable for us both that I should labour with you today, and that you should aid me tomorrow. I have no kindness for you, and know you have as little for me. I will not, therefore, take any pains upon your account; and should I labour with you upon my own account, in expectation of a return, I know I should be disappointed, and that I should in vain depend upon your gratitude. Here, then, I leave you to labour alone: you treat me in the same manner. The seasons change; and both of us lose our harvests for want of mutual confidence and security.' The device of promising exists in order to overcome impasses of this sort. But, Hume insists, a single act of justice, considered on its own, may do more harm than good; 'it is only the concurrence of mankind, in a general scheme or system of action, which is advantageous'.

3. The form of the device

Protagoras, Hobbes, Hume, and Warnock are all at least broadly in agreement about the problem that morality is needed to solve: limited resources and limited sympathies together generate both competition leading to conflict and an absence of what would be mutually beneficial cooperation. But there are some differences in their sketches of the solution which are instructive and call for further discussion.

Hobbes speaks of laws of nature, that is, basic moral rules which are unchangeable because the essential outlines of the human predicament do not change. But, he argues, they are not unconditionally valid as rules of action. They 'bind to a desire they should take place: but ... to the putting them in act, not always'. One cannot afford to obey these rules unless one has some guarantee that others will do so too; but if one has such a guarantee, then one is obliged to obey them; for obeying them then gives one the best chance of preserving one's life. Consequently in Hobbes's view such rules, working merely as moral rules, are not enough. They must be supplemented by the political device of sovereignty. Only if each agent knows that these rules will be enforced, that violations of them by others to his detriment will be discouraged by an effective threat of punishment, will he have a good reason for obeying them himself. Hume also speaks of three fundamental laws of nature, 'that of the stability of possession, of its transference by consent, and of the performance of promises'. ' 'Tis,' he says, 'on the strict observance of those three laws that the peace and security of human society entirely depend ... Society is absolutely necessary for the well-being of men; and these are as necessary to the support of society.' He too sees the institution of government, magistrates, and their officers to enforce the laws as a necessary supplementary device, but he is either less clear-headed or less candid than Hobbes about the reason why it is necessary. Hume writes as if it were to everyone's long-term interest to obey the rules that make society and cooperation possible, and as if it were only the human weakness of preferring smaller immediate advantages to greater but more distant ones that needed to be counteracted by creating a special group of persons to whose immediate advantage it would be to enforce what would be for the long-term advantage of all. He does not point out, as Hobbes does, that though general conformity to these rules will benefit everyone, my unilateral conformity will be not even to my long-term advantage: however far-sighted and prudent men were, they would still need an enforcement device to give each man a selfish motive for obeying these moral rules. But Hume also raises the question 'Why [and how] we annex the idea of virtue to justice, and of vice to injustice,' which on his theory of virtue and vice means 'why and how we feel approval for just actions and disapproval for unjust ones even when they have no effect on our interests'; virtue and vice are objectifications of disinterested approval and disapproval. He suggests that the sorts of interested calculations already indicated will induce men to 'lay themselves under the constraint of such rules, as may render their commerce more safe and commodious'. But it is not such a simple matter for a group of selfish individuals to lay themselves under rules. He then suggests that it is sympathy, a natural tendency to share the feelings of those who are directly affected, that makes us extend what are initially interested approval and disapproval to cases remote from our interests. This natural tendency is further encouraged by 'the artifice of politicians', who, seeing that such moral sentiments are beneficial, deliberately foster them, and by private education, because parents, realizing that a man is 'the more useful, both to himself and others, the greater degree of probity and honour he is endowed with', inculcate these sentiments in their children.

Though these last points are correct, the explanation as a whole is inadequate. Both its foundations – men's interested laying of themselves under rules, and natural sympathy – are too weak. But Hume points out that conventions can grow up gradually as men repeatedly experience the advantages of conforming to them and the disadvantages of violating them. And we can develop this hint. For the reasons given, moral sentiments which 'annex the idea of virtue to justice' will enable social groups in which they take root to flourish. Consequently the ordinary evolutionary pressures, the differential survival of groups in which such sentiments are stronger, either as inherited psychological tendencies or as socially maintained traditions, will help to explain why such sentiments become strong and widespread. Since evolution by natural selection is the standard modern replacement for divine providence, we could arrive at this account by an almost mechanical reinterpretation of Protagoras's myth.

Thus filled out, Hume's solution adds something important to that of Hobbes. Though, as I have said, Hobbes's laws of nature can be taken as moral rules, the motive that binds (always) to 'a desire that they should take place' and (when there is an adequate enforcement device) to 'the putting them in act' remains a selfish one; Hobbes does not allow for the development of what we might call secondary instinct in favour of morality. But having seen what beneficial function morality performs we can well understand how there should be, as indeed there plainly are, such secondary instincts or persistent social traditions. If Hobbes's account is supplemented by the recognition of them, the social structure he describes becomes less like a house of cards, which stands up, indeed, but precariously, each part being supported by another which can do so only so long as it is in turn supported by something else.

Whereas both Hobbes and Hume speak of laws of nature, that is, of rules, Warnock argues that the morality whose task it

113

is to counteract limited sympathies cannot be a matter of rules, that is, of rigid or absolute requirements: in moral thinking we have to weigh reasons, not simply follow rules. Rather, Warnock argues, the central content of morality must be a set of moral virtues. If things are not to go so badly as they are inherently liable to do four sorts of things are required: knowledge, organization, coercion, and good dispositions. He concedes to Hobbes that coercion is needed, but he argues, I believe rightly, that it would not be sufficient without the good dispositions, and he gives these a certain priority. But among good dispositions he separates the non-moral virtues – industriousness, courage, and self-control – which merely counteract various kinds of human weakness, from the distinctively moral virtues – non-maleficence, fairness, beneficence, and non-deception. It is the latter that are the core of morality.

We can certainly take such moral virtues, a sub-class of the beneficial dispositions, as having the same sort of value and as open therefore to the same evolutionary sort of explanation as the moral sentiments. On the other hand there seems no good reason for excluding from morality such rules as those listed by Hobbes and Hume; we can postpone (until Chapter 7) the question whether we want any of them as absolutely rigid and inflexible rules. Warnock also understresses the part played by obligations. He treats the obligation to keep promises as a special case of the virtue of non-deception, but it is surely Hume's explanation of this that is more correct; promising is a device which enables people whose motives are mainly selfish to give one another reciprocal non-simultaneous assistance with consequential benefits to all, and in general enables one person to rely on future actions of another. Again, something analogous to Hume's explanation of the point of the institution of promising is needed to account for other, non-contractual, obligations which arise out of special relationships, like those of parents to children and children to parents. In fact, Protagoras was right in outline, though not explicit enough in detail, to sum up the morality with which the gods supplied men under the headings of *aidōs* and *dikē*; for *aidōs* could cover the moral

114

sentiments and dispositions and the respect for various obligations, while *dikē* could cover the more formal rules along with politico-legal devices for law enforcement and the making of positive law. Both of these are essential and complementary parts of the device of morality.

4. Game theory analysis

A more abstract analysis with models drawn from the theory of games may confirm the theses we have collected from these accounts. The natural starting point is what is known as the Prisoners' Dilemma; but its significance and its connections are brought out better by one of the other variants of the story. Two soldiers, Tom and Dan, are manning two nearby strongposts in an attempt to hold up an enemy advance. If both remain at their posts, they have a fairly good chance of holding off the enemy until relief arrives, and so of both surviving. If they both run away, the enemy will break through immediately, and the chance of either of them surviving is markedly less. But if one stays at his post while the other runs away, the one who runs will have an even better chance of survival than each will have if both remain, while the one who stays will have an even worse chance than each will have if they both run. Suppose that these facts are known to both men, and each calculates in a thoroughly rational way with a view simply to this own survival. Tom reasons: if Dan remains at his post, I shall have a better chance of surviving if I run than if I stay; but also if Dan runs away I shall have a better chance if I run than if I stay; so whatever Dan is going to do, I would be well advised to run. Since the situation is symmetrical, Dan's reasoning is exactly similar. So both will run. And yet they would each have had a better chance of survival, that is, of achieving the very end they are, by hypothesis, aiming at, if both had remained at their posts.

At first sight this may seem to be a paradox; but in fact there is nothing paradoxical about it. Why should it be surprising if two men, making separate, uncoordinated choices of action, aimed, however rationally, at separate, private goals, should fail to achieve them, or that they would have a better chance of each achieving his private goal if only they could coordinate their choices of action? But how can they do this? The best result for each is that the other should somehow be induced to stay while he runs away; but since this is asymmetrical it could be achieved only by some kind of trickery or exploitation. The best symmetrical result, and therefore the best that could be achieved by any device which both could freely accept, is that both should stay. But how can this be achieved? What they need is something that will literally or metaphorically tie their actions together. If they both know that the only options open are that both should stay or both should run, then, calculating rationally but selfishly as before, both will stay. But what will serve to tie their actions together? Suppose that they make a bargain; each says 'I will remain at my post if you remain at yours.' But still, if they are rational egoists, each will have the same motive for breaking this agreement that he originally had for running away before there was an agreement. If each can see the other, and each knows that the other will know the moment he abandons his post, will this make him more likely to keep the agreement? It may, if Tom believes that Dan is more likely to break the agreement if he sees Tom breaking it, and more likely to keep it as long as he knows that Tom is keeping it, and vice versa; but as yet, on the assumptions so far introduced, neither has any reason to believe this.

On the other hand, it would be effective, and in the supposed situation rational, for both men to agree to be literally chained to their posts. It would be rational for each to accept this loss of his own freedom of choice provided that his comrade's freedom was similarly taken away. Almost equally effective would be some external discipline, if each knew that any man who ran away would be severely punished. But what is important for our purposes is that there can be psychological substitutes for physical chains and external penalties. Military traditions of honour and loyalty to comrades can serve as invisible chains.

The stigma of cowardice, with the disgrace and shame associated with it, can be as effective as external penalties. Also, given the hypothetical situation, it is rational to prefer to be encumbered with these psychological fetters, provided that one's comrades are so too. If you have to fight, it is better, even from a purely selfish point of view, to be a member of a disciplined unit with good morale than a member of a rabble.

But it is also clear that if Tom and Dan have a general tradition of keeping agreements, they will be able to achieve much the same result. They will then be able to make a bargain that each will remain at his post, and the agreement-keeping tradition will then hold each man there. Moreover, since it is a bargain, each will feel bound to keep it only so long as the other does, and each will know that the other feels this; and then if each can see whether the other is remaining at his post, each will have a further motive for doing so himself, namely the knowledge that by remaining he encourages his comrade to remain. It is true that in practice a general agreement-keeping tradition is likely to be rather less effective, in situations of extreme danger (such as our hypothetical one) than more specialized military traditions of honour and loyalty; but it has the advantage of being more flexible; it can be applied to support the making and keeping of all sorts of useful bargains. Hume was quite right in saying that a man is the more useful, both to himself and to others, the greater degree of probity and honour he is endowed with.

The particular example we have used here to illustrate this form of two-person game has the advantage of being both dramatic and realistic, but it has the disadvantage that it does not lend itself to repeated trials by the same two players. Let us think of some other example, where even if Tom, say, comes off badly at the first trial he will still survive to play with Dan again. Let us assume that each man has only a weak agreement-keeping tendency, and that neither can see, on any one occasion, whether the other is keeping the bargain until he himself is committed either to keeping it or to breaking it. Let us make the further reasonable assumptions that if both men keep the agreement on one occasion, each is more likely to keep it next time, whereas if either or both men break the agreement on one occasion, each is less likely to keep it next time, that all these tendencies are known to both men, and that each time Tom and Dan play this game they know that they will have to play it again with one another. These assumptions alter the form of the game, and bring it about that if, on any one occasion, Dan is going to keep the agreement, it will be to Tom's selfish advantage, with a view to the future, to do so too, though if Dan is going to break the agreement this time, it will be to Tom's advantage also to break it. And of course the situation is still symmetrical. Self-interest no longer unambiguously urges each man to break the agreement on any one occasion: consequently only a fairly weak agreement-keeping tendency will be needed to tip the balance. Fairly obvious and natural assumptions lead to a similar conclusion if we extend the game in another direction as well, and assume that there are more than two players. It will be to each man's selfish advantage to keep the agreement if most of the others are going to keep it and to try to enforce it, though not if most of the others are going to break it. This is, of course, the pattern of relationships that Hobbes envisaged; again in any situation of this sort only a fairly weak agreement-keeping tendency is needed to tip the balance, because it does not have to overcome any clear, one-sided counsel of self-interest. But the balance still needs to be tipped: no rational calculation of self-interest alone will even now clearly direct each man to keep the agreement.

It would be irrelevant to our purpose to go far into the endless variety of types of situation that can be studied by the theory of games, but one complication at least must be mentioned. In our examples so far both the initial situations and the agreements considered have been symmetrical, but of course they need not be so. Even if Tom and Dan are initially placed alike, there may be several possible agreements between them, each of which is better for each man singly than the results of failure to agree or of failure to keep the agreement, but some of which are in various degrees more advantageous to Tom than to Dan, and vice versa. In these circumstances the man who is, or gives the appearance of being, the more reluctant to make, or to adhere to, an agreement is likely to get more advantageous terms. Though complete intransigence in either party is disastrous for both, incomplete relative intransigence is differentially advantageous to its possessor. This holds, as I have said, even if the initial situation is symmetrical; but if one party has less to lose by failure to agree, or less to gain from a stable agreement, further possibilities of unequal agreements arise. Rational bargaining can result in exploitation. Beneficial though the invisible chains of which we have spoken are, they may not be an unmixed blessing.

There can be no doubt that many real-life situations contain, as at least part of their causally relevant structure, patterns of relationship of which various simple 'games' are an illuminating description. An international arms race is one obvious example: another is the situation where inflation can be slowed down only if different trade unions can agree to limit their demands for wage increases. One merit of such simplified analyses is that they show dramatically how the combined outcome of several intentional actions, even of well-informed and rational agents, may be something that no one of the agents involved has intended or would intend. Even purely descriptive social sciences have as a large part of their subject matter, as Popper has neatly put it, the unintended effects of intentional actions. But from our point of view the game theory approach merely reinforces the lessons that we have extracted from the arguments of Protagoras, Hobbes, Hume, and Warnock. The main moral is the practical value of the notion of obligation, of an invisible and indeed fictitious tie or bond, whether this takes the form of a general requirement to keep whatever agreements one makes or of various specific duties like those of military honour or of loyalty to comrades or to an organization.

One moral that we might be inclined to draw from the game theory analyses is that prudence is not enough, that the rational calculation of long-term self-interest is not sufficient in itself to lead men to make mutually beneficial agreements or, once made, to keep them. But here some caution is needed. This is true of the particular 'games' we have described. But nothing in the game theory analyses rules out the possibility of what Hobbes suggests, agreement backed by a coercive device (the sovereign), where the motives of the sovereign himself, those who obey him, and those whose support constitutes his power, are exclusively prudential. It is indeed hard to see how such a construction could be brought into existence by the operation of selfish motives, however rationally directed; but it is not so hard to see how once in existence it could be maintained by such motives alone. The real weakness of the Hobbesian solution lies not in anything that the game theory models show, but in what, just by being models, they leave out. Real situations always incorporate, along with the skeletal structure of some fairly simple game, other forces and tendencies whose strength varies through time. The Hobbesian solution is, as I have said, like a house of cards – each bit is held up by others – and it is inflexible in the same way. A structure is more likely to be able to bend in response to changing forces without collapsing if it is held together by ties of which some are less conditional than those of prudence.

5. The content of the device: conservatism or reform?

I have made some very general remarks, in Section 3, about the form of the device with which we are now equating morality in the narrow sense, but I have said very little about its content. Of the thinkers to whom I have referred, Protagoras, Hume, and Warnock are all concerned to explain the point of an already existing morality, though they select and emphasize particular parts of it. Hobbes writes as if his task were to create a morality from scratch, but most of the provisions he builds into it are in fact parts of the conventionally accepted body of moral ideas. His condemnation of retributive punishment is only a partial exception, since traditional Christian morality contains conflicting suggestions about this.

But is it so obvious that what is conventionally accepted as morality is exactly what is required? As all our writers have stressed, the device of morality is beneficial because of certain contingent features of the human condition. But if they are contingent they may also have changed. The contrast between Protagoras and Hobbes points at least to a change in the scale of the problem. Protagoras was looking for the ordering principles of a city, a *polis*, and in Greece a *polis* could be pretty small: his problem was how men could form social units large enough to compete with the wild beasts. But for Hobbes the problem was how to maintain a stable nation state. Today the scale has changed again: we can no longer share Hobbes's assumption that it is only civil wars that are really a menace, that international wars do relatively little harm. Warnock thinks it is slightly improper for a philosopher to take any account at all of contingent empirical facts about the human predicament; but we might argue that, given this general approach, he should have taken more account of them, not less.

Changes in the human situation which may well be relevant to morality have occurred in the last hundred and fifty and particularly in the last fifty years. Though they are obvious and well known, they should at least be summarized. One is the growth of worldwide mutual dependence. This is partly economic: an increased proportion of what people see as their needs is supplied directly or indirectly by goods from distant countries. It is partly a matter of possibilities of assistance: in 1700 the inhabitants of Europe would not have known, at least till much later, of an earthquake or a famine in India, and even if they had known they could have done nothing about it; but this is no longer so. It is partly, also, that there are worldwide political movements, and that local wars and changes of government can have repercussions far away. Again, technological advances of many kinds have put greatly increased powers into the hands of some men and some organizations. These include powers to

121

do harm; for example, to wage nuclear war. Also, powers to do at least apparent good. As Belloc said:

> Of old, when folk were sick and sorely tried
> The doctors gave them physic, and they died;
> But here's a happier age, for now we know
> Both how to make men sick and keep them so.

Again, powers to do at once both good and harm, especially powers to produce economic goods at the cost of permanent depletion of resources and radical changes in the biological and physical environment. Again, developments in the means of communication (for information, entertainment, or persuasion, or mixtures of the three) have given some men increased powers over the minds of others, and probably there will be before long possibilities of genetic engineering applied to the human race itself.

It is tempting to speak of all these as increased powers that mankind (or 'Man') now has and may use in one way or another or refrain from using. But this is utterly misleading. Mankind is not an agent; it has no unity of decision; it is therefore not confronted with any choices. Our game theory examples have made even plainer what should have been plain enough without them, that a plurality of interacting rational agents does not in general constitute a rational agent, and that the resultant of a number of choices is not in general a choice. These powers are scattered about: they are possessed, and may be exercised, by some men or groups of men or organizations, not by Man.

However, there is one kind of change that the technological increases in power have not produced. They have not falsified Hume's description of 'the scanty provision nature has made for [man's] wants'. What men see as their needs have increased, in the economically developed countries, at least as fast as their ability to satisfy them, and in the less developed countries the growth of production has been matched by growth of population.

It may be argued that such changes as these, though of great importance for political philosophy, have little bearing on morality. Moral principles rest upon the basic general structure of the human predicament, and this does not change. Against this, it is clear that these changes at least extend the range and scope of moral issues. It is not so easy for us as it was for Hume to say in one breath 'an Indian, or person wholly unknown to me'. If we were thinking of loving all our neighbours, there are a lot more of them to take into account. Nor is it quite so easy to prescribe a theoretical universal concern when we have some possibility of implementing it. New powers raise embarrassing moral questions about their exercise. If we can keep people alive, or half alive, at certain costs, the question whether we should do so is not idle. Questions about the relative claims of present and future generations are no longer purely academic, since things that are done now can radically affect, in not wholly unforeseeable ways, the prospects of future generations, and control of the numbers of the inhabitants at least of particular countries, and as a more remote possibility, of the world as a whole, is becoming a conceivable political objective. These facts, and the threats of psychological manipulation and genetic engineering, introduce a bewildering circularity into the relation between moral principles and human welfare. The human race is no longer something determinate whose members have fairly fixed interests in terms of whose satisfaction welfare might be measured and decisions thus morally assessed. Some of the decisions that come up for moral assessment can themselves determine what those interests are and even what the race itself is to be.

At the beginning of this chapter I said that morality is not to be discovered but to be made; we cannot brush this aside by adding 'but it has been made already, long ago'. It may well need to be in part remade. Of course only in part. Nothing has altered or will alter the importance of being able to make and keep and rely on others keeping agreements. Hobbes's third law of nature, that men perform their covenants made, is an eternal and immutable fragment of morality. But some more specific obligations traditionally attached to status, not created by contract, are dispensable; patriotism, for example, may have outlived its usefulness.

If we cannot be wholly satisfied with the content of what we can recognize as the main stream of moral tradition, we must be even less satisfied with the alternative of leaving the whole content of morality to be determined by the conscience or moral sense of each individual agent. As Anscombe says, 'A man's conscience may tell him to do the vilest things,' and this is not surprising when we realize how consciences are formed and how they work. They are based on the taking into the individual's mind, in childhood, of outside moral demands, but they are modified, usually unconsciously, by many motives, and can serve as an outlet for otherwise repressed desires. Even if we took the most optimistic view possible, and assumed that in general men's consciences have been appropriately moulded by evolutionary forces, the best we could hope for is that they should lay down principles which *have been* useful. Unlike the God it has replaced, natural selection cannot be supposed to possess or to embody foreknowledge.

This is not to deny that moral sense, and moral virtues, are essential parts of the *form* of the device of morality. Since prudence is not enough, even when combined in the Hobbesian solution with a coercive device, it is important that there should be a widespread tendency to act on moral grounds. But what I am now denying, and this does not imply, is that the best possible *content* for the device of morality is supplied by the specific moral sense that each agent happens to have acquired.

Chapter 6   Utilitarianism

1. Act utilitarianism

At the beginning of Chapter 5 'morality in the narrow sense' was roughly distinguished as a particular sort of constraints on conduct, and the remainder of that chapter discussed why such constraints were needed for the flourishing of human life. The view sketched there of morality in the narrow sense was therefore utilitarian in the very broad sense that it took general human well-being as in some way the foundation of morality. However, it is not very illuminating to use the term 'utilitarianism' as broadly as this; it is better to restrict it, or qualified variants of it, to more specific views about the way in which moral conclusions are to be derived from or founded upon human happiness, to specific methods of determining the content of the first order moral system.

One such view is extreme or act utilitarianism. This holds that where an agent has a choice between courses of action (or inaction) the right act is that which will produce the most happiness, not just for the agent himself but for all who are in any way affected. The greatest possible total happiness or 'utility' – or, as it is sometimes rather misleadingly put, 'The greatest happiness of the greatest number' – is proposed as the criterion of right action, and happiness is usually interpreted hedonistically as a balance of pleasure over pain. The suggestion is that for each alternative course of action it is possible in principle to measure all the amounts of pleasure it produces for different persons and to add these up, similarly to measure and add up all the amounts of pain or distress it produces, and subtract the sum of pain from the sum of pleasure; then the right action is that for which there is the greatest positive or the least negative balance of pleasure over pain; presumably if for two or more actions the balances are equal, but better than the balances for all others, each of them is *a* right action.

This proposal has several obvious merits. It seems reasonable that morality, if it is to guide conduct, should have something to do with happiness. It seems natural to seek pleasure and to avoid pain and distress, but it also seems sensible to balance these against each other, to put up with a certain amount of pain in order to achieve a quantity of pleasure that outweighs it. In taking the *general* happiness as the standard of right action this proposal seems to satisfy at once the presumptions that moral actions should be unselfish and that moral principles should be fair. It seems to provide a coherent system of conduct; all decisions about what is right or wrong would flow directly from a single source, whereas in other proposed first order moral systems we find a multiplicity of independent rules and principles, perhaps arbitrarily thrown together, possibly conflicting with one another in certain circumstances. Also it has been argued, particularly by Sidgwick, that if we confront utilitarianism with common-sense or intuitionist morality, utilitarianism can swallow up its rival. We can explain many of the common-sense or intuitive rules as being in general justified by their tendency to promote the general happiness, but where two common-sense rules come into conflict we need to appeal directly to utility to decide what to do. Common-sense morality can be seen as a practically convenient approximation to utilitarianism, but not, therefore, something whose requirements can resist those of utility in the rare cases where there is an open conflict between them.

Closer examination, however, reveals cracks in this apparently unitary structure. There are difficulties for and indeterminacies in utilitarianism. What are we to include in 'all who are in any way affected'? Does this mean 'all human beings' or all sentient beings'? Are non-human animals included? A theory that equates good with pleasure and evil with pain would appear to have no non-arbitrary reason for excluding from consideration any creatures that are capable of feeling either pleasure or pain. Does it include only those who are now alive, or also future generations; and if so, only those who will exist or also those who might exist? We may have to compare alternative courses of action one of which would lead to there being a large population each of whose members was only moderately happy, and another of which would lead to there being a smaller population each of whose members was very happy; in the former there will be more total utility or happiness, in the latter a higher average utility or happiness. For a fixed population, the maxima of total utility and of average utility must coincide, but if the size of the population is itself variable they can fall apart. Which of the two, then, is it whose maximization is to be the criterion of right action? Again, is it really possible to measure quantities of pleasure and pain even for the same person at different times and in different sorts of experience? Is pleasure even sufficiently of the same category as pain to be measurable on the same scale and so to allow a quantity of one to balance a quantity of the other? Interpersonal measurement presents even greater difficulties, and the problem becomes still more acute if the pleasures and pains of non-human animals are to be taken into account. It can be argued that utilitarianism only appears to avoid the arbitrariness of some rival methods of ethics. It only pretends to provide a unitary decision procedure, and arbitrariness breaks out within any serious attempt to implement it, in whatever decisions are made in answer to some of these questions and in estimates of the comparative amounts of pleasure and pain that various courses of action will produce.

Again it can be asked whether the proposed criterion is simply the greatest total happiness (or perhaps average happiness), or whether it matters how happiness is distributed. Is a state of affairs in which one person is supremely happy and nine are miserable better than one in which all ten are equally happy, provided only that the total balance of happiness is greater? Are we to interpret utilitarianism as being founded on an aggregative principle alone, or as including a distributive principle as well – and if so, what distributive principle: should happiness be distributed equally or in proportion to some kind of merit?

Bentham's remark that 'everybody [is] to count for one, nobody for more than one' has been taken as a distributive thesis; but it offers no clear principle of distribution, and is more naturally taken simply as an instruction that there is to be no unequal weighting, that the happiness of an aristocrat is not more important than that of a peasant, which would, however, leave us with only the aggregative requirement that total utility so calculated should be maximized.

There is even a problem about the distribution of happiness within the life of one person. A period of misery followed by one of happiness seems preferable to a period of happiness followed by one of misery, even if the quantities of misery and happiness are respectively equal. However, it could be argued that order as such is indifferent; what makes the difference here is that when one is unhappy the anticipation of future happiness is itself pleasant, whereas the recollection of past happiness is not (but is even, according to Tennyson and Dante, 'sorrow's crown of sorrow') while the reverse holds for the anticipation and recollection of misery when one is happy. One can enjoy troubles when they are over. When we take into account these joys and sorrows of anticipation and recollection, the aggregate of happiness is greater when the order is right, even if the quantities of misery and happiness were *otherwise* equal.

The utilitarian might try to deal analogously with problems of interpersonal distribution. Thus the familiar rule that happiness should be proportionate to merit is merely an incentive device for increasing the aggregate of happiness, merit being measured by a person's contribution to the happiness of others. Material goods have a diminishing marginal utility, so a more equal distribution of whatever goods there are is (apart from the just-mentioned incentive requirement) likely to produce a greater aggregate utility. Less plausibly, the utilitarian might say that it is not possible for a less equal distribution (even of happiness as opposed to material goods) to yield a higher aggregate (still apart from incentive effects) on the ground that (starting from a position of equality) one person's happiness cannot be pushed up much by any procedure that essentially involves reducing the happiness of others. A case, though not, I think, in the end a very convincing case, could thus be made out for a utilitarianism based on an aggregative principle only, without any independent principle of distribution.

All these difficulties and indeterminacies tell, in the first place, only against the claim that utilitarianism offers a peculiarly unitary and systematic basis for morality. A utilitarian can simply decide which of the various options to take up, and he can plausibly argue that rival views are subject to similar indeterminacies. In particular, many thinkers would give some weight to utility, even though they differ from utilitarians in that they recognize other moral requirements as well; such thinkers will obviously have the same problems about how to calculate the utility of which they propose to take account.

2. The ethics of fantasy

However, even if all the difficulties and indeterminacies mentioned in the last section were resolved, by argument or by decision, there would still be a fatal objection to the resulting act utilitarian system. It would be wholly impracticable. The system can, indeed, be looked at in several different ways, but this charge can be sustained against each interpretation in turn. Suppose, first, that it is considered as a morality in the broad sense, as an all-inclusive theory of conduct. Then, when utility or the general happiness is proposed as the immediate criterion of right action, is it intended that each agent should take the happiness of all as his goal? This, surely, is too much to expect. Mill himself conceded this, and replied to this objection by saying that it confuses the rule of action with the motive of it. 'The great majority of good actions,' he said, 'are intended not for the benefit of the world, but for that of individuals ... and the thoughts of the most virtuous man need not ... travel beyond the particular persons concerned, except so far as is necessary to assure himself that in benefiting them he is not violating the rights, that is, the legitimate and authorized expectations, of any one else.' But even if we accept this clarification, and take utilitarianism to be supplying not the motive but only a test of right actions, the charge of impracticality still stands. We cannot require that the actions of people generally should even pass the test of being such as to maximize the happiness of all, whether or not this is their motive. Even within a small village or commune it is too much to expect that the efforts of all members should be wholly directed towards the promoting of the well-being of all. And such total cooperation is out of the question on the scale of a nation state, let alone where the 'all' are to be the whole human race, including its future or possible future members, and perhaps all other sentient beings as well. The question, which moral philosophers sometimes discuss, 'What would happen if there were a society of pure act utilitarians?' is purely academic. We can indeed work out an answer, though only with difficulty, because this hypothesis is so far removed from anything within our experience that it is difficult to envisage it consistently and thoroughly. But the answer would have no direct bearing on any policies of practical importance. All real societies, and all those which it is of direct practical use to consider, are ones whose members have to a great extent divergent and conflicting purposes. And we must expect that their actions will consist largely of the pursuit of these divergent and conflicting purposes, and consequently will not only not be motivated by a desire for the general happiness but also will commonly fail the proposed test of being such as to maximize the general happiness.

Act utilitarianism is by no means the only moral theory that displays this extreme of impracticality. The biblical commandment 'Thou shalt love thy neighbour as thyself,' though it has its roots in a mistranslation of a much more realistic rule, is often taken as prescribing a universal and equal concern for all men. So interpreted, it is, as Mill says, effectively equivalent to the utilitarian principle. And it is similarly impracticable. People simply are not going to put the interests of all their 'neighbours' on an equal footing with their own interests and specific purposes and with the interests of those who are literally near to them. Such universal concern will not be the actual motive of their choices, nor will they act as if it were.

In Chapter 4 I argued that an ethics based on the universalizability of moral judgements would come close, in its specific demands, to some kind of utilitarianism only if it included what I there called the 'third stage of universalization', taking account of all different tastes and rival ideals, or looking at things from all actual points of view at once. Only this – indeed only this pushed to an extreme – and not the first and second stages on their own, would give equal weight to the interests of all. With the extreme form of this third stage included, universal prescriptivism would be open to the same charge of impracticality as utilitarianism and the doctrine of neighbourly love, but if only the first and second stages were incorporated, or only these with a modest version of the third, it would not.

But why have moralists and preachers thought it worthwhile to propound rules that obviously have so little chance of being followed? They must surely have thought that by setting up such admittedly unattainable ideals they might induce at least some movement towards them, that if men were told to let universal beneficence guide all their conduct, they would not indeed do this, but would allow some small admixture of universal beneficence to help to direct their actions.

This would amount to proposing utilitarianism (or the doctrine of neighbourly love) no longer as a morality in the broad sense but indirectly and in effect as one in the narrow sense: not as an overriding guide to conduct in general, but as a check or corrective on conduct which was very largely otherwise motivated and otherwise directed. I shall discuss utilitarianism, explicitly so presented, in the next section. Here I would remark only that if this is what is intended, it would be much better if it were explicitly so presented. To put forward as a morality in the broad sense something which, even if it were admirable, would be an utterly impossible ideal is likely to do, and surely has in fact done, more harm than good. It encourages the treatment of moral principles not as guides to action but as a fantasy which accompanies actions with which it is quite incompatible. It is a commonplace that religious morality often has little effect on the lives of believers. It is equally true, though not so frequently pointed out, that utilitarian morality is often treated as a topic of purely academic discussion, and is not taken any more seriously as a practical guide. In both cases the mistake is the same. To identify morality with something that certainly will not be followed is a sure way of bringing it into contempt – practical contempt, which combines all too readily with theoretical respect.

But why, it may be asked, are such moralities of universal concern impracticable? Primarily because a large element of selfishness – or, in an older terminology, self-love – is a quite ineradicable part of human nature. Equally, if we distinguish as Butler did the particular passions and affections from self-love, we must admit that they are inevitably the major part of human motivation, and the actions which express and realize them cannot be expected in general to tend towards the *general* happiness. Even what we recognize as unselfishness or benevolence is equally incompatible with *universal* concern. It takes the form of what Broad called self-referential altruism – concern for others, but for others who have some special connection with oneself; children, parents, friends, workmates, neighbours in the literal, not the metaphorically extended, sense. Wider affections than these usually centre upon devotion to some special cause – religious, political, revolutionary, nationalist – not upon the welfare of human beings, let alone sentient beings, in general. It is much easier, and commoner, to display a self-sacrificing love for some of one's fellow men if one can combine this with hostility to others. It is quite implausible for Mill to argue that such an array of limited motives can express themselves in actions which will conform to the utilitarian standard, provided only that the agent assures himself that he is not violating the rights of anyone else. As a proposed general pattern of conduct, there is indeed much to be said for the pursuit of some such array of special and limited goals within bounds set by respect for some 'rights' of others. But it is misleading to present such a pattern as a consequence of the act utilitarian standard of right action, and to suggest that each choice that is a component in such a pattern could be validated as that which, out of the options available to that agent at that time, would contribute more than any other to the happiness of all men or of all sentient beings.

But could not human nature be changed? I do not know. Of course, given the techniques of mass persuasion adolescents can be turned into Red Guards or Hitler Youth or pop fans, but in each of these we have only fairly superficial redirection of what are basically the same motives. It is far more doubtful whether any agency could effect the far more fundamental changes that would be needed to make practicable a morality of universal concern. Certainly no ordinary processes of education can bring them about.

Besides, if such changes could be effected, they might well prove self-defeating. Thus Bernard Williams has argued that in becoming capable of acting out of universal concern, people would have to be stripped of the motives on which most of what is of value in human life is based – close affections, private pursuits, and many kinds of competition and struggle. Even if our ultimate goal were the utilitarian one of maximizing the general happiness, the cultivation of such changes in human nature as would make an act utilitarian morality practicable might not be the most sensible way of pursuing it. But in any case this is at most a remote possibility, and has little relevance to our present choice of a first order moral system. For the present our terms of reference can be summed up in words close to those of Rousseau: we are to take men as they are and moral laws as they might be.

It may be objected that if we trim down moral demands to fit present human capacity, we bring morality into contempt in another way. But I do not mean that moral demands are to be so minimal that they are likely to be fulfilled by most people pretty well at once. We may well advocate moral principles that are in conflict with established habits of thought and behaviour, that prescribe a degree of respect for the claims of others – and

133

of distant others – which can flourish only by overcoming in-grained selfishness and limitations of generosity that are author-ized by the existing law and the real conventional morality (as contrasted with the fantasy moralities of utilitarianism and neighbourly love). All I am insisting upon is that we should advocate practicable reforms, that we should look for rules or principles of conduct that can fit in with the relatively per-manent tendencies of human motives and thought.

3. Morality in the narrow sense

Act utilitarianism, then, is not viable as a morality in the broad sense – an all-inclusive theory of conduct – nor is it wise to propound it as such in the hope that it will then operate as a morality in the narrow sense, as a counterpoise to selfishness or excessively narrow sympathies. But this leaves open the possi-bility of supporting it explicitly as a morality in the narrow sense. Could it not be one factor among others which we allow to influence choices, but the factor which has the special func-tion of countering the bad effects of limited sympathies? War-nock states, before going on to criticize, this suggestion:

The essential evil to be remedied ... is the propensity of people to be concerned in practice, if not exclusively with their own, yet with some restricted range of, interests and ends; and surely the *direct* way to counter, or to limit, the evils liable to result from this pro-pensity is to counter it *itself* – to inculcate ... a directly remedial propensity to be concerned with, and in practice to take into ac-count, the welfare, needs, wants, interests of *all*.

Plausible though this suggestion is, I would agree with Warnock in rejecting it, though for reasons other than the ones on which he chiefly relies. My main reason is that such a pro-pensity is too indeterminate to do the trick. It is not now being proposed that an agent should either take the general happiness as his overriding aim or act as if he were doing so, but only that he should give it some weight against the more special interests to which he is primarily attached. But how much weight? When should the one consideration override the other? The utilitarian principle now gives no answer. The function we are now assigning it is to set a boundary to the pursuit of selfish or special or narrowly altruistic aims. Now a boundary may be blurred, uncertain, disputed, wavering, and yet still fulfil to some extent its function as a boundary; but it must be at least roughly indicated, at least dimly visible. The utilitarian principle sets up no visible boundary at all.

Mill himself, however reluctantly, implicitly concedes this. Recognizing that notions of justice are the main obstacle to the acceptance of utilitarian views, he argues that the moral force of the various rules and principles which we are inclined to put under the heading of justice is derived from their utility, but he admits that they form a special sub-class of utilitarian considerations:

Have mankind been under a delusion in thinking that justice is a more sacred thing than policy, and that the latter ought only to be listened to after the former has been satisfied? By no means ... Justice is a name for certain classes of moral rules, which concern the essentials of human well-being more nearly, and are therefore of more absolute obligation, than any other rules for the guidance of life ... The moral rules which forbid mankind to hurt one another (in which we must never forget to include wrongful interference with each other's freedom) are more vital to human well-being than any other maxims, however important, which only point out the best mode of managing some department of human affairs ... It is their observance which alone preserves peace among human beings ... in inculcating on each other the duty of positive beneficence [men] have an unmistakable interest, but far less in degree; a person may possibly not need the benefits of others; but he always needs that they should not do him hurt.

That is, Mill recognizes that there are certain principles not indeed wholly determinate nor quite invariable from one society to another, but still far more determinate than an expression of a general propensity to show concern for the welfare of all, which play a more vital part than any such general propensity either does or can play in checking the bad effects of limited sympathies. Unlike it, the rules of justice do set a boundary to the pursuit of special goals.

A related argument springs from what Mill says about the ultimate sanction of the principle of utility. 'I see nothing embarrassing to those whose standard is utility, in the question, what is the sanction of that particular standard? We may answer, the same as of all other moral standards – the conscientious feelings of mankind.' And again, 'The principle of utility either has, or there is no reason why it might not have, all the sanctions which belong to any other system of morals.' But this is not true. Conscientious feelings can attach themselves far more readily and more firmly to such specific rules as those of justice – for example, rules against invading what are recognized in a particular society as someone's rights, of keeping agreements, of not punishing the innocent, and in general of making judicial and other analogous decisions impartially, by reference to relevant considerations alone. There are, then, good reasons why such specific rules, rather than a general utilitarian principle, should form the core of morality in the narrow sense.

4. Rule utilitarianism

These objections to act utilitarianism as a determination of the content of a first order morality, whether in the broad or in the narrow sense, leave open and indeed naturally lead on to the consideration of rule utilitarianism. This differs from act utilitarianism in that it makes the general happiness not directly but only indirectly, by way of a two-stage procedure, the criterion of right action. It is summed up in Austin's dictum: 'Our rules would be fashioned on utility; our conduct, on our rules.' To find out whether an individual act is right or not, we must, Austin says, discover its 'tendency', that is, we must consider the probable effect upon the general happiness if acts of the class to which this one belongs were generally done rather than generally omitted.

We must not suppose, however, that if a utilitarian gives any place at all to rules he is therefore a rule utilitarian. Act utilitarians regularly admit the use of rules of thumb: the great majority of ordinary decisions will be guided by rules which sum up what has been found or is reasonably believed usually to conduce fairly well to the general happiness, since it would often be either impossible or absurdly laborious to calculate in any detail the likely effect on utility of each available alternative in an individual case. What is distinctive of rule utilitarianism is the suggestion that the two-stage procedure, and the rules which in it intervene between utility and the individual choice, have some substantial merit over and above the economy of quick decision. It has often been suggested that rule utilitarianism can escape some of the more violent conflicts that break out between act utilitarianism and common moral beliefs or 'intuitions'. It is easy to construct imaginary examples, and not impossible to find real concrete ones, where an act utilitarian would have to say that it is right to kill innocent people, to invade their rights, to torture political opponents, to break solemn agreements, to cheat, or to betray a trust. But the rule utilitarian can say that each such individual act is wrong because the general performance of acts of each of these classes would plainly have a very bad effect on the general happiness. And in the last section we have followed Mill in recognizing the importance of respect for rules which are justified ultimately by their utility.

But before rule utilitarianism can be considered seriously, it has to defend itself against the criticism that it can make no practical difference, that it is extensionally equivalent to act utilitarianism in that the outcome of its two-stage procedure, consistently carried out, will always coincide with that of a direct test of an individual act by reference to its own utility. The essence of the argument for this equivalence can be given as follows, in *reductio ad absurdum* form.

Suppose that the two methods are not extensionally equivalent, and consider some case where there is a discrepancy between them. That is, some individual act *A* would in itself have a higher utility than any alternative, but it is forbidden by a utility-based rule R, because it is of a sort S – the sort which R forbids – the general performance of which would diminish the general happiness. Since the general performance of acts of sort S is harmful, whereas the performance of A would be beneficial, there must be something distinctive about A or its circumstances which explains this contrast. Let this causally relevant difference be D; then all acts that are not only of sort S but also have this difference D – SD acts – will be beneficial although the other acts of sort S – S non-D acts – are generally harmful. There is then a possible rule R' which will forbid S non-D acts but enjoin SD ones, and R' will serve utility better than R, since it will still forbid everything harmful that R forbids, while enjoining the beneficial acts that R forbids. Hence a consistently worked out rule utilitarianism, basing its rules on utility, will incorporate R' instead of R, and so will agree with act utilitarianism in prescribing A. Any apparent discrepancy between the two methods can be similarly resolved.

It may be objected that there are kinds of acts such that each act on its own is harmless and perhaps also beneficial, but the general performance of acts of that very same kind is harmful – for example, when too many people cross a flimsy bridge at once or visit the same remote beauty spot at the same time. But we can still find a difference D which marks off the beneficial from the harmful examples, namely 'at a time when not more than n others are doing so'. The argument for equivalence stands, therefore: it cannot be that A is beneficial while there is *no* difference D such that all SD acts are beneficial.

This proof of equivalence is decisive, however, only if the rules in rule utilitarianism are treated as purely abstract entities, which can be formulated at will in order to fill in a stage in a theoretical two-stage procedure by which actions are tested in terms of utility. The argument may fail if the rules are to be social realities, rules more or less consciously accepted, followed, appealed to in criticism of violations, backed by public opinion, explicitly taught or unobtrusively passed on from one generation to another – that is, if they are to form what Hume called 'a general scheme or system of action' that has 'the concurrence of mankind'. To flourish in this way a rule does not need to be absolutely simple and inflexible; it may not even be neatly formulable in words; but still there are limits to the complexities and qualifications it can incorporate. It may well be that R meets these requirements (indeed it may already exist as a social reality) but that the R' required to instantiate the proof of equivalence does not.

Rule utilitarianism, thus understood, can therefore resist the threatened collapse into act utilitarianism. Nevertheless I would not defend it, and would not attempt to justify on rule utilitarian grounds the first order moral system that I support. Utilitarian theory is still plagued by the difficulties and indeterminacies mentioned in Section 1. We cannot in any strict sense fashion our rules on utility. There is no such common measure of all interests and purposes as happiness or utility is supposed to be. Utilitarians commonly speak as if there were some entity, happiness, which is in some respect homogeneous and in principle measurable, that the different parts or constituents of happiness can somehow be reduced to a single scale and weighed objectively and decisively against one another. They may, indeed, also admit that this can be done only in principle, that in practice we can achieve only very rough estimates and comparisons of utility. But I doubt whether it can be done even in principle. The utilitarian calculus is a myth, and not, I think, a helpful one. There are and no doubt always will be considerable differences between people about what they value or think worthwhile in human life, about what could be called their concepts of happiness or *eudaimonia*; and if we say, with Aristotle, that everyone aims at *eudaimonia* we run the risk of deceiving ourselves by a mere verbal trick into thinking that human purposes are more unitary than they are or ever will be. We can hope to get much more genuine agreement about certain specifiable evils, about the respects in which, as Warnock says, things are liable to go very badly, and it is more realistic to consider morality in the narrow sense as a device for countering such specific evils than to regard morality, in either the broad or the narrow sense, as a system of rules whose function is to maximize a fictitious agreed or objectively determinable positive value, happiness or utility.

In any case, there is no cogent reason why we should want to justify by reference to utility whatever first order morality we support. Utility or the general happiness is not, as has often been supposed, a peculiarly authoritative or self-justifying starting point for moral reasoning. This becomes plain when we examine the kind of proof that is often offered for the principle of utility.

5. The 'proof' of utility

Mill's difficulties over the proof of this principle are notorious. He is probably not guilty of all the fallacies of which he has been accused, but there are problems enough in even the most favourable possible interpretation of what he says.

Mill hesitates between two basic theses. One is that proof and reasoning generally apply only to means, not to ultimate ends. We can inquire rationally into the means to health, for example, but we cannot prove that health is a good, that it is to be taken as an ultimate end: we simply take it as such, and reason from that starting point. 'Whatever can be proved to be good, must be so by being shown to be a means to something admitted to be good without proof.' We would expect him, consistently with this, to say bluntly that he just takes the general happiness as an ultimate end. But he does not. Instead he states a second thesis, not easily reconcilable with the first, that even for an ultimate end like pleasure or utility something 'equivalent to proof' can be given: 'Considerations may be presented capable of determining the intellect either to give or withhold its assent to the doctrine.' What are these considerations?

No reason can be given why the general happiness is desirable, except that each person ... desires his own happiness. This, however, being a fact, we have not only all the proof which the case admits of, but all which it is possible to require, that happiness is a good: that each person's happiness is a good to that person, and the general happiness, therefore, a good to the aggregate of all persons.

How are we to interpret the key phrases 'is desirable', 'is a good', 'is a good to'? We might take the last as equivalent to 'is desired by' or 'will tend to satisfy' – these are not indeed equivalent to one another, but the difference between them does not now matter – and 'is desirable' and 'is a good' as merely elliptical for one or other of these, reference to the person by whom the thing in question is desired, or whom it will satisfy, being suppressed. Then to say that each person's happiness is a good to that person is merely to restate the assumption that each desires his own happiness. But what, on this interpretation, can be made of 'the general happiness is a good to the aggregate of persons'? This would have to mean 'The aggregate of persons desires the general happiness,' or 'The aggregate of persons will be satisfied by the general happiness.' The first of these is non-sense, since the aggregate of persons is not a possible subject of desire. The second is almost as bad, since this aggregate is not strictly speaking a possible subject of the experience of satisfaction. But if we speak less strictly, and say that an aggregate is satisfied in so far as its members in general are, our conclusion is the near tautology that when people in general are happy people in general are satisfied. No progress towards any principle of utility has been made. If on the other hand we take the aggregate of persons distributively to provide genuine subjects of desire or receivers of satisfaction, the conclusion will mean that each person desires the general happiness or that each is satisfied by the general happiness. But this conclusion in either form plainly does not follow from the premiss and is, moreover, blatantly false. With these 'naturalistic' interpretations of the key terms, then, the proof gets nowhere.

Alternatively, we might follow hints that Mill gives both in *Utilitarianism* and in the last chapter of his *System of Logic* that 'is desirable' and 'is a good (to)' mean rather 'is a proper object of pursuit and/or approbation'. But then there seems to be an unwarranted move from 'Each person desires his own happiness' to 'Each person's happiness is a proper object of that person's pursuit and/or approbation' followed by an invalid move – an example of the fallacy of composition – from this to 'The general happiness is a proper object of each person's pursuit and/or approbation.'

However, this second interpretation leaves room for a more charitable understanding of Mill's line of thought. Perhaps he is just assuming that there is *some* proper object of pursuit and approbation: something or other is intrinsically desirable or good. Then each person's desire for his own happiness can be taken as showing that he believes that his own happiness is objectively good. The first step in Mill's argument is an inference from this widespread belief to its truth – a genuine inference, that is, for Mill, one that is not even meant to be deductively valid. It is not likely that such a widely held belief is completely wrong; so each person's happiness *is* objectively good, intrinsically desirable. We can each recognize the intrinsic goodness of happiness in the instance of it with which we are most immediately acquainted, namely our own. Then the second step is merely an integration: the sum of all these particular happinesses, the general happiness, will also be objectively good, intrinsically desirable. Hence it is a proper object of pursuit for everyone.

The problem for any attempted proof of the principle of utility, any considerations that are intended to determine the intellect in the way Mill wants, is to make the transition from individualistic hedonism (psychological or ethical) to universalistic hedonism. Sidgwick therefore appropriately presents the argument in the form of a debate between an Egoist and a Utilitarian:

If the Egoist ... confines himself to stating his conviction that he ought to take his own happiness or pleasure as his ultimate end, there seems no opening for any line of reasoning to lead him to Universalistic Hedonism ... When, however, the Egoist offers, either as a reason for his Egoistic principle, or as another form of stating it, the proposition that his happiness or pleasure is objectively desirable or Good; he gives the ground needed for such a proof. For we can then point out to him that *his* happiness cannot be more objectively desirable or more a good than the similar happiness of any other person ... Hence, starting with his own principle, he must accept the wider notion of Universal happiness or pleasure as representing the real end of Reason, the absolutely Good or Desirable: as the end, therefore, to which the action of a reasonable agent as such ought to be directed.

Here Sidgwick is exactly right. Once the disputants start using the concept of something objectively good, the transition from egoism to utilitarianism can be effected; but as long as the egoist is content to speak in terms only of what is objectively right (or rational), he can claim that it is right (or rational) for each to seek his own happiness, and he cannot be dislodged from that position and pushed into utilitarianism. What I have suggested is that Mill was thinking implicitly along the lines that Sidgwick makes explicit, that he was in effect relying on a notion of the intrinsically desirable, the introduction of which would make cogent such an argument as he was trying to present.

This argument is not blatantly fallacious. But it is not cogent for us, because the key assumption that something or other is intrinsically desirable, objectively good, has been undermined by the rejection of all objective values in Chapter 1. In any case, Mill's proof requires a further stage. He has to show not merely that the general happiness is desirable (for everyone) but also that nothing else is so. His argument for this rests on the claim that nothing but happiness is desired. But this seems patently false. There are, as Butler said, particular passions as well as self-love, and self-love could hardly operate unless there were particular passions. Mill gets round this difficulty by arguing that everything that is desired is desired either as a means to happiness or as a part of happiness. But in this way he scores only a verbal success which is really fatal to his main argument. He is in effect emptying the word 'happiness' of all specific content: it is no longer the name of a distinct condition, a state of an individual person made up, perhaps, of recognizable feelings of pleasure or well-being that outweigh contrasting feelings of pain or distress, but a name for whatever anyone wants. But if happiness thus ceases to be any distinctive sort of thing, the suggestion, in my interpretation of Mill's earlier argument, that our desire for our own happiness is evidence for its intrinsic goodness, collapses. We cannot be recognizing the intrinsic, objective, goodness of happiness if there is no specific thing or condition, happiness, to be objectively good. If 'each person's happiness' is only shorthand for 'anything and everything that each person desires or aims at', we are left with nothing whose intrinsic desirability could be indicated by the widespread occurrence of a desire for it.

It is often suggested that utilitarianism would be better restated not in terms of happiness but in terms of the satisfaction and non-frustration of desires. The ultimate criterion of right action (whether in an act or a rule utilitarian scheme) would then become the maximum satisfaction and minimum frustration of desires, and if the words 'happiness' and 'utility' were retained, they would be understood as referring to this, not any balance of pleasure over pain as specific states. But whatever the merits of this reformulation, it cannot be combined with what I have taken to be the reasoning implicit in Mill's proof. The sense in which any desire at all aims at its own satisfaction cannot be taken as a sign that the desirer is recognizing satisfaction as such as intrinsically desirable or objectively good.

These difficulties tell not against mere mistakes in Mill's argument, but against the possibility of any cogent argument of this general sort. There are no considerations that can reasonably determine the intellect to assent to a utilitarian principle. As I have said, the general happiness is not a peculiarly authoritative or self-justifying starting point for moral reasoning.

6. Utility as desire-satisfaction

Would the version of utilitarianism suggested at the end of the last section stand up better to our criticisms? If utility is identified with the amount of satisfaction of desires, the measurement and interpersonal comparison of utility becomes somewhat easier. But there are still some puzzles. Do we simply lay it down that each person is to be considered as having the same total force of desire, though different persons distribute their desires differently between objects? Or do we allow that one person may have stronger desires all round than another, so that his satisfactions and frustrations contribute more, positively or negatively, to general utility? If so, how is overall strength of desire to be measured?

But what is of more fundamental importance is that our other objections apply equally to this version of utilitarianism. The indeterminacies mentioned in Section 1 have still to be resolved. An act utilitarianism on this basis, considered as a morality either in the broad or in the narrow sense, would still be impractical. And as we have just seen, the interpretation which would give the greatest plausibility to Mill's proof of the principle of utility is incompatible with this account of utility. There is, then, no good reason why we should take the general satisfaction of desires as a peculiarly authoritative goal, even in a rule utilitarian system.

This version, indeed, brings out particularly clearly what is one of the characteristic features of utilitarianism, its allowing of replacements. If all that matters, in the end, is the total amount of satisfaction of desires, the satisfying of one desire can be replaced by the satisfying of another. And, more dramatically, the satisfying of one person's desires can be replaced by the satisfying of another's. It is this that leaves room for the charge that utilitarianism not merely allows but enjoins, in some circumstances, that the happiness of some people should be purchased at the cost of the undeserved and uncompensated misery of others.

145

As was suggested in Section 1, the utilitarian can meet this charge in either of two ways. He may add to his aggregative principle an explicit principle of distribution. Alternatively, he may be able to argue that in practice the system of rules whose application is likely to maximize utility will be one which protects people against exploitation and prevents at least the extremes of unfairness in the sacrifice of some for the sake of others.

The utilitarian may, then, be able to get out of this difficulty. But there was no need to get into it. There is no good reason for taking the general human well-being which it is the function of a working morality to protect or promote as consisting of a sum of in principle interchangeable satisfactions.

Mill himself, when setting out to defend liberty on the basis of utility, insisted that 'it must be utility in the largest sense, grounded on the permanent interests of a man as a progressive being'. My own approach, as I have admitted, could also be called utilitarian in a very broad sense. But I think that it is less misleading to give up the terms 'utility' and 'utilitarian' than to use them in senses so broad that their characteristic association with quantitative measurement and calculation and interchangeable satisfactions is lost.

7. The malleability of morality

If the arguments of the last six sections have any force, the content of the first order moral system is more malleable, more a matter of choice, than utilitarianism, in any form, makes it appear. It may not, indeed, be more malleable than it really is within a utilitarian view, because of the indeterminacies that are concealed within such terms as 'pleasure', 'happiness', and 'utility'; but there is no merit in pretending that our choices are rationally constrained in ways that they are not. We are, then, free to mould or remould our moral system so as better to promote whatever it is that we do value.

An extreme illustration of this is provided by Smart's science fictional pleasure machine. Suppose that there were developed a convenient and easily-operated device for stimulating the pleasure centre in one's brain; people might well spend most of their time hooked up to – and hooked on – such a machine, obtaining pleasure directly instead of obtaining it, as they do at present, only indirectly through sex or sport or social intercourse or books or music or controversy or country walks or a host of other activities and entertainments. In this manner happiness, considered as a balance of pleasures over pains, might be maximized: but would this be a desirable state of affairs? We are free to say firmly that we do not so regard it, whereas for the utilitarian this is at least an embarrassment. If he is unwilling to accept this, he has to find some plausible reason for rejecting it. This is, of course, only a variant of Mill's problem about whether it is better to be a fool satisfied or Socrates dissatisfied, which he solved by arguing that pleasures differ in quality as well as in quantity, and that the higher pleasures are preferable to the lower ones. But this is a dodge to escape from a trap in which we need never get caught; there is no good reason for even pretending that our moral system is founded on the maximizing of happiness or pleasure.

Corresponding embarrassments can be created for the desire-satisfaction version of utilitarianism. We can think of devices – physiological or psychological or propagandist – for generating easily-satisfied desires and suppressing awkward and expensive ones. People will be able more fully to get what they desire if they are made to desire what they are going to get. But we need not equate human well-being with such artificially-maximized satisfaction of desires.

It does not follow, on the other hand, that an individual is free to invent a moral system at will. If a morality is to perform the sort of function described in Chapter 5, it must be adopted socially by a group of people in their dealings with one another. Of course, there can be and are larger and smaller social circles. The rules and principles that govern relations within a relatively small group will in general be more detailed than those that govern relations between people who are less intimately involved with one another. The morality, or fragment of a morality, of a small group for its internal relations needs to be accepted, on the whole, by the members of that group: but they can change it as long as they manage to keep fairly well in step with one another. The fragment of a morality that regulates dealings between people who are more remote will be not only less detailed but also much less open to change. But in either case a fragment of a morality has to be a social reality, a going concern, and therefore something that some number of people jointly know of and understand, so that each can rely to some considerable extent on the others' observance of it. Privately imagined rules or principles of action are worthless. It is idle to point out how good (or how bad) would be the results of everyone's doing such-and-such if there is no likelihood that they will. What counts is rules that are actually recognized by the members of some social circle, large or small, and that thus set up expectations and claims. Innovations and reforms are not excluded, but they must be possibly actual, not purely utopian.

The prescription 'Think of a set of rules and principles the general adoption of which would best promote what you value and see as worthwhile, and then follow them yourself, regardless of what you think others will do' may well be a recipe for disaster. The prescription 'Think of such a set of rules, and try to secure their general acceptance' may be impractical. What the individual can do is to remember that there are, in the different circles of relationship with which he is concerned, various fragments of a moral system which already contributes very considerably to countering specifiable evils which he, like others, will see as evils; that he can at once take advantage of this system and contribute to its upkeep; but that he may be able, with others, to put pressure on some fragments of the system, so that they come gradually to be more favourable to what he sees as valuable or worthwhile.

Chapter 7 Consequentialism and Deontology

1. Conceptions of the good

Having rejected utilitarianism, we could move in either of two directions. We could retain the consequentialist structure of utilitarian theory, but replace the goal of utility or happiness, conceived as a balance of pleasure over pain, or of the satisfaction over the frustration of desires in general, with some other concept of the good which is to be achieved or realized or maximized. Alternatively we could reject the consequentialist structure, and develop a moral system built not round the notion of some goal that is to be attained but rather round the notions of rules or principles of action or duties or rights or virtues, or some combination of these – in a very broad sense, some kind of deontological system. Of course a consequentialist theory will usually give some place to items of all these sorts, but a subordinate place: a utilitarian takes virtues, for example, to be good just because and in so far as they tend to issue in behaviour that increases the general happiness. But in a deontological theory actions of the kinds held to be virtuous are seen as being intrinsically obligatory or admirable, and goodness of character too may be seen as having intrinsic value; actions and characters may have a merit of their own not wholly derived from what they bring about.

In fact I want to move in both these directions, to introduce both some non-utilitarian consequentialism and some deontological elements. Indeed I find very great difficulty in distinguishing and separating these. For example, I should take as one component of the good to be realized the non-existence of extreme unfairness in the distribution of advantages among persons. But the fairness or unfairness of a distribution cannot

149

be completely distinguished from the fairness or unfairness of the procedures and actions that have led to that distribution, and yet cannot be completely identified with these either. But fairness of distribution would be a non-utilitarian consequential good, while the fairness of procedures and actions would fall naturally under deontology.

Other components of the good may well include many of the particular kinds of activity and experience that a utilitarian would list as pleasures or as parts of or means to happiness – activities which are naturally pursued and found satisfying. But the vital difference is that we can now take these in their specificity as components of the good, not merely as means to or representatives of some one thing, pleasure or happiness, which is alleged to be the sole good: we are not now committed to the suggestion that the loss or absence of some specific 'pleasure' can be fully compensated for by the provision of another.

Also, when we put forward our conception of good, we need not hesitate to include in it things for which Mill, indeed, was as much concerned as anyone, but which he had great difficulty in squeezing into the utilitarian scheme either as higher pleasures or as indirect means to happiness – liberty of thought and discussion, thought and discussion themselves, understanding of all sorts of things, including ourselves and other human beings, a self-reliant, enterprising, and experimental spirit and way of life, artistic creation and craftsmanship of many sorts, the enjoyment and appreciation of beauty, and general participatory self-government both in smaller institutions and in the determination of large scale social policies and laws.

But when we frame our conception of the good, it is just as that. We need neither submerge our specific values in a supposed general happiness nor claim that our values are objectively authoritative and expect everyone to join us in endorsing them. No-one can demand that his view of the good life should be accepted by everyone else; but equally there is no reason why anyone should abandon his own view and accept as authoritative some resultant or highest common factor of all (or most) current conceptions. Rather it is to be expected that different individuals and different groups should have different ideals and values. Each person's special values will help to determine his morality in the broad sense; his actions will be guided not simply by what he wants but also, to some extent, by the endeavour to realize in some degree whatever he sees as good.

It must be admitted that such endeavours may not contribute much to morality in the narrow sense. The promotion of a particular set of values will do something to harmonize the activities of those who share those values, but may well bring them into conflict with those who have radically different ideals. We must look elsewhere for contributions to morality in the narrow sense. On the other hand the latter need not be taken as ruling out adherence to different systems of positive values, but only as imposing some constraints on the ways in which they are promoted as well as on the ways in which other interests are pursued.

2. The rationale of universalization

The view I am here propounding can also be reached by reflecting on the three stages of universalization distinguished in Chapter 4. We may hope at the same time to explain why universalization plays the part it does in characteristically moral reasoning, and why there are the difficulties noted in Chapter 4 for the logical theses about the universalizability of moral judgements.

I argued in Chapter 4 that it was the third stage of universalization that would be needed to bring us anywhere near the utilitarian scheme in which particular ideals and values are submerged in and subordinated to a resultant general happiness. But it was the first stage, at most, that could be presented as being required by the meaning of moral terms and the logic of moral statements, and it was only the second stage that, failing this, could be seen as being involved in a traditionally accepted and widely influential pattern of moral reasoning. The third stage can claim neither of these supports; but only it, and not the two more defensible stages, would tell against the diversity of systems of values. But why are there these differences between the three stages? Also, why is there the asymmetry noted in Chapter 4, that we can more easily recognize as moral the variety of asceticism which says 'I cannot allow myself such indulgences, but I do not condemn them in others' than the corresponding variety of egoism which says 'This is permissible for me, though not for you in exactly similar circumstances'?

The first stage of universalization, the elimination of purely individual reference to persons, nations, and so on, and hence the denial of moral privilege for an individual moral speaker or for what he belongs to, seems necessary if morality is to fulfil the sort of function discussed in Chapter 5. When Hobbes put forward his laws of nature as articles of peace, he reasonably required, in his second law, that a man should 'be contented with so much liberty against other men, as he would allow other men against himself'. Naturally fairly selfish, and therefore in the circumstances competitive, individuals and groups just will not accept as principles of compromise and adjustment of conflicting claims any that give a totally unsupported preference to one individual or group. But for this purpose it does not matter if a man is contented with *less* liberty against other men than he would allow others against himself. If the function of morality is to counter the bad effects of limited sympathies, it would be undermined by proper name egoism, but not by proper name asceticism. This asymmetry seems to figure in our ordinary moral thinking; it conflicts with a simple ascription of first stage universalizability to moral terms as a logical feature; but is easily understood when we look beyond the proposed logical thesis to a practical function.

The second stage of universalization, the elimination of principles which differentially favour those who happen to have certain characteristics or certain positions, is supported by similar considerations, but less strongly. As we saw in Chapter 4, this stage amounts to looking for and adopting principles which one would be prepared to endorse no matter what one's actual condition was. Such principles have obvious merits as those that are to govern the adjustment of claims between fairly selfish competing individuals. On the other hand, the history of moral thought and practice make it all too plain that it is not a necessary condition for a working moral system that it should pass this test *as we would apply it*. Almost all actual societies have been and are, in various ways and in various degrees, inegalitarian, and it is not surprising that they should have had inegalitarian moral codes which have no doubt contributed to their harmony and stability. Morality has sustained socially established privilege. Game theory models, as we saw in Chapter 5, can illustrate the acceptability, in some circumstances, of unequal agreements: an unequal agreement may be better for each party than no agreement at all. Such agreements, or the equivalent arrangements, may be advantageously maintained by such invisible chains as moral rules and principles provide. Thus moral codes which seem to us to resist the second stage of universalization can grow up and survive: they serve a social function. But they can do so only because they seem to most members of the societies in which they are in force to pass this test. They are viable as moral codes only because most members of these societies *do* endorse them, whatever their actual condition may be. Differences of rank or race or sex, and so on, are accepted as morally relevant grounds of privilege not only by those who enjoy these privileges but also by many who do not. But an unequal rule can also be used to defend an existing arrangement against attempts by some of the underprivileged to change it: the latter will naturally criticize the rule by appealing to arguments of the sort covered by this second stage of universalization -- How would you like it if you were in this position? -- but since such criticisms will be resisted it is not surprising that this second stage has, as we found in Chapter 4, an equivocal status. It is supported by widely used and traditionally influential patterns of moral argument, but it is not established as a logical constraint on the meanings of moral terms and statements.

The third stage of universalization is less strongly supported again by what we have identified as the object of morality. No doubt if everyone gave equal weight to all currently held ideals and values, and hence to all actual interests, conflicts would be very thoroughly resolved; but this is not necessary in order to counter the evils which it is the function of morality in the narrow sense to check, nor is it practicable. People do have specific and divergent ideals and values, and it is not possible genuinely to adhere to an ideal and at the same time to subordinate it completely to some resultant of all ideals.

There is still force, however, in the argument that principles which are to govern the adjustment of conflicting claims, and so check the bad results of the confined generosity of mankind, had better be ones that can be endorsed from all points of view – not only no matter what one's actual condition is, but also no matter what one's actual ideals and values are. This may be too much to hope for. Some actual disagreements about values are so extreme that they react against any principles that are proposed for the adjustment of claims: it may be impossible to agree even about the procedures for reaching agreement. Those who subscribe wholeheartedly to some ideal may be unwilling to tolerate any constraint upon the methods by which they strive to achieve their goal. Nevertheless the realistic moral aim is to maintain or establish such constraints, not to reach or impose agreement about goals or ideals.

3. The need for secondary principles

The issue between deontology and consequentialism is often raised by asking 'Should we always act so as to bring about the best possible results on the whole, or are there some things that must be done, and/or others that must not be done, whatever the consequences?' But if the main line of my argument is accepted, the question in that form will be seen as misleading. There are no objective moral prescriptions of either sort. Our question must rather be, 'Are all the guides to conduct that we want people to adopt, and all the constraints on conduct that we want them to accept, of the form "Act so as to bring about x as far as possible", or are some of them of the form "Do" (or "Do not do . . .") "things of kind y"?'

Once we put the question in this form, it seems easily answered. Even those who would be called consequentialists – for example, utilitarians like Mill – accept deontology at this level. 'Secondary principles' framed in terms of kinds of action that are, or are not, to be performed will often be our immediate guides. There are several reasons why this must be so.

In general any calculation of the consequences of an action beyond the most immediate and obvious ones, even if it were possible, would be absurdly wasteful of time and effort. Besides, even where a choice is serious enough to warrant careful consideration, the question about *all* the differential consequences of this or that alternative is almost always intractable. Even after the event, and even if all the facts were known, there would be serious theoretical problems about what to assign as consequences of my having done this rather than that, particularly when this act is overlain by many others, and what has happened can be traced causally not only to my choice but also to many independent or partly independent choices of other agents. Perhaps these theoretical problems can be solved; but it will still be impossible in practice for an agent to be guided by consideration of all the consequences of alternative actions where these consequences will depend upon many factors that are inevitably unknown to this agent, some but not all of these being the independent or partly independent simultaneous or later choices of other agents. Nor is it illuminating to say that the agent can be guided by the totality of the probable consequences of each alternative; in most cases there will be only a few fairly definitely likely consequences, but our knowledge of the kind of act that a proposed act will be, some description of it as kindly or cruel, honest or dishonest, candid or deceitful, generous or mean, will have to do duty for the practically impossible weighing of a long but utterly obscure train of other 'probable consequences'. If we restate the utilitarian principle as 'Do what can *with reasonable safety* be predicted to maximize satisfaction,' we shall still in practice have to rely on secondary principles as guides to what we can reasonably predict to be beneficial.

Again, where it is to some extent possible to calculate consequences, the attempt to do so may well not lead to good results. In calculating about a particular case, subject to the necessity of acting straight away on the decision, one is liable to give undue weight to claims or considerations that are somehow more vivid, that seem immediately more pressing, at the expense of others which calmer and more detached judgement (such as one may have the leisure for when it is too late) would treat as having greater relative importance. There are in practice great advantages in acting on principle, and in having predetermined principles on which to act. We are rightly sceptical about a man of principle who has a new principle for every case. His decisions are likely to show just that undue deference to what is immediately vivid or pressing which it is one function of principles to counteract.

Anything that I can see as a good life for myself will include the bringing about of certain results by my choices, activities, and endeavours. Such purposive actions of mine will be performed in what is largely a human, social, environment. They presuppose, therefore, some degree of regularity and reliability in the behaviour of other people. What makes it possible for me to live my life as I choose, to any extent, is that very many other people do their jobs, refrain from invading what I regard as my rights, and respond in standard ways when I seek to buy goods or services. There are many relations and transactions in which I treat other persons as means. Of course it may be that these other persons are also fulfilling some of their purposes in or by these transactions; but it is important from my point of view that they are doing so, if at all, in standardized ways. Life is, fortunately, not a continuous application of game theory. My variably purposive actions presuppose respects in which the actions of others, whether purposive or not, are relatively non-variable. But the demands that I thus make on others are not unfair if there are other transactions in which I am content that other persons should treat me as a means, if there are respects in which my behaviour is sufficiently standardized to help to constitute a reliably responsive human environment for the freely variable purposive action of others. This pattern of interaction, in which for each person there is some body of relations and transactions with respect to which his choices are the variable factor and the behaviour and responses of others are fairly reliable, requires that the majority of human actions should be guided either by habit or by conscious attention to the kind of action that any envisaged alternative would be, that is, to some description under which the action can be easily recognized as falling by others, as well as by the agent himself, rather than by the calculation of any considerable range of consequences.

These points are so obvious that it is unlikely that consequentialists would deny them, though their writings might sometimes suggest this. If there is a real dispute, it is on other issues.

4. Special relationships and the form of moral principles

There is an important formal difference between consequential and deontological guides to action, if they are stated in a universalized form or, *a fortiori*, if they are seen as objective requirements. A consequential principle will say merely that such-and-such is (or is not) to be brought about: it leaves no room for any essential mention of who is (or is not) to bring it about. But a deontological principle can make essential mention of the agent, and so of various sorts of special relation between him and what he does or particular things or persons on whom his action impinges. We noted in Chapter 6 that egoism could not be defeated by appeal to the notion of what is objectively right – it could be objectively right for everyone to seek *his own* happiness – but only by appeal to the consequentialist notion of something objectively good as an end. This form of egoism is also universalizable, or rather already universalized. But it is

157

only one of many sorts of deontological principle that make use of this formal feature. Deontology leaves room also for the self-referential altruism that builds, sensibly, on widespread tendencies in human nature: one may have the right, or the duty, to look after *one's own* children (or other relatives) in preference to persons who, apart from this relationship to oneself, would have equal claims. But if all that mattered was consequences, then, in so far as these counted morally, all similar cases would count alike, regardless of any special relationships. Deontology similarly leaves room for duties arising from the agent's own previous actions, or from the actions of others that have affected him, such as the duty to fulfil a contract or promise, or to show gratitude, or to repay benefits, or to compensate for harm done. (It also formally leaves room for a right to take revenge for injuries, and for retributive principles of punishment, but we may not want our moral system to make use of these formal possibilities.) Of course there will often be a consequentialist case for actions that fulfil one or other of these duties, but this case would need to be made out in each instance, and might be rebutted by other considerations of the same consequentialist sort: what deontology can do, while consequentialism cannot, is to make actions described in terms of such special relations to the agent obligatory or wrong as such. A consequentialist would have no difficulty in pointing out the good consequences that flow from there being such 'institutions' as gratitude, compensation, promising, several kinds of self-referential altruism, and even a moderate amount of egoism. But it is more embarrassing for him to have to admit that these good consequences can come about only if these 'institutions' stand, in practice, on their own feet, if those whose actions exemplify and maintain them are themselves observing principles of a non-consequentialist form, and taking some special relations as in themselves reasons for action.

5. Ends and means

Discussion between consequentialists and deontologists has often centred on Machiavelli's dictum that the end justifies the means. If this meant that any end which could be seen in itself as good would justify the use, to bring it about, of any means, however bad, then the consequentialist who adopted this maxim would have to explain how ends differed from means and why this difference was of such moral significance that only an end matters, that a means counts for nothing at all. But not even Machiavelli held this, nor is it the usual consequentialist view, which is rather that there is no morally relevant distinction between means and ends, that any badness in the proposed means has to be balanced fairly against the expected goodness of the end, with no special weighting for either, but that it is possible even for a means which is in itself very bad to be outweighed and therefore 'justified' by a sufficiently good end. If consequentialism thus requires that everything known to be involved in a course of action – the chosen end, the means adopted to achieve it, side effects of that means, and further consequences that will follow from the chosen end – should be taken equally into account, then a deontological view could clash with it in either (or both) of two ways. It could hold that factors of these four types – end, means, side effects, further consequences – are *not* all of equal weight, that some play a bigger part than others in determining the moral quality of an action (or, in our way of looking at the matter, that action-controlling principles are to be framed with more regard to some of these factors than to others). Again, it could hold that some aspects of some actions determine their moral quality absolutely, that there are some descriptions such that if an action or proposed action falls under one of them it can thereby be judged either obligatory or wrong without further ado, no matter what else it involves (or, in our way of looking at the matter, that people are to adopt such action-controlling principles as that justice is to be done though the heavens fall, or that truth is to be told, or agreements

159

kept, or that innocent human beings are not to be deliberately killed, no matter what else the action involves or carries with it). Leaving this second, absolutist, view on one side for a moment, we can see some point in giving special prominence to one of our four types of factor, the chosen end. It is naturally in terms of the objects to which they are directed that actions are primarily characterized. The first line of moral defence is the attempt to set limits to what ends people pursue. Though we admit that the way to hell may be paved with good intentions, we are very sure that the way to heaven is not paved with bad ones. Consider two people who together plant a bomb in a railway station, knowing (or believing firmly and with good reason) that this will both promote some intrinsically defensible political cause and do damage to property, inconvenience many travellers, and endanger some lives. There is a sense in which each of them 'intends' both these results: each acts with the full expectation that what he is doing will bring both results about. But suppose that one of the two has the promotion of this political cause as his chosen end and accepts the foreseen harm as an unavoidable accompaniment of this, while for the other the foreseen harm is itself his chosen end, and the promotion of the political cause merely incidental; are we not inclined to view the two rather differently? We certainly evaluate differently the motives and the characters of the two men. It is a primary requirement of a morality that is to serve the purpose sketched in Chapter 5 that people should not foster and satisfy a love of gratuitous harm. Such a morality no doubt also needs somehow to limit the harm that may be tolerated as a side effect or used as a means to an intrinsically worthy end; but that is a further, secondary, matter.

6. Absolutism and the principle of double effect

It is a more difficult question whether a similar distinction should be drawn between a means on the one hand and either a side effect or a further consequence on the other – we can call either of them a second effect. Such a distinction is drawn by the principle of double effect which is used and defended by Roman Catholic moralists and which can be traced back at least to Aquinas. For example, a man defending himself against an attacker may do something which has two effects: the saving of his own life and the death of the attacker. Aquinas says that if he intends the former, his action is right, provided that he does not use more force than is needed for this. But unless he is acting with public authority for the common good, a man is not permitted to kill another; so if a man who lacks this authority intends the death of his attacker and kills him, his action will be wrong, even though his ultimate aim was to save his own life and the killing of the attacker was a means to this. A well-known modern example is that it is held that a doctor may give pain-killing drugs to a patient who would otherwise die in agony, although as a side effect his death is accelerated; but he must not give a drug that will kill the patient as a way of preventing further pain.

There undoubtedly is a distinction between the way in which a means is related to a chosen end and the ways in which a side effect and a further consequence are. It is recognized, for example, by Bentham, who says that an agent 'directly intends' not only his actual goal but also whatever he chooses as a means to that goal, but only 'obliquely intends' a known second effect. But is this distinction morally relevant?

The main reason why it has been thought important by Catholic moralists is that it seems necessary if there are to be absolute moral rules, for example ones which forbid murder, adultery, or apostasy in any circumstances. If an agent is equally responsible for all the foreseen consequences of an immediate action (or failure to act) as well as for that action itself, there will be conflict cases where different rules, or even different applications of the same rule, require incompatible actions, so that the rule (or rules) cannot (both) be absolute. As Anscombe says, 'If someone innocent will die unless I do a wicked thing, then on this view I am his murderer in refusing, so all that is left to me is to weigh up evils.' I might be forced to

161

kill one innocent person to save the lives of several others. Again, if a doctor can save the life of an unborn child only at the cost of the mother's life, and can save the life of the mother only at the cost of the child's, then if we do not invoke the principle of double effect we shall have to say that whatever the doctor does, even if he does nothing, he is morally responsible for the death of one presumably innocent person. But if we use the principle of double effect we can retain absolute moral rules; for example, we can say that the doctor can save one of the two persons at the cost of the death of the other, provided that this death is a second effect and not a means. Even under duress, I can refuse to kill an innocent person, though I know that others will die as a result of my refusal, for this too will be a second effect.

In other words, we could have a system of absolute prohibitions about directly intended actions – chosen ends and means – whereas we could not maintain absolute prohibitions if their scope were extended to include obliquely intended actions – side effects and further consequences.

There is, indeed, one other way in which absolute prohibitions could be maintained even if their scope were thus extended: we could distinguish positive acts from omissions, and frame absolute rules only about positive acts. No conflict cases could then arise, because in any conceivable set of circumstances all prohibitions of kinds of positive act (including the bringing about of certain evils as known second effects) could be obeyed at once by complete inaction.

But do we want to maintain absolutism in either of these ways?

There is at least one important difference between a means on the one hand and a side effect or further consequence on the other. Suppose that a chosen end is good, while each of the other three (means, side effect, further consequence) is bad. It may be fairly certain that what the agent immediately does will achieve the chosen end, while the side effect or further consequence is uncertain. Then even a consequentialist will allow, in his calculation of the total goodness or badness of the proposed course of action, for this uncertainty: he will discount, to some appropriate extent, the badness of the uncertain side effect or consequence, and therefore not allow it to weigh so heavily as it otherwise would against the goodness of the chosen end. But the badness of a means cannot be thus relatively discounted. For since it is a means, it is only through it, if at all, that the chosen end will be achieved. So any uncertainty in the coming about of the (bad) means will carry with it at least the same uncertainty in the achievement of the (good) end; any discounting of the badness of the means for uncertainty is matched by an at least equal discounting of the goodness of the end. To put the same point slightly differently, if there is an evil which we only obliquely intend, which we accept as a second effect, we may still hope that it will not come about – or, if we have religious beliefs, pray that it will not or trust that God will avert it; but it would be absurd to do any of these with what we intend directly, as a means to our chosen end. It is true that this sort of consideration will not allow a consequentialist to give any different weight to a second effect, as compared with a means, where the second effect is known to be as likely to come about as the means and the end to which it is a means: he will not downgrade second effects as such. Yet if second effects are often less certain, reluctance to use a bad means may in general be more beneficial than a similar reluctance to tolerate a bad second effect, so that we can understand how a moral system which fostered the former reluctance more than the latter might thereby better achieve what we have taken to be the object of morality. Besides, to be effective a moral constraint must be attached to what the agent sees himself as doing, to some description under which the agent recognizes his proposed action as falling. An agent cannot fail to be fully aware of what he chooses as an end or as a means; but he may not attend in the same way to second effects even if they are to some extent foreseen.

Similar considerations apply where the side effects or further consequences come about partly through the choices of other agents. Here a simple ruling would be that if a bad second effect

of A's action would come about only through some later decision of B, then, even if this second effect is foreseen by A,
responsibility for it can be assigned to B and not to A, so that
the prohibition of the bringing about of such an effect would
not forbid A's action. But this would be too simple. It is more
natural to say that if B's action would be a legitimate or even
morally required response to A's action or to the situation created by it, any evil involved in or produced by B's action must
be charged against A's action, whereas if B's action is, in the
circumstances created by A's, unreasonable or wrong, the evil is
not to be charged against A's action; but further that if A's
action somehow tempts B to do what produces the bad result,
the responsibility for this result is to be assigned both to A and
to B, or perhaps shared between them. Briefly, the more defensible or excusable B's action is, given the situation created by
A's, the more the bad effect is to be counted against A's action
and, consequently, the more any prohibition of the bringing
about of such an effect is to be taken as prohibiting A's action.
However, even this principle seems to call for further
qualification: if B's action, though neither defensible nor excusable, could be confidently anticipated as a response to A's, then
A must take some responsibility for the result, and the more
automatic B's response could be foreseen as being, the more of
the responsibility for the result must be referred back to A's
action. Of course, to say this is to deal hastily with considerations of kinds that lawyers weigh carefully in concrete
particular cases; here and elsewhere moral philosophy appears
as a poor relation of law. But for us the more important aim is
not to improve further the formulation of such a principle and
qualification, but to see the rationale behind them. And it is
surely this. The object of the exercise is to reduce the likelihood
of a certain kind of evil being brought about by a pattern of
two-agent performances of which A's action followed by B's
response to it is an instance. The rationale of our principle is
that if actions of the kind to which B's belongs morally cannot
be discouraged (because they are of some generally defensible
or excusable sort), then the evil has to be opposed by dis-

couraging such actions as A's, but that where such actions as B's morally can be discouraged there is no need to discourage such actions as A's. The rationale of our qualification is that where actions such as B's practically cannot be discouraged, even though there is no moral obstacle to discouraging them, it may still be necessary to discourage such actions as A's.

To understand this argument, we must recall what is the form of the problem of morality in the narrow sense. We must think of a 'game' in which most, perhaps all, of the 'players' are largely selfish, or have limited sympathies, in a situation where scarce resources and the like tend to produce conflicts of interest; further, it is important for most of the 'players' that certain roughly specifiable evils (which, other things being equal, would result from the basic situation) should be prevented or reduced; we are asking what are the possibly acceptable principles of constraint on action the general encouragement of and widespread respect for which will do most to counter these evils, subject to the assumption that these constraints will not be respected by all the 'players' all the time. Within this framework the considerations mentioned are sufficient to show that we might want these principles of constraint to include absolute prohibitions against the taking of certain sorts of result as chosen ends and yet not to include similar absolute prohibitions with regard to obliquely intended second effects. But it is still not clear whether we want them to include the corresponding absolute prohibitions with regard to means.

In support of such absolutism, it may be argued that a non-absolutist who accepted our above-stated qualification could be blackmailed into doing something which would be absolutely ruled out as a chosen end – for example, into killing some innocent people to avert the worse evil of the blackmailer killing a larger number. An absolutist could not be thus pushed around, and a potential blackmailer, knowing this, might not even try to do so. This is a good argument for resistance to such pressure, provided that such resistance can be systematically displayed by some recognizable class of persons, so that potential blackmailers may know when it will be useless for them to exert pressure. It is not a good argument for resistance in a particular case which will not contribute to such a systematic practice of resistance. Nor, of course, can it be used to support absolutism about means where the proposed end is the averting of an evil which will come about (if the means we are thinking of prohibiting is not adopted) by natural causes rather than by the choice of someone who is using this threat to put pressure on another agent.

Against absolutism about means, it can be argued that though the distinction between a means and a side effect can be drawn formally, the distinction is sometimes too fine and, in our ordinary thought about actions, too artificial to carry much weight in a practically viable moral system. It seems absurd to say that I must not use someone's death as a means to some end – say, the saving of many other lives – and yet that I may use as a means to that end something which will inevitably, and to my certain knowledge, carry his death with it. To lay stress on such artificial distinctions is not merely implausible but also morally corrupting. Anscombe has herself said that, while the rejection of the principle of double effect has been the corruption of non-Catholic moral thought, its abuse has been the corruption of Catholic thought. I suggest that such corruption follows automatically from the view that a second effect *as such*, however certain and however well known to be certain, and apart from the special considerations introduced by the actions of other agents, has less moral weight than a means. Yet the devaluing of a second effect as such is required if absolutism is to be maintained in the face of some extreme problem cases.

The same charge of artificiality can be brought against the other device that we mentioned as a way of defending absolute prohibitions, the distinction of positive acts from omissions. It is not of course artificial to distinguish evils that I directly bring about from some which I fail to prevent, even though it would have been remotely possible for me to prevent them. Any workable morality must make some distinction of spheres of responsibility, and hold me specially responsible for evils, whether produced by positive acts or by omissions, within my special sphere. But the distinction between what is and what is not within my sphere of responsibility is quite different from one between positive acts and omissions, and unlike the latter would not provide a defence for absolutism.

I conclude that strict absolutism about means cannot be reasonably maintained, and that, given our approach to morality, it is not to be maintained at the expense of the above-mentioned qualification, that even where a bad second effect results from the action of another agent *B*, the more automatic *B*'s response can be foreseen as being, the more the responsibility for this effect must be referred back to *A*'s action. To neglect this qualification would be an evasion of responsibility. Absolutism has the dramatic appeal and, associated with this, the real practical merit of a straightforward and clear-cut, though severe, system of constraints. But against this are the artificiality into which it is forced at some points and its indefensible rigidity in some extreme cases.

However, to reject absolutism on these grounds is not to go over to a simple consequentialism. Not only do all the points made in Sections 3 and 4 above in favour of action on principles, including some that take account of special relations, remain in force; it is also true that there are certain descriptions of actions (including 'murder', 'unjust judicial decision', and 'treachery', though not 'adultery' or 'apostasy') such that in an already existing (though of course not universally respected) morality actions that fall under these descriptions are very nearly out of the question, whatever other favourable descriptions may also apply to them, and that this must be so in a morality that is to serve the purpose we have sketched. Given what we have found to be the general form of the moral problem, respect for these nearly absolute principles is a feature of existing morality which it is reasonable to preserve. But only nearly absolute; regrettably, such actions cannot be seen as completely out of the question.

To put the issue crudely, consider three possibilities with regard to the moral constraints that most people might observe: first, that they should be act consequentialists, each with respect

167

to his own conception of the good; second, that they should be strict absolutists, adopting some plausible set of absolute prohibitions, with regard to what they directly intend, as chosen ends and means, but not with regard to what they obliquely intend, as foreseen second effects, however closely and certainly these are causally linked with what they directly intend; third, that they should adopt principles that are absolutist with respect to chosen ends, but only very nearly absolutist with respect to means, allowing some weight to second effects in such ways as I have indicated. Which of these three possibilities will best serve the object of morality, given that the general situation is as we have described it and that in any case not everyone is going to observe these constraints? Certainly not the first. But also, I think, the second is inferior to the third. The most plausible absolute prohibitions must be violated where strict adherence to them would result in disaster.

The religious believer may concede that this is as far as human reasoning will carry us, but still insist that God's moral commands are absolute, and that we have simply to obey them, calculating consequences only within the limits they set, and trusting that God himself will avert or put right the disastrous consequences which otherwise seem certain to result from our obedience to these absolute rules. Yet we know of appalling tragedies that God has not averted. And why should a believer ascribe to a presumably rational and benevolent God an absolutism more extreme than any moral reasoning of ours could justify without begging the question by recourse to a morally absolutist God? To find a religious basis for moral absolutism, he must appeal not to reasonable inference about God's will but to revelation. But what revelation? It would, for example, be intolerable to take the Christian Bible as a whole and literally as an authoritative moral guide, but once we select from and interpret its messages they can support non-absolutist as easily as absolutist views.

Chapter 8 Elements of a Practical Morality

1. The good for man

When we set out to sketch a practical system of morality in the broad sense, the question which we naturally begin by asking is Aristotle's: 'What is the good life for man?' And, remembering the discussion in Chapter 2, we may willingly admit that 'good' here is indeterminate. The good life will be such as to satisfy the interests in question; that is, the interests of those who participate in the good life – and hence, when we think of any specific activities, the interests both of those who engage in them and those who are affected by them – but also ours: what we call the good life must be one that we can welcome and approve. But though we can ask this question, it is not so easy to answer it, for two reasons. First, different people have irresolvably different views of the good life – not only at different periods of history and in different forms of society, but even in our own culture at the present time. Such differences may be correlated with various political views, with attachments to different religions or to none, and simply with what as individuals we enjoy and admire. But, secondly, a specific answer cannot be given in any brief, abstract, way. It is in imaginative literature – including those parts of it which pass for history and biography – that what may be good in human life is concretely represented, both directly and by contrast with what is not good. Not, of course, that the authors of such literature commonly label as good or bad what they display; it is sufficient if they show real possibilities of life in some detail, rather than romanticized impossibilities – or, if these are shown, that they are labelled as what they are – leaving the reader to draw his own moral conclusions. But this is obviously not a work of that

169

sort. I can write only in general terms, and hope that specific content will be supplied from other sources.

We can, however, say firmly that for any individual a good life will be made up largely of the effective pursuit of activities that he finds worthwhile, either intrinsically, or because they are directly beneficial to others about whom he cares, or because he knows them to be instrumental in providing the means of well-being for himself and those closely connected with him. Egoism and self-referential altruism will together characterize, to a large extent, both his actions and his motives. The happiness with which I am, inevitably, most concerned is my own, and next that of those who are in some way closely related to me. Indeed, for any reasonably benevolent person these cannot be separated: he will find much of his own happiness in the happiness of those for whom he cares, or in what he and they do together, where the enjoyment of each contributes so essentially to that of the other(s) that it will be more natural to say 'We had a good . . .' (whatever it was) than to speak of a mere sum of individual enjoyments.

But the altruism that thus forms part of the good life is self-referential. Confined generosity, in Hume's phrase, is what we can expect and all that we can reasonably hope for. There is nothing wrong with self-love and confined generosity in themselves. We have already noted that they can have bad effects which the special device of morality in the narrow sense is needed to counteract; we need some constraints on the pursuit of these narrower interests. Nevertheless the pursuit of them is a large and central part of the good life. Of course there can be, and there plainly is, cooperation of many sorts that extends far beyond the range of self-referential altruism. It is the main function of any economic system to produce cooperation that is quite independent of affection or goodwill, and it is one function of political organizations to maintain conditions in which this is possible. But if we accept the centrality of self-love and confined generosity, we must, as a corollary, accept competition and some degree of conflict between individuals and between groups. Rival social and political ideals offer different ways in which cooperation, competition, and conflict may be institutionalized and regulated, but every real alternative includes some combination of all three of them.

This would be obvious if it were not that moralists in both the Christian and the humanist traditions have fostered an opposite view, that the good life for man is one of universal brotherly love and selfless pursuit of the general happiness. I have already argued, in Chapter 6, that this is quite impracticable; I would now add that it has little plausibility even as an ideal.

Points of this sort were very forcefully made by Fitzjames Stephen in opposition to what he saw as the dominant trend in Mill's later work. He rejects Mill's belief 'that this natural feeling for oneself and one's friends, gradually changing its character, is [to be] sublimated into a general love for the human race'. Against this 'transcendental utilitarianism' he sets 'common utilitarianism' which tells us to love our neighbours and hate our enemies – but with qualifications:

'Love your neighbour in proportion to the degree in which he approaches yourself and appeals to your passions and sympathies. In hating your enemy, bear in mind the fact that under immediate excitement you are very likely to hate him more than you would wish to do upon a deliberate consideration of all his relations to yourself and your friends, and of your permanent and remote as compared with your immediate interest'.

He contrasts 'The man who works from himself outwards, and who acts with a view to his own advantage and the advantage of those who are connected with himself in definite, assignable ways' with 'a man who has a disinterested love for the human race' – which Stephen suspects to be 'little, if anything, more than a fanatical attachment to some favourite theory about the means by which an indefinite number of unknown persons ... may be brought into a state which the theorist calls happiness' – and 'who is capable of making his love for men in general the ground of all sorts of violence against men in particular'.

The alternative to universalism is not an extreme individualism. Any possible, and certainly any desirable, Human life is social. We can see each individual as located in a number of circles – smaller and larger, but sometimes intersecting, not all concentric – and so united with others in a variety of ways. Within any circle, large or small, we must expect and accept not only some cooperation but also some competition and conflict, but different kinds and degrees of these in circles of different size. Within a family, within a group of scientists or philosophers, between the members of some department or of any other group of people who are working together, between employees and whatever it is that employs them, between business firms, and between states there will be differentially appropriate sorts of cooperation and differentially appropriate sorts of competition and conflict. Also, individuals belong vitally to diachronic social wholes as well as to these synchronic ones. Each individual is linked not only to his biological ancestors but also to traditions of activity and information and thought and belief and value; nearly all of what anyone most distinctively and independently is he owes to many others. The taking over and passing on – with perhaps some changes – of a cultural inheritance is itself a part of the good life, and this too is a social relation to which there belong appropriate sorts of conflict as well as cooperation.

2. Egoism, rights, and property

Any plausible view of the good for man, any viable concept of happiness, will, I believe, have this general form. But, as I have said, there will be many irresolvably different specific views, different contents with which this form may be filled. We might suppose that each ideal of life would carry with it its own distinct set of moral principles. To some extent this is true; but it does not follow, as one might suppose, that there is nothing more to be said in general terms. Something further can be inferred from the general form, on which there should be a considerable measure of agreement. Widely different ideals may still need, for their support, some common basic moral principles.

When I said that egoism and self-referential altruism would form a central part of the good life, I was of course using these terms themselves to describe kinds of activity and kinds of motivation. But it follows that we shall want egoism also as a moral principle: we want people to see it as not only legitimate but right and proper that they should pursue what they see as their own well-being. In the same way we shall want some self-referentially altruistic moral principles. But which ones? Will that have to be left to be determined by the choice of a specific ideal? Not wholly, because we can say that there is at least a *prima facie* case for each person's adopting those principles that conventionally belong with whatever relationships he finds himself in, or enters more or less voluntarily, and in which he hopes to remain.

Also, it is a consequence of the general form I have ascribed to the good life that the notion of *rights*, both of individuals and of groups, will be valuable and indeed vital. Rights can be, formally, of several different sorts, but the most basic distinction is that between a liberty and a claim-right. To say that someone has a right, of whatever sort, is to speak either of or within some legal or moral system: our rejection of objective values carries with it the denial that there are any self-subsistent rights. To say that someone has a certain liberty, then, may be to say that the system in question, whatever it is, does not forbid him to act in the way indicated – or (speaking within the system) it may be to give him permission so to act, or explicitly to refrain from forbidding him to do so. To say that someone has a certain claim-right may similarly be to say that if he claims (or if someone representing him claims on his behalf) whatever it is that he has this right to, the system will support his obtaining what he claims – or (speaking within the system) to say that he has this right may be to give him this support, typically by imposing on one or more or indefinitely many others the duty of fulfilling the claim if it is made. A liberty and a related claim-right may go together: for example, it will often be natural to associate with the liberty to do something the claim-right not to be impeded by others in doing it. There often are clusters of rights, of which the ownership of property is an example. Now one function that a system of rights can fulfil is to secure, for individuals or groups, areas of freedom of action. This is not the only function that rights can serve, but it is one that could not be served nearly so well by anything else. Then, given that each individual's pursuit of what he sees as his own happiness is a large and central part of the good life, he needs an area, and preferably a secured area, in which he is free to make choices that contribute to that pursuit.

Such general considerations support the view that there should be some rights, but they do not determine what rights should be recognized. Jefferson's formulation of a right to the pursuit of happiness is too vague: it does not specify any definite content of a right, but rather sums up what I have offered as the general reason why there should be some rights. In fact I would defend two negative theses, that specific rights cannot be determined *a priori*, on general grounds, and that whatever rights are recognized should not be absolute.

The first thesis entails that even in theory rights can be determined only by reference to a particular ideal or conception of happiness, or to some system of rights that is already recognized, or by some interplay between the two, and that in practice rights have to be determined by a politico-legal process, typically by partial modification of an existing system through conflict and compromise between rival ideals.

It is difficult to establish such a universal negative thesis as this, but I shall illustrate it by criticizing one kind of attempt at an *a priori* derivation. A particularly important right would be the right to the ownership of property. It was maintained by John Locke, and the view has recently been revived in a modern form by Robert Nozick, that there is a natural law of property, that we can decide, independently of any positive law or positive morality, that there is a way in which a man can legitimately acquire property to which he then has a right, and that there are also legitimate methods of transferring property (for example, voluntary exchanges and gifts and bequests) and hence that if someone now holds property either by legitimate initial acquisition or as a result of a series, however long, of legitimate transfers from someone who initially acquired it legitimately, then he is entitled to keep it, and any move to take any of it from him – for instance, to redistribute it to others who are less well off – would be unjust.

Locke's basic principle is that everyone has an exclusive right to his own person and to his own labour; and he argues that this carries over into an exclusive right to whatever portion of what God gave originally to all men in common to enjoy he mixes his labour with. Now even if we grant Locke's premisses, this will not follow without qualification. If a man has mixed his labour with some apples by picking them, or with some ore by mining it, or with some land by clearing and fencing it, it would be natural to say that the value of what he then has derives from two sources, part indeed from his labour, but part also from what was there at the start – the apples on the tree, the ore in the ground, the wild forest or scrub. Only the first of these two parts belongs exclusively to the man: the second is, on Locke's assumptions, the common property of all men. To forestall this objection, Locke says that one can acquire something by mixing one's labour with it only 'where there is enough, and as good left in common for others'. If the common property is not effectively diminished, the rights that others have in what a man annexes by mixing his labour with it can be ignored: what I have called the second part of the thing's value can be rated at zero, and all its final value ascribed to the labour of the man who has acquired it.

It is plain that this vital proviso, that there should be enough and as good left for others – which Nozick echoes – cannot in general be satisfied now, nor could it have been satisfied, in many countries, even hundreds of years ago. If we are thinking of the acquisition of land, it can be satisfied only where there is an indefinitely extensible 'frontier', and if we are thinking of removable but lasting goods like metals or stone or wood it can be satisfied only where there are large unused but accessible resources. In a world where nearly all resources are short and are the object of competition, Locke's theory has no application. Nor could he argue that acquisition which was legitimate at the time, because the proviso was *then* satisfied, confers a lasting right to property which persists even when the proviso is no longer satisfied. On Locke's principles, God must be presumed to give the whole earth *at any time* in common to all the men there *at that time*. Therefore, when the vital proviso is no longer satisfied, goods once legitimately acquired can no longer be retained in exclusive possession, but revert to common ownership.

The same follows if we shift the discussion from the theological setting Locke gives it to, say, that of a Rawlsian choice of principles. It would probably be reasonable for persons in Rawls's initial position to adopt Locke's rule of property acquisition *with the proviso*. But where the proviso cannot be satisfied, where there is a problem of the division of scarce resources, it will not be reasonable to adopt any simple principle that one can acquire goods by mixing one's labour with them.

But perhaps we can develop the labour theory of property rights in another way: a man is the rightful owner of whatever part of a thing's value has been contributed by his labour. This principle simply sidesteps the problem of the distribution of scarce resources, leaving that to be dealt with in some other way. What it says about what it does deal with is plausible (for example from either Locke's point of view or Rawls's). But there would be insuperable difficulties in applying it in most cases. Almost all goods that are produced by labour (as opposed to natural resources as they are *in situ*) embody directly or indirectly the labour of indefinitely many people, and even what we see as the labour of one man may embody techniques, skills, and knowledge provided by others. Besides, goods that have already been produced may acquire more value through changes in circumstances; such increases in value cannot be ascribed to the labour of the producer of these goods (but perhaps to that of the producers of other goods). Equally,

176

changing circumstances may reduce market value. When goods are eventually exchanged, therefore, their exchange value may bear little relation to the value of which the producer is, by our revised Lockean principle, the rightful owner. Nor is it obvious that inheritance is, without restrictions, a legitimate way of acquiring ownership. It seems reasonable to say that if A is the rightful owner of some piece of property, one of the things he may do with it is to give it to B; but when A, being dead, is no longer there, *his* rights surely lapse automatically; so A's rights can no longer license B's enjoyment of the property. There is indeed a case for recognizing some right to bequeath and inherit property, but it has to be made out on its own merits and in competition with other considerations: no absolute right to bequeath follows from the labour theory of property rights alone. Our revised principle, then, however intrinsically plausible, does not lend itself to direct application, and there is certainly no reason to suppose that the outcome of any ordinary process of production by private enterprise, exchanges at market prices, gifts, and inheritance will reflect it with any semblance of accuracy. Neither actual property holdings nor holdings in any workable system can be justified by this principle alone. At most, the thought behind it is one consideration among others that may reasonably be brought into the debate about what concrete property rules and rights there are to be.

In any case, the ownership of property is itself a cluster of rights. It is not simple and absolute: it has to be determined what the 'owner' can and cannot do with various sorts of property. It is, then, hardly to be expected that there should be any simple *a priori* way of assigning what is itself complex and variable.

However, the conclusion to be drawn from this is not that there can be no rights to property (or in particular private property) but only that such rights cannot be derived from self-evident first principles. They have to be worked out and created and modified through time by the interplay of various considerations and various pressures. Indeed there is a strong general case, founded on the legitimacy of a considerable degree of

177

egoism and self-referential altruism, and connected with what I have offered as the basic case for rights as the essential device for securing areas for the free pursuit of happiness, in favour of some private property. This is one point among many where our grounds for dissatisfaction with at least the cruder forms of utilitarianism have practical consequences. If we see the good for man as happiness, conceived as a single, undifferentiated commodity, we may also suppose that it could be provided for all, in some centrally planned way, if only we could get an authority that was sufficiently powerful and sufficiently intelligent, and also one that we could trust to be uniformly well-disposed to all its subjects; and then the natural corollary would be that all property should be owned by all in common, collectively, and applied to the maximizing of the general happiness under the direction of this benevolent authority. But if we reject this unitary notion of happiness, and identify the good for man rather with the partly competitive pursuit of diverse ideals and private goals, then separate ownership of property will be an appropriate instrument for this pursuit. From a very simple utilitarian point of view, with the general happiness as an objectively identifiable and supposedly agreed goal, individual (or group) rights and private property would appear as mere obstacles to the most efficient pursuit of this goal; but this no longer holds once we recognize that men's real goals are irresolvably diverse. Briefly, then, there is no natural law of property; but there is at least in Hobbes's sense a natural law that there should be some law of property.

If we turn from the individual ownership of property to the occupation of territory by national groups much the same applies. The Norwegian people, say, have a right to continue to occupy and control the territory known as Norway; but that they have this right is not a consequence of any absolute law of nature but an uncontroversial application of principles to which national groups commonly appeal and which they are usually ready to recognize by allowing claims made in terms of them by other national groups. But not everything in this field is uncontroversial. It is still a matter of international dispute and negotiation how much of the sea around Norway belongs to the Norwegian people and what kinds of restrictions they can place on its use by others. Does the right of a nation as it is at present to its territory include the right to forbid or to limit immigration, or to deny full citizenship to immigrants and even to the locally born children of immigrants? Obviously this raises the question just what is to count over time as the same nation, the potential bearer of the rights we are now considering. Also, notoriously, there are disputed territories – for example, border areas and regions occupied by groups which are not independent nations, but many of whose members wish that they were. Again, there are territories like that which used to be called Palestine; here the principles which in the case of Norway point univocally to one national group as that to which the area belongs diverge, some supporting the claims of the Israelis and others the claims of the Palestinian Arabs. Cyprus and Northern Ireland are two other obvious examples of conflicting *prima facie* rights of distinguishable national groups.

In such cases the appeal, by both parties to a dispute, to supposedly absolute rights is disastrous. It reduces the readiness to negotiate and compromise, and it seems to justify any atrocities against the enemy, and any resulting losses and suffering for one's own side, that are needed to vindicate those rights. But it is almost equally unhelpful to ask what solution will maximize total utility in the area, or happiness summed over all the people concerned. That is not a goal at which the conflicting groups can be expected to aim. Nor is a compromise which is merely a compromise, based simply on the relative military strength of the parties at the present time, likely to be a stable solution. The only approach to these intractable problems that is at all hopeful is to acknowledge the reality and the probable persistence of the conflict of aims, to try to get both parties to recognize their conflicting *prima facie* rights as such, and to look for a solution which can be seen as a reasonable compromise between these *prima facie* rights, and which can therefore be defended morally, not merely politically, in the court of international opinion in terms of principles which are already recognized and confidently relied upon in uncontroversial cases.

3. Liberty

Mill argued eloquently in favour of the principle that 'the only purpose for which power can be rightfully exercised over any member of a civilized community against his will is to prevent harm to others' and that 'The only part of the conduct of any one for which he is amenable to society is that which concerns others. In the part which merely concerns himself his independence is of right, absolute.' A person's 'own good, either physical or moral, is not a sufficient warrant' for any interference with his liberty, and Mill made it clear that he was excluding interference by 'the moral coercion of public opinion' as well as 'legal penalties'. On the other hand he said that a person's own good might provide a reason for 'remonstrating with him, or reasoning with him, or persuading him, or entreating him', and the line drawn between all these and 'moral coercion' is rather fine.

This principle is not easily defended on utilitarian grounds. Though Mill was careful to confine its application to civilized communities, and explicitly excluded the subjects of Akbar and Charlemagne and any modern nations at similar (or lower) stages of cultural development, he explicitly included 'all nations with whom we need here concern ourselves'; but it would be very hard to deny that many members of these nations, in Mill's time and later, are not the best judges or guardians of their own good, if this is reckoned in terms of quantity and quality of pleasures and freedom from pains. If the object were simply to maximize what is ordinarily called happiness, paternalism would often be justified. But it would be easier to defend the principle of non-interference in terms of Mill's 'utility in the largest sense, grounded on the permanent

interests of a man as a progressive being', or of the view of the
good for man sketched in Section 1 of this chapter.

What is more important, however, is that even if this principle can be defended it is far too weak a foundation for liberty.
Hardly any part of anyone's conduct concerns only himself.
Above all it would be absurd to defend the liberty of thought
and discussion on this ground (and Mill does not in fact do so).
The thought and discussion – political, moral, religious, or anti-
religious – the freedom of which it is especially important to
defend can have, in time, very great effects on the way of life of
innumerable people. Mill himself defends this freedom not on
the ground that such thought and discussion concerns only
those who engage in it, but on the ground that its effects are
likely to be beneficial rather than harmful. But it is by no means
plain that this will always be so if benefit and harm are
reckoned in a traditional utilitarian way. It is more plausible to
say that the kind of interference represented by free speech and
discussion, which affects other people in the first place by persuading them to change their views and policies, fits in with the
view of the good life sketched in Section 1. Yet even this does
not hold without qualification. It is all too clear that people can
be persuaded to destroy not only the freedoms of others but
also their own, including the freedom of discussion which that
persuasion exemplifies. The most we can say is that whatever
excuses are used, it is unlikely in practice that, if restraints on
freedom of discussion are imposed, this will be in even the long-
term interests of such freedom itself.

The general conclusion to be stressed, however, is that we
need not a supposedly self-evident principle of non-interference,
but principles of legitimate interference, rules which distinguish
acceptable from unacceptable ways of affecting other people –
perhaps quite radically – where the acceptable ways are those
that in the concrete situation harmonize with the general form
of conditions for the good life.

Liberties conflict with one another, and almost any policy
whatever can be represented as a defence – direct or indirect –
of some sort of liberty. What we need, therefore, is not a

general defence of liberty, but adjudication between particular rival claims to freedom. For example, parents commonly claim the right to bring up their own children as they think fit, and in particular to bring them up as adherents of whatever religion they themselves profess, and to hand on to them, if they can, their own beliefs and their own moral outlook. But this may constitute a very grave interference with the freedom of the children to make up their own minds about these matters. Was Rousseau right, then, in holding that parents and teachers alike should refrain from any pre-rational indoctrination, leaving all these subjects to be discussed rationally after the children are old enough to take part critically and intelligently in such discussion? This is an attractive ideal. But it is unrealistic to demand the postponement of all consideration of morals and religion in a world where from their earliest years children are confronted with all sorts of information and influences and opinions. Still, we could insist that children should not be subjected to the one-sided teaching of any single set of doctrines, and above all that there should not be one-sided teaching coupled with the view that it would be wicked even to consider any contrary opinions. That is, we can object to indoctrination in the sense of a style of teaching that tends to preclude any subsequent rational reconsideration of the issues, and we can object to it as an interference with a legitimate freedom of the children – though one which others may have to claim on their behalf.

4. Truth-telling, lies, and agreements

On an assumption that the normal and proper state of affairs is that people should live as members of various circles, larger and smaller, with different kinds and degrees of cooperation, competition, and conflict in these different circles, the appropriateness of telling the truth becomes disputable. Truth-telling naturally goes along with cooperation; it is not obviously reasonable to tell the truth to a competitor or an enemy. A question may well be seen as an intrusion, backed perhaps by an assumption of a right to intrude, which the person questioned may deny and resent. Where, for one reason or another, it is not possible to tell the inquirer to mind his own business, a lie may be an appropriate defence of privacy.

There is an important difference between telling the truth and keeping an agreement. There is no question of keeping an agreement unless one has first made it, and making an agreement is voluntary and in general deliberate, whereas one often gets quite involuntarily into a position where one has to decide whether or not to tell the truth. Saying nothing may well be no real option: to give no answer to a question may well be, by implication, to give one answer rather than another, and a round, confident, lie may be the only practicable alternative to an undesirable revelation of the truth.

On the other hand lies, in any particular circle of relationship, are parasitic upon truth-telling within that same circle. Your enemies will believe what you say only if you generally tell even your enemies the truth. And if doctors habitually tell seriously ill patients what are meant to be reassuring lies, not only will their lies fail to reassure but even a true statement that the patient is not as ill as he fears will also be unconvincing. Since a fair proportion of lies will in time be discovered to be such, anyone's credibility in falsehood, in any particular circle, is an expendable asset. A prudent man will not squander his limited stock of convincing lies, but use it sparingly to the best effect.

Agreements, however, are in a different position, not only, as I have said, because they are entered into voluntarily, but also because they are an essential device for regulating conflicts and bringing them to an end. All that I have said about the inevitability and acceptability of various kinds and degrees of competition and conflict, as well as cooperation, between individuals and groups with naturally divergent aims, merely adds to the importance of being able to make agreements and to rely upon their being kept. In fact, it is important to have the notion of agreements with different degrees of bindingness or solemnity – some which contain, as it were, the implied clause 'provided that no strong reason for doing otherwise turns up', and others on which one can rely no matter what happens.

5. How princes should keep faith

It is a consequence of this approach, which will be paradoxical only at first sight, that the most solemn agreements will be those between parties whose normal relationship includes the most conflict and the least spontaneous cooperation. But this has often been denied. It is not only Machiavelli who holds that 'a prince, and especially a new prince, cannot observe all those things which are considered good in men, being often obliged, in order to maintain the state, to act against faith, against charity, against humanity, and against religion', and that 'a prudent ruler ought not to keep faith ... when the reasons which made him bind himself no longer exist'. Hume too says that 'There is a maxim very current in the world, which few politicians are willing to avow, but which has been authorized by the practice of all ages, *that there is a system of morals calculated for princes, much more free than that which ought to govern private persons.*' Hume does not assert 'that the most solemn treaties ought to have no force among princes'. Treaties between princes serve the same kind of purpose as agreements between individuals, and are therefore binding in the same sort of way. But, he argues, they are less binding, and 'may lawfully be transgressed from a more trivial motive'. The reason he gives is that 'though the intercourse of states be advantageous, and even sometimes necessary, yet it is not so necessary nor advantageous as that among individuals, without which it is utterly impossible for human nature ever to subsist'. This was no doubt true in Hume's time, and if it was true it was a good reason for the conclusion that he drew from it. But it is evidently no longer true, and the same line of argument would now support the opposite conclusion. It is now utterly impossible for human nature to go on subsisting unless there are some limits to aggression between states. We can still agree with Hume that 'we must necessarily give a greater indulgence to a prince or minister who deceives another, than to a private gentleman who breaks his word of honour'. Deceit is all very well as a possibly appropriate move in the competitive game; but breaking the most solemn treaties is another matter; that corrupts a device without which conflicts which in themselves are acceptable and inevitable can hardly be kept within tolerable bounds.

But as well as the agreements that terminate conflicts, there are international agreements whose fulfilment extends hostilities. What if the rulers of country A have promised those of country B that if country C attacks B then A will go to war with C? If C does attack B, should the promise be kept? On a particular occasion, this may be very hard to decide. Nor is it easy to say when, if ever, it will be right to give such assurances. But once again it is better to turn from the problem of deciding in a particular case to the choice of a regular pattern of conduct. One fairly clear point is that as a standing practice the giving of shaky assurances of this sort, promises which may or may not be fulfilled, is likely to be worse than either giving no such assurances or giving only ones which will be fulfilled, and of which it is known that they will be fulfilled, if the occasion arises. For where there are shaky assurances, the opposing parties are likely each to interpret them optimistically from their own point of view. That is, the rulers of C are likely to believe that A will not go to war if they attack B, while the rulers of B are likely to believe that A will do so. The rulers of B are then likely to take greater risks than they otherwise would in their dealings with C, while those of C will not be correspondingly restrained. It is easy to find historical illustrations of the conclusion to which this reasoning points, that unreliable promises are more likely than either reliable promises or none at all to turn a conflict of interests into open war.

6. Virtue

Aristotle tells us that the well-being or *eudaimonia* which is the good for man is an activity in accordance with virtue; each virtue is a disposition for making (right) choices, and one that is trained or developed by experience rather than inborn; with most virtues, the right sort of choice which it enables its possessor to make is somehow intermediate between two wrong sorts of choice; one can do or show too little or too much of something, one can go too far or not far enough; what constitutes the right amount, the virtuous choice, is determined as the man of practical wisdom would determine it; and he is the man who is good at choosing the means to the end of *eudaimonia.*

As guidance about what is the good life, what precisely one ought to do, or even by what standard one should try to decide what one ought to do, this is too circular to be very helpful. And though Aristotle's account is filled out with detailed descriptions of many of the virtues, moral as well as intellectual, the air of indeterminacy persists. We learn the names of the pairs of contrary vices that contrast with each of the virtues, but very little about where or how to draw the dividing lines, where or how to fix the mean. As Sidgwick says, he 'only indicates the whereabouts of virtue'. We must, then, take this mainly as a formal sketch of the structure of the good life, which leaves the specific content still to be filled in. To fill in this specific content, to mark off each virtue from the contrasting excesses and defects, we can draw on three sources. One will be the ways of behaving that are, at a particular place and time, conventionally admired; another will be one's own conception of the good. The third is at once more objective and less often noticed. When Hume maintained that reason alone can never be a motive for or against any action, that it can neither oppose nor support any passion or preferences, he was right in so far as he was stressing the logical independence of preferences on the one hand and factual information and valid inferences on the other. Yet we must also admit that in practice some degrees of emotion, some states of feeling and spirit, harmonize with seeing things as they are, and some do not. The man who 'thinks with his blood' cannot think with his mind at the same time on the same subject. Yet it is not being completely 'dispassionate' or detached, a total absence of feeling, that fits in best with seeing things as they are. It is rather a certain degree of enterprise and involvement that goes along with understanding. Also, some states of feeling can, and others cannot, survive an honest scrutiny and clear-sighted realization of their causes. As Spinoza says, 'An emotion which is a passion ceases to be a passion as soon as we form a clear and distinct idea of it.' This gives us a possible ground of distinction between a virtue and the contrasting vices of excess and defect: a virtue is a disposition which harmonizes with understanding, with seeing things as they are, while a vice is one which distorts appreciation of the qualities of the relevant situation, which needs such distortion in order to maintain itself, and which is manifested by states of mind which cannot stand honest reflection on the ways in which they have themselves arisen. This approach would define courage, for example, as a disposition for choice in relation to danger which neither cultivates nor depends upon either the exaggerating or the minimizing of those dangers, and which is compatible with self-awareness. We may compare this with, for example, Locke's definition of courage as 'For a man to be undisturbed in danger [which he perceives], sedately to consider what is fittest to be done, and to execute it steadily.' Other traditional virtues could be defined in systematically analogous ways. Though there is a lot of sophistry in the details of the argument by which Plato, in the *Protagoras*, tries to establish the unity of the virtues by assimilating them all to knowledge or wisdom, there is considerable force in the general suggestion that the virtues can be identified as dispositions that harmonize with knowledge. It must be conceded, however, that this approach would not narrowly determine the sort of choice to which a virtue would lead: it equates each virtue (or rather the corresponding choices) with a broad band rather than with a

187

particular point on some scale; it leaves room, therefore, for reference to one's own conception of the good or to what is conventionally admired (or to both) to help to determine just how much of this or that can go into what is to count as an action in accordance with virtue.

But however this specific content is to be filled in, there is merit in Aristotle's formal sketch taken simply as such. The good life will consist in activities that manifest and realize developed dispositions for choice. To say this is to avoid two contrary errors. These activities will manifest *dispositions*; that is, the good life is not just a collection of separate choices (either separately calculated or arbitrary) or of equally separate pleasures and satisfactions, or of both. But on the other hand these are dispositions *for choice* – preferential choice – not just instincts or habits.

Though dispositions can change and develop, they are fairly persistent. They cannot be switched on and off at will. Also, though dispositions can be discriminating, there are practical limits to the fineness of the discriminations they can make. A disposition for choice can express itself in differential choices only if the agent not only judges but also feels the cases to be significantly different. One can have a complex disposition, say of being honest with friends and deceitful towards enemies. It is more difficult to be deceitful on a particular occasion towards someone who is normally a friend but who has now taken on the role of an enemy. On the other hand being poker-faced is itself a disposition that can be cultivated. One can treat a special class of persons, or persons in some special setting, as opponents towards whom one is not honest by disposition, but to whom one offers a judicious mixture of truth and falsehood without betraying which is which.

The part that virtues play in the good life depends crucially on the fact that they are dispositions of this sort: fairly persistent and not too finely discriminating. The virtues that go with a particular conception of the good will be dispositions which, given that conception, it is advantageous for their possessor to have. But not every choice in which they are manifested will be advantageous considered on its own.

For example, courage – in a fairly conventional sense which is included in but more narrowly defined than that given by the above-mentioned third approach – is a kind of strength. It makes its possessor more likely to achieve whatever he sets out to do, whereas the foolhardy man is likely to destroy himself or his enterprise or both, and the timid man is too easily turned aside. Besides, most worthwhile enterprises involve risks of some kind, and the courageous man can enjoy the activity, risks and all, whereas the coward cannot. Again, both vice and virtue in this area are hard to conceal, and the brave man will be a more acceptable partner for others than either the foolhardy man or the coward. There can be no doubt that such courage is in general advantageous to its possessor – more advantageous than a tendency to calculate advantage too nicely. In so far as one can choose one's dispositions – say by cultivating them – this is one which it would be rational, even on purely egoistic grounds, to choose. Admittedly there will be particular occasions when rashness would be rewarded, and others when only the coward would survive. But it is hard to calculate which these are, and almost impossible to switch the dispositions on and off accordingly. To be a coward on the one occasion when courage is fatal one would have had to be a coward on many other occasions when it was much better to be courageous. The real alternatives are the various persisting dispositions, courage and those that contrast with it, and it is clear which of these the rational egoist would prefer. A far from negligible part of discretion is valour.

7. The motive for morality

It is easy to brush aside the question 'Why should I be moral?' by pointing out that if the 'should' is a moral one, 'You should be moral' is tautological, and if it is anything else, say a prudential one, this statement is sometimes false, so that our question either answers itself or, having a false presupposition, admits of no answer. But this reply is superficial and evasive. The real question is whether there is, as Sidgwick, for example, thought, an unresolvable tension between moral reason and the rationality of self-interest, between any recommendations that we could defend as moral and the advice that anyone could be given about his own well-being.

What I have already said, both in this chapter and particularly in Chapter 5, does much to reduce this tension. I have argued that egoism is not immoral, but forms a considerable part of any viable moral system. I have also given abundant reasons why almost everyone should, in his own interest, welcome the fact that there is, and hope that there will continue to be, some system of morality, and why, even if the existing system does not suit him, his aim should be to modify it, at least locally, rather than to destroy it. But this does not completely resolve the tension. It leaves unanswered the question 'Why should I not at the same time profit from the moral system but evade it? Why should I not encourage others to be moral and take advantage of the fact that they are, but myself avoid fulfilling moral requirements if I can in so far as they go beyond rational egoism and conflict with it?' It is not an adequate answer to this question to point out that one is not likely to be able to get away with such evasions for long. There will be at least some occasions when one can do so with impunity and even without detection. Then why not? To this no complete answer of the kind that is wanted can be given. In the choice of actions moral reasons and prudential ones will not always coincide. Rather, the point of morality, and particularly of that branch of it which I have called morality in the narrow sense, is that it is necessary for the well-being of people in general that they should act to some extent in ways that they cannot see to be (egoistically) prudential and also in ways that in fact are not prudential. Morality has the function of checking what would be the natural result of prudence alone.

When Plato raises this question in the *Republic*, the answer that he puts into the mouth of Socrates is that the just man is happy because his soul is harmoniously ordered, because, as we would say, he has an integrated personality, whereas the unjust man's personality is disintegrated, and the man who represents the extreme of injustice is psychotic, his soul is a chaos of internal strife. This is a forceful argument against the extreme of injustice; but perhaps injustice in moderation will do no harm. However, though Plato is wrong in suggesting that there is only one sort of leading motive around which a personality can be integrated, we can concede that one who, in the pursuit of apparent self-interest, evades on special occasions a morality which he not only professes and encourages but allows ordinarily to control his conduct will probably be incurring costs in the form of psychological discomfort which he may not have taken adequately into account when calculating his self-interest. But we must not make too much of this. A completely harmonious soul, a fully integrated personality, is in any case an unattainable ideal, and in the post-Freudian era we know that an appearance of harmony is likely to be achieved only by pushing the conflicts out of sight. In particular the man who, commendably, develops and retains moral ideals which are at variance with those currently dominant in the society in which he lives will also thereby incur psychological costs which a merely conventionally well-behaved person does not.

Should we, then, abandon the attempt to show that it is always – and not merely for the most part – prudentially rational to act in ways that one sees as morally defensible in terms of one's own ideals? We can the more easily reconcile ourselves to this when we reflect that even the rationality of prudence – in the sense of equal concern for the interests and welfare at all future times of this same person, oneself – is not quite as self-evident as is commonly supposed. Personal identity is not absolute, as it is believed to be: as I argued in Chapter 3, our concept of personal identity through time itself functions as a sort of institution, aided by a contingent present desire for one's own future welfare. We can, then, fall back on the comparable fact that nearly all of us do have moral feelings and do tend to think in characteristically moral ways, and that these help to determine our real interests and well-being. Why we are like this is in the first place a psychological question, to be answered, perhaps, as Hutcheson, Hume, and Adam Smith suggested, by reference to 'sympathy'; but more fundamentally it is a sociological and biological question to be answered, as I have said, by an evolutionary explanation. If someone, from whatever causes, has at least fairly strong moral tendencies, the prudential course, for him, will almost certainly coincide with what he sees as the moral one, simply because he will have to live with his conscience. What *is* prudent is then not the same as what would be prudent if he did not have moral feelings. But if someone else has only very weak moral tendencies – or, if that is possible, none at all – then it may be prudent for him to act immorally.

About the choice of actions there may be no more to be said. But as both Plato and Aristotle remind us, behind the choice of actions lies the choice of dispositions, of characters, of overall patterns of life. If it is asked what action will be the most prudent or the most egoistically rational, we must answer that that depends partly on what sort of person you are, and consequentially on what sort of person you want to be. And what was said at the end of the last section about courage applies also to other virtues, including those that are not as purely self-regarding as courage can be: dispositions cannot be switched on and off in deference to the calculation of likely consequences on particular occasions, and there are limits to the fineness of the discriminations they can incorporate. The practical choice will be between one fairly persistent disposition and others, equally persistent, that contrast with it. If we then ask what sort of person it is in one's own interest to be, what dispositions it is advantageous to have, there is little doubt that it will be ones that can be seen as virtues, as determined at least in the way emphasized in Section 6, as dispositions that harmonize with knowledge, but also more specifically in the light of some conception of the good and with some respect for the way of life of the society in which one lives.

8. Extensions of morality

Morality as I have described it is concerned particularly with the well-being of active, intelligent, participants in a partly competitive life, and the constraints summed up as morality in the narrow sense have been introduced (especially in the Hobbesian line of thought and the game theory models in Chapter 5) as necessary limits on competition for the benefit of all the competitors. This approach would seem to provide for no duties towards non-participants, and to assign no rights to beings who do not need to be drawn into a quasi-contractual scheme, who have no benefits which they are free either to confer upon others or to withhold, and no powers to do harm. Classes that we ordinarily see as having morally valid claims to consideration, but which seem to be wholly or partly excluded from consideration by this approach, include young children, the unborn, members of future generations, the aged, the sick, the infirm, the insane, the mentally defective, and non-human animals.

However, my approach is not quite equivalent to a contractual one. It takes general human well-being or the flourishing of human life as the foundation of morality, and its instruments are not purely consequential principles of action but include rules, duties, rights, and dispositions. It is clear that a morality that is to promote the flourishing of human life over time must include elements that look after the well-being of children and that ensure some respect for the needs of future generations. Also some of the special classes just mentioned are ones that individuals move into and out of: everyone who is old has been young, and many of those who are sick or infirm or insane have previously been fit and some of them will be fit again. Even something like a contractual approach would provide consideration for those who are only sometimes powerless. I shall be more willing to give you help which at present I can either give or withhold if there is something that provides me with a fairly firm assurance that I shall still be recognized as having rights and claims to consideration when I am no longer in a position to bargain for them.

The difficult question, then, is the more restricted one about the moral claims, first of human beings who through mental or physical defect are never, at any time in their lives, independent active participants in the cooperation, competition, and conflict of normal life, and secondly of non-human animals. We could afford to ill-treat members of both these classes: they are never in anything even analogous to a position where we should need to bargain with them. Consequently a moral system which ignored their well-being could still achieve what I have said to be the object of morality.

The claims of these classes, then, lie outside what I must regard as the core of morality. It is only extensions of morality that cover them. Moreover, these are gratuitous extensions of morality. They are different from the sort of extension by which morality has been applied more and more widely, not just between members of some small closed social group such as a clan or tribe, but also between members of neighbouring tribes, and foreigners, and people of different races and different religions. Actual contacts, wider intercourse that brings with it possibilities of mutual help and mutual harm, make it necessary that some moral considerations at least should be applied throughout these larger circles. But no such practical need explains the extension of moral consideration to those who are never in a position deliberately to help or to harm us.

It is the role of dispositions in morality that explains these gratuitous extensions. A humane disposition is a vital part of the core of morality; it would surely have been an element in the *aidōs* that the gods, in Protagoras's myth, gave to men. Such a disposition, if it exists, naturally manifests itself in hostility to and disgust at cruelty and in sympathy with pain and suffering wherever they occur. If we are people of the sort that we need to be, and that – no doubt in consequence, but spontaneously and uncalculatingly – we want to be, we cannot be callous and indifferent, let alone actively cruel, either towards permanently defective human beings or towards non-human animals.

But there are important differences between these two classes. Though non-human animals are in one obvious respect less close to us, they can call upon a different kind of sympathy. Most of them are in no way defective; they are capable of flourishing in their own way which, though different, will still bear a significant analogy with whatever we take to be the good life for man. If we admire and enjoy the flourishing of human life, we shall naturally delight also in the flourishing of animal life. The prominence of this factor will affect the kind of concern we have for animals. Wild animals suffer pain and inflict pain on one another in the ordinary course of the struggle for survival; we may sympathize with this suffering, but any attempt to interfere is likely to do more harm than good. We can do more about the suffering that human beings cause to wild animals directly, when they hunt them for food or for sport; but even this may well be seen as less important than the suffering they cause indirectly, through pollution. With domesticated animals it is perhaps factory farming that involves the greatest impoverishment of life, but there are many other forms of cruelty, including frivolous 'scientific' tests and experiments.

9. The right to life

We can speak coherently of a right to life only as a claim-right, correlative to a duty not to kill and not to do things that are likely to cause death. Fundamental though such a right is, it cannot be absolute. As the world is, wars and revolutions cannot be ruled to be morally completely out of the question. The death penalty, I believe, can. The prearranged killing of someone at a stated time is a special outrage against the humane feelings which are a central part of morality, and this is not outweighed by any extra deterrent effect; in fact the use of the death penalty is likely to increase criminal violence. But long terms of imprisonment are probably at least as inhumane. There are, indeed, many activities that involve known risks to life – mining, bridge-building, cricket, road travel. No doubt we should take precautions to reduce such risks, but we tolerate a certain amount of risk for the sake of other advantages. It is certain that far fewer people would be killed on the roads if there were a speed limit of, say, twenty miles an hour for all vehicles except those dealing with emergencies. Since we would not tolerate the deliberate killing of a comparable number of people in order to secure whatever advantages can be ascribed to travel at higher speeds, it seems paradoxical that we accept the statistical certainty of this number of deaths so long as for each individual it is (until he is actually killed) only a risk. But it becomes less paradoxical if we reflect that what matters is not just the result – so many deaths – but rather the flourishing of human life in certain ways, sustained by the appropriate dispositions. From this point of view risks are acceptable whereas deliberate killing is not, at least so long as people who know the dangers are taking risks, for the sake of known benefits, only with their own lives. What is not fair, but also occurs, is that people should take risks with the lives of others who do not and would not willingly make this choice. However, if the different parties cannot be isolated, a morally acceptable solution will be some compromise between those who want to take risks and those who do not.

The right to life has as a corollary the right to end one's life, though this, too, is not absolute: others may have claims that tell against suicide when it would be preferable from the agent's own point of view. Still, there is no difficulty in describing circumstances in which suicide would be permissible. Nor can there be anything morally wrong in assisting a genuinely voluntary suicide. The same principle would allow euthanasia where someone really wants and seriously asks to be killed, with some understandable reason. It is a more difficult question whether it is ever legitimate to act on someone's merely presumed desire for his life to be ended: I think the grounds for the presumption would need to be very strong. Where, however, someone can be kept half alive only by the continued use of elaborate support mechanisms or by repeated operations, and where the life thus maintained is plainly of no value to him, it will be right to let him die.

These may seem to be hasty judgements about highly controversial questions. I agree that these questions should be discussed more thoroughly. But I think that they should be considered neither in terms of slogans about murder and the sanctity of life nor in terms of an attempt to calculate the effects of actions on the total general happiness, but more concretely in terms of the values, rights, and dispositions involved, our under-standing of these being taken over from more normal and less controversial cases. Also, these are matters for intelligent public discussion: they should not be left for doctors to decide privately in one way while professsing to act on different prin-ciples. We do not want medical (or other) experts to shield us from moral choice.

Abortion is another controversial question. There are three main grounds that are held to justify abortion: it may be needed to prevent a grave risk to the mother's life or health; there may be good reasons to expect that if the child is born it will suffer from some serious permanent defect; or the mother simply may not want a child – or another child, or this particular child, for example if it has been conceived as a result of rape – and it may be held that she has a right not to have her body used by or for what she does not want. (This third ground has sometimes been smuggled in under the first heading by questionable references to the mother's mental health, but it would be better to consider it separately on its own merits.) The basic argument against abortion, on which all others build, is that the unborn child is already a human being, a person, a bearer of rights, and that abortion is therefore murder. This is essentially a continuity argument. Given that we want to regard a newly-born baby as a person, and to forbid the killing of it as murder, it seems arbitrary to distinguish between this and the killing of an un-born child almost at full term, and then the argument can be carried back step by step until immediately after conception.

It is, of course, quite implausible to carry it back any further. Though ova and sperms are, taken in pairs, potential human beings, nature is far too lavish in its production of them, particularly the latter, for us to accord them a right to life. But why should conception or fertilization be taken as the point of distinction? It is true that it is the only salient point, the only discontinuity between the ovum and sperm that have no right to life and the baby just before birth, which has. (Birth itself is, of course, another salient point.) But this discontinuity is a very inadequate ground for the required moral distinction. It would be more reasonable to think of the right or claim to life as growing gradually in strength, but as still being very slight immediately after conception. Then we might well conclude that the third ground for abortion is valid early in pregnancy – the mother's right to the control of her own body then outweighs the child's right to life – but not late in pregnancy. The first ground, however, according to the graveness of the risk to the mother's life, might be valid at any time up to birth.

The second ground, the likelihood of serious permanent defect, also seems to be valid at any time up to birth. In saying this I am relying on the presumption that not only is it much against the interests of the parents (or whoever else will have to look after it) and the other members of the family that the child should survive, but it is also against the child's own interest. Of course this brings us back to the question of euthanasia: if a child is born with such a severe defect, should it then be killed? The view that it should is supported by the reflection that it is only by a fiction that we regard a newly-born child as a person. It is surely not yet conscious of itself as itself, as a distinct and potentially continuing being. It cannot be seen as making even an unspoken demand that it should continue in existence which would need to be weighed against any other presumptions about its interests. Nor can we appeal against this view to what was said in Section 8 about a humane disposition: in this case reflective humanity would require that the child should be killed. What does tell against this view is that this rule cuts across the classifications that are most natural to us and very well established in ordinary thought: this would be seen as the deliberate killing of an independent human being, not at his own request. Here birth is a salient point, a popularly acceptable ground of distinction: abortion is seen as different from the killing of what is now a separately existing human being. In principle, therefore, I think that a baby born with a very severe permanent defect should not be allowed to survive; but recognition of this principle must be conditional upon widespread appreciation of what makes this distinct from other cases of killing – that is upon its being seen and felt why this is not murder. In particular, since the elimination of the unfit has been advocated on simple utilitarian grounds, which would have other implications that we may well want to reject, it is important that the present principle should not be taken as an endorsement of simple utilitarianism, as just one particular case of an individual's claims being rightfully sacrificed to the general happiness.

10. Conclusion

This chapter, and indeed the whole of this part of the book, has done no more than sketch the outlines of a first order moral system. A more adequate treatment would have required not only discussion of particular issues at much greater length, but also a more specific determination of the good life for man, and hence the explicit intrusion of what those who are joining in the discussion subjectively prefer and value. I am less concerned, however, about any particular conclusions that I have suggested than about the method implicit in my treatment. My hope is that concrete moral issues can be argued out without appeal to any mythical objective values or requirements or obligations or transcendental necessities, but also without appeal to a fictitiously unitary and measurable happiness or to invalid arguments that attempt to establish the general happiness as a peculiarly authoritative end. No doubt my approach could be called, in a very broad sense, a rule utilitarian one, since any specific development of it would be based on some conception of the flourishing of human life, but it would be utilitarianism without its characteristic fictions, and it would be not just a rule-utili-tarianism but a rule-right-duty-disposition utilitarianism. It might also be called a rule-right-duty-disposition egoism; in the light of our stress on dispositions and the arguments of Sections 6 and 7, these two approaches will very largely coincide.

Part III : Frontiers of Ethics

Chapter 9   Determinism, Responsibility, and Choice

1. Voluntary or intentional actions

Moral principles and ethical theories do not stand alone: they affect and are affected by beliefs and assumptions which belong to other fields, and not least to psychology, metaphysics, and religion. An extreme view is that of Kant, that the existence of God, the freedom of the will, and the immortality of the soul are all necessary presuppositions of moral thought. It can hardly be doubted that belief or disbelief in religion will make some moral difference. Also, morality is concerned not only with good and bad, right and wrong, virtues and vices, duties and rights. Closely linked with these concepts are those of choice, voluntary action, intention, responsibility, regret, and remorse. It is hard to see how anything that we could recognize as a moral system could dispense with the notions of what a person does, of the choices he makes and hence of what he takes credit or discredit for. Yet these notions are not clear in themselves; besides it has been argued that causal determinism is, or may be, true, and that if it is true it undermines the reality of choice and responsibility.

In examining these matters, it is essential to distinguish three sorts of question which are often run together: the first, whether we can draw a coherent and systematic distinction between intended and unintended and also between voluntary and non-voluntary actions; the second, how we are to assign moral (and legal) responsibility, blame, and credit; the third, in what circumstances rewards and punishments, and in particular legal penalties, are appropriate. It is also best to tackle these problems on two levels, trying first to clarify and systematize distinctions drawn in everyday and legal thought, and only later going to the deeper level of the metaphysical issues between determinism and free will.

Praise and blame, Aristotle remarks, are commonly confined to voluntary actions, while actions are made non-voluntary by compulsion or ignorance – or rather, he goes on to explain, by only certain kinds of compulsion and ignorance. However, these bear most clearly upon the intentionality of actions. The key to the understanding of the role of ignorance is that an action may be intended under one description but not under another. A woman whose husband has gone off on a journey shoots, intentionally, a supposed intruder; in fact the intruder is her husband, who has returned unexpectedly; but perhaps she does not intentionally shoot her husband. If an agent does not know, at the time when he does something, that a certain description applies to what he is doing, then his action is not intended under that description.

This principle need not be confined, as Aristotle suggests, to ignorance of particular facts and circumstances. If I grow cannabis in my garden, knowing that it is cannabis, but not knowing that this is against the law, I am not intentionally breaking the law. If Eichmann believed that everything he did was his patriotic duty, he did not intentionally do anything wrong, though we may judge that what he did intentionally was wrong. Nor does it matter what has caused the ignorance. If someone is so drunk that he literally does not know what he is doing, then his actions are not intended under the relevant description. It is another question whether people are to be held responsible or liable to punishment in any such cases; but we should not distort our account of intentional action to make it fit more closely with our views about responsibility and punishment.

What I am in a literal sense physically compelled to do is not an intentional act of mine under any description – for example, if someone much stronger than I am pushes my hand, or if I remain where I am because I am tied up. A more difficult problem is that of duress and 'necessity', of compulsion by threats and dangers. In Aristotle's all too modern example, if a tyrant has a man's children or parents in his power, and threatens to torture or kill them unless the man does something that he would otherwise be extremely reluctant to do, and the man yields to this threat, is his action intentional? The same question arises if the captain of a ship jettisons his cargo to save the ship from sinking in a storm. In any such case, the agent is faced with some range, usually a pair, of alternatives: jettison the cargo and save the ship, or keep the cargo on board and have the ship sink; do what the tyrant wants and have one's relatives safe, or defy him and have them tortured or killed. The agent does not choose or intentionally accept this range of alternatives: it is simply imposed upon him. But he does intentionally adopt one alternative rather than the other. It will be true to say, then, that the captain intentionally jettisons the cargo, or that the man intentionally does what the tyrant demands: but it will be misleading to say just this without mentioning the restricted alternatives open to either agent. What he does intentionally is not just X, but X-rather-than-Y.

This account has appropriate moral and legal corollaries. Even if X is in itself wrong or bad or illegal or dishonourable, it does not follow that X-rather-than-Y is so. It may be foolish, or a breach of contract, or professional misconduct for a captain to throw cargo overboard in ordinary circumstances, but it may be a wise, justifiable, and commendable action when the ship would otherwise sink. To have chosen X-rather-than-Y may be something for which the agent has no need to escape responsibility, something of which he can be proud rather than ashamed. Even if we think he made the wrong choice of evils, we could regard his doing X-rather-than-Y as less wrong or less bad than doing X in general is. A plea of duress or 'necessity', therefore, should not be seen as cancelling an agent's responsibility, but only as modifying the description of the action for which he is responsible, and so claiming either justification or mitigation. In evaluating any such plea, we must take account of the relative badness (of whatever sort) of the alternatives X and Y.

It may be objected that if we are required to complicate the descriptions under which we call actions intentional that result from duress or 'necessity', we should do likewise in all cases: every deliberate action, at least, is a choice between alternatives. It is true that there will always be complicating conditions, accompaniments as well as alternatives: the agent may not have done just X, but X-rather-than-Y, X-for-the-sake-of-this-bribe, X-in-response-to-that-provocation, X-in-self-defence (or in defence of others), or X-in-the-belief-that-(such and such). But these complications may or may not be relevant: an adverse moral judgement on X would not be altered by the introduction of harmless alternatives or, in general, of merely attractive accompaniments.

I conclude that the only kind of compulsion that makes an act unintentional is simple physical compulsion or constraint, which really makes it not an act of this agent at all. Everything else, in the way of duress, dangers, temptation and the like will at most complicate the description under which it will be most relevant and least misleading to say that it was intended. I shall discuss later the sorts of mental disturbance that have led people to speak of 'irresistible impulses' as a species of compulsion.

A third factor which can affect the intentionality of actions is lack of skill or defective control. When I first try to drive a car I zigzag along the road; I am driving intentionally, but not zigzagging intentionally. On the other hand if I know that I am zigzagging and accept this as unavoidable in the first stage of learning to drive, my zigzagging is, in Bentham's terminology, obliquely though not directly intended, in the way that known second effects are.

The central case of an intentional action is that of an act which is both directly intended under the description in question and carried out. Such an act is both the object and the causal product of the same desire: it fulfils the desire which motivates it; but the intending includes, along with the desire, the belief that it will lead straightforwardly to the fulfilment of the desire which it includes. One can intend to do only something that one believes one can and will do.

However, this is only the central case. One can directly intend

– aim at – something not itself desired but seen as a means to a desired end. An intention need not be preformed, but may merely accompany the activity that it makes intentional. On the other hand there can be a bare intention to act, where the appropriate combination of desire and belief occurs but the causal process stops short before it issues in action. One can attempt to do something, where the causal process issues in some action, but not in the fulfilment of the intention. There can be intentions to do something at some future time, and one can do something with a further intention. A full account of all these matters would take a long time, but I am confident that they can all be understood as complex structures which involve desires, beliefs, movements, activities, and outcomes in various patterns of causal relationship.

The notion of something's being obliquely intended can be understood in terms of an admittedly ideal picture of a fully deliberate action. Here every feature of which the agent is aware will have been brought into consideration, and so forms part of the action-as-known which he has chosen as a whole. This whole action as known has been intentionally brought about under the corresponding complete description: any description under which the agent sees it as falling represents a feature which the agent either has sought or has accepted for the sake of accompaniments he has sought or to escape alternatives he has been avoiding. The action will be directly intended under any description that represents a feature he has sought, either as an end or as a means, but obliquely intended under any that represents one that he has not sought even as a means but has thus accepted. But this is an ideal picture. Actions which are not fully deliberate, but are impulsive, or result from passion, or rage, or terror, and so on, conform to it imperfectly. An agent may then know that a certain further consequence will result from what he is doing, and yet not explicitly include it in any action which he chooses as a whole: he can thus bring something about knowingly but without intending it even obliquely.

Voluntariness is less firmly tied to descriptions than intentionality is. We might suggest that an action considered as a concrete performance, irrespective of any particular description, is voluntary if it is directly intended under some description. We can in this way develop the hint given by the etymology of the word that a voluntary action is one that issues from and somehow carries out the agent's 'will'; it results from and either fulfils or makes some appropriate moves towards fulfilling some intention. But again we must admit that actions that do not quite satisfy this description are called voluntary in weaker senses. An action that arises from and immediately expresses a desire, without involving any intention or the sort of belief that is needed, along with desire, to constitute an intention, still counts as voluntary; and so does an habitual action or a mere omission, a failure to act, which did not positively result from any desire or intention, but which was subject to the agent's will in the negative sense that if he had so willed, he would have done otherwise.

2. The straight rule of responsibility

It is a factual, psychological, question whether an action is intentional or voluntary, but it is a moral or legal question whether or in what ways an agent is to be held responsible. But an initially plausible proposal would relate these matters directly, yielding what we may call the straight rule of responsibility: an agent is responsible for all and only his intentional actions.

This proposal agrees with the legal tradition which sees *mens rea* – literally, a guilty mind – as the essential condition for criminal responsibility. But both the law and ordinary moral judgements diverge somewhat in both directions from the straight rule: we hold people responsible for some unintended actions, and we tend to excuse certain classes of people from responsibility even for their intentional actions. But before we discuss such divergences, we might inquire whether there are any general grounds for adopting the straight rule.

An objectivist in ethics might appeal simply to an intuition that what the straight rule prescribes is just and that it would be unjust to hold someone responsible for unintended aspects or results of his actions. But this could be further explained. What is unintended because it is brought about by physical compulsion is not really anything that the agent does: it is done by some outside force which acts, perhaps, through his body. Similarly, features of my action which result from my lack of skill or defective control, though they are actions of my body, are not actions of me as a conscious agent – though if I go on doing what produces these features, knowing that they will be produced by my lack of skill, they are *then* actions of me as a conscious agent, but equally, as explained above, they are then obliquely intended. And in general in so far as I am ignorant of what I am doing or bringing about, the actions which are for this reason unintentional can be seen not as belonging to me as a conscious agent, but to have been foisted upon or obtruded into my course of action by the facts or circumstances of which I was unaware. However, this argument only develops the notion of an action's belonging to a conscious agent, and does not explain why we should build (exclusively) upon it in our assignments of reward and punishment, blame and praise.

Bentham, and many utilitarians following him, have offered such an explanation. The purpose and justification of punishment is deterrence, but it is only intentional actions that people can be deterred from performing, so it is only these that it can be rational to punish. Blame is seen as a kind of informal punishment, and therefore as subject to the same rational restrictions. Analogous accounts can be given of praise or moral credit and reward; and responsibility is interpreted simply as liability to blame or punishment or eligibility for credit or reward.

But this argument is unsound. It is true that only intentional actions can be deterred, and hence that a penalty is deterrently effective only in so far as a rational agent sees it as being attached to some possible intentional action. But it is not true that his so seeing it can result only from its being legally annexed to actions of just that sort. Though an unintentional killer, say, could not himself have been deterred, it is quite possible that potential intentional killers should be more effectively deterred by the punishing of all killers than by the punishing only of the intentional killers and the excusing of the unintentional ones. For there are practical difficulties in implementing such a distinction, so there are liable to be mistakes and uncertainties in the enforcement of the law, and potential intentional killers might well have more hope of evading the penalty if they knew that the law excused unintentional killers.

But though Bentham's argument, framed as it is in the context of legal penalties, is unsound, a related moral argument has much more force. In Chapter 5 and elsewhere I have discussed morality in the narrow sense as a particular sort of system of constraints on conduct. It works by modifying an agent's view of possible actions, by attaching to them a moral characterization, favourable or adverse, which has prescriptive entailments, and carries with it a corresponding characterization of the agent himself if he performs those actions. It thus brings pressure to bear upon intentions, but in a peculiarly direct way. Moral wrongness is a bit like a penalty, but moral sense, *aidōs,* attaches it more tightly than any penalty to the wrong act, and discourages such acts more directly than by way of deterrence. There is now no room for the mistakes and uncertainties of enforcement that may make it useful to apply deterrent legal penalties more widely than to intentional acts. The attachment of moral wrongness to actions or aspects of actions that were unintended, that did not, in the sense explained above, belong to the conscious agent, would always be idle.

If we can thus explain and underpin our 'intuition' in favour of the straight rule for moral responsibility, we can understand, as an extension of this moral principle, the feeling that this rule should also control legal penalties. We see a legal penalty as just, as immediately morally appropriate, only if the act to which it is attached is morally wrong. (It need not, of course, have been antecedently wrong: the law does, and may justifiably, make into offences acts that are not antecedently immoral; but if we accept the legal system we shall consider it at least *prima facie* morally wrong to do what the law forbids.) It may, indeed, be expedient sometimes for the law to diverge from the straight rule, but we shall then feel that there is a conflict with justice, since it is punishing someone for something for which he cannot be blamed.

This provides an initially plausible case for the straight rule. But what are we to say about divergences from it? There is, indeed, some tendency for the law to move closer to the straight rule. In England, since the Criminal Justice Act of 1967, a man is no longer presumed to intend or foresee the natural and probable consequences of his acts: the crucial question is whether he in fact intended the harm that has occurred. The Homicide Act of 1957 abolished the doctrine of constructive malice, by which killing in the course of a felony counted as murder, even though there was no actual intention to kill. Yet there is also a contrary tendency to add to the list of offences for which there is strict liability, where someone is held responsible for actions or results which he did not intend and was perhaps not even negligent in performing or bringing about.

First, should we go against the straight rule by imposing responsibility for negligence? If an agent foresees as likely certain harmful results of what he is thinking of doing, but still goes ahead, and those results come about, then they are obliquely intended. But if he is only vaguely aware that harm of a certain sort could result from his carelessness, the particular bad results that come about are not even obliquely intended; but since he knows that he is being careless, his negligence itself is obliquely intended, and the straight rule would still hold him responsible for that. The controversial question is whether someone can be held responsible not only thus for inadvertent negligence itself, but also for its unforeseen results. Morally we do often blame ourselves for what we bring about thoughtlessly. But it would be more rational, more in agreement with the general system of moral thought, only to blame ourselves for the thoughtlessness itself. Similarly 'causing death by dangerous driving' is a more serious offence than 'driving without due care and attention', and gross negligence that results in death may count as manslaughter whereas similarly gross negligence that does not result in death is not even punished as a crime. But this surely is unfair, since it means that mere chance may make a great difference in the treatment of two people who are equally negligent – for example, they drive equally recklessly, but it just happens that someone gets in the way of one but not of the other.

Aristotle and many others have held that drunkenness is no excuse even if, as a result of it, the agent is not acting intentionally because he literally does not know what he is doing. This harsh principle is defended on the ground that he had it in his power not to get drunk. But it would be more reasonable to follow the straight rule and say that since getting drunk (or perhaps rather starting to get drunk) is something that one does intentionally, one can be held responsible for doing this, and perhaps for doing so in circumstances in which one foresees that it is likely to lead to harm, but not for the further things that one does non-intentionally after one is drunk.

If, say, selling dirty or adulterated milk is made an offence of strict liability, the purpose is to encourage a particularly high standard of care; the legislation is directed against what in this context amounts to negligence, even if similar behaviour would not count as negligence in other spheres. If the seller has really not been negligent at all and has taken every reasonable precaution, he cannot morally be blamed if some dirt has got into his bottles in some way over which he had literally no control. If he is held legally responsible, this is not just in the particular case, but it may be expedient to have such a law for the reason indicated in our criticism of Bentham's argument, that the imposing of a penalty on all acts of a certain class, even the unintended ones, may constitute a more effective deterrent, or in this case a stronger incentive to milk sellers to take all the precautions they can.

All these are cases where there is some tendency to hold people responsible for unintended acts. We also hold certain sorts of people non-responsible, or less responsible, for acts that are intentional by the account sketched in Section 1. There is no general lack of intentionality in the actions of children, except very young ones, yet we see them as being both legally and morally less responsible for what they do. We expect people only gradually to become responsive to the pressures that constitute morality in the narrow sense. The intensity of the moral colouring of actions grows gradually as agents become more mature, along with the expectation that that colouring will be effective as a control. This carries over into the sphere of legal responsibility, but this may be further limited by the considerations that where parents and schools have some control over children, the direct intervention of the law may be unnecessary, and that the actual imposition of legal penalties seems more likely to turn juvenile offenders into habitual criminals than to reform them.

The psychopath of the kind that is quite lacking in sympathy and shows no capacity for moral feeling or moral reasoning simply stands outside the system of control which we have identified as morality in the narrow sense: he is permanently in the condition from which a child normally grows gradually into that of a full moral agent. Moral characterization of his actions would be idle because he is quite unresponsive to it, even though he knows, intellectually, that certain kinds of action are forbidden or are called wrong. Other considerations of policy, of the best way of handling such cases, will bear upon the question of legal responsibility, but the psychopath's lack of moral responsibility removes the most obvious foundation for legal penalties.

Many other kinds of mental defect or disturbance raise a different problem – for example, when someone acts impulsively, or is in a rage, or terrified, or carried away by passionate desire or by the mass hysteria of a crowd, or is drunk or drugged (though not to such an extent as not to know what he is doing), or is of very low intelligence, or is a kleptomaniac or compulsive drinker or drug addict, or is carrying out instructions given under hypnosis. All of these seem to be acting not only voluntarily but also intentionally by the account given in Section 1, yet we have some inclination to assign to them at most a

213

somewhat lower degree of responsibility. This can be explained by reference to one or other of three models.

First, in impulsive action, rage, and so on many aspects that the agent knows of will simply not be attended to, and low intelligence may permanently prevent someone from bringing a set of diverse considerations into account. The resulting action may not be fully intentional in that aspects which the agent in some sense knew of were not even obliquely intended at the time.

Secondly, even where an act under a certain description was one which I deliberately chose at the time, and was therefore intentional for me as I then was, a temporary disturbance may have made this phase of me less than normally continuous with and representative of my relatively permanent character and personality. 'I did it, but I wasn't myself at the time'; the action therefore belongs less than it normally would to me as I am now.

This second explanation presupposes that the identity of persons through time (like that of other things) rests only upon various continuities which are themselves matters of degree. It goes along with the view that the ownership even of fully intentional actions fades out gradually even in ordinary circumstances; mental disturbances merely accelerate this fading.

A third explanation correspondingly impugns the contemporaneous unity of the agent. If we follow Freud, or Plato, in comparing the mind of an individual to a society, we can recognize an action as the fulfilment of a desire that has indeed arisen within the agent as a human being but that may nevertheless be outside the boundaries of his central personality or ego or self. What is an intentional act of the human being may not be an intentional act of the parliament of co-conscious motives which ordinarily works as a whole and acknowledges as its own the thoughts and actions that originate anywhere within it. We can thus clarify the obscure distinction between 'irresistible impulses' and those which are simply not resisted. Irresistible impulses are ones which arise outside the central personality and are seen by it as alien, but which are strong enough to get their way not through the parliamentary procedure of deliberation but in defiance of it.

The same action may fit more than one of these models. An addict's taking of his drug is partly intentional, but may be less than fully intentional in all three ways. It is an empirical question how well particular actions or classes of actions fit these models, but we can see how, if they fit, the ascription of something as an intentional action to an agent, and hence the moral characterization of the agent with respect to it, becomes less apt. Though legal responsibility is not completely tied to moral responsibility, we can see how it may reasonably also be affected. These three models formulate questions which we should like psychologists to answer about particular cases or types of case.

I suggest, then, that the straight rule can on the whole be defended for the ascription of moral responsibility. Most apparent exceptions can be explained away in terms of one or other of these models, and this rule can itself be understood in the light of our account of the nature and point of morality in the narrow sense. (One surviving exception, which can be similarly understood, concerns responsibility for obliquely intended second effects, and particularly those which come about through the choices of other agents: it was argued in Chapter 7 that responsibility for these should be restricted.) There is, in consequence, a case for adhering fairly closely to the straight rule for legal responsibility too, but here other considerations may justify some divergences from it: as we have seen, unjust penalties can be useful, and inversely penalties may be useless even where they are not unjust.

3. Causal determinism and human action

We do not know whether causal determinism holds or not, in particular whether it holds for all or most human actions, or whether, even if strict determinism does not hold, there is yet some close approximation to it. It is not, however, as difficult as some have thought to say what the determinist thesis means. I have argued elsewhere that causation 'in the objects' (as opposed to our concept of causation) can be analysed in terms of complex regularities together with certain kinds of continuity of process and (to provide for the direction of causation, the asymmetry of cause and effect) the notion of an effect becoming fixed only by way of its cause. Then the determinist thesis is that for every event there is an antecedent sufficient cause, that is, a temporally prior set of occurrences and conditions which is sufficient, in accordance with some regularity, for just such an event and which leads to it by a qualitatively continuous process.

This thesis would be falsified if there were two antecedent situations which were alike in all relevant respects, but had different outcomes. We make progress towards confirming it in so far as we find what appear to be satisfactory causal explanations of more and more kinds of occurrence. It is an empirical thesis, which only the progress of science will either gradually confirm or perhaps more dramatically disconfirm. This view of the problematic status of determinism can be supported by an examination of some of the *a priori* arguments or general outlines of argument that have been advanced on either side.

Determinism has been said to be a necessary presupposition of science; but falsely: some scientific theories, such as quantum mechanics, get along very nicely without it. The truth is only that determinism about particular ranges of phenomena is often a working hypothesis. In any case, if science did presuppose determinism, this would weaken rather than strengthen the thesis, by making it impossible for science to test and so confirm it.

Determinism with regard to voluntary human actions has been supported by the argument that such actions require motives and that an explanation of an action by reference to its motives is a causal explanation. The account of voluntariness offered in Section 1 would agree with this. But such an explanation might be in terms of a cause which is necessary in the circumstances for the action as well as leading on to it: it is not clear that this cause must also be sufficient in the circumstances for the action in accordance with some true regularity. And even if every action had an antecedent sufficient cause in the form of a desire, this would merely shift the question: do desires always have antecedent sufficient causes, or do they spring up randomly, or are they formed in some other way? The determinist may then appeal to psychological, perhaps psychoanalytic, theories of mental working and development; but in this area we have only a small amount of evidence in favour of very rough outline accounts, which leave us miles away from a complete deterministic explanation. Theories of social or historical determinism are also speculative in the extreme. Their best chance of being even approximately correct is as statistical theories which might explain trends of development or the general patterns of behaviour in large groups without requiring deterministic behaviour in their individual members. The suggestion that either psychological or social theory, either as it is now or as it is at all likely to be in the near future, confronts us with a deterministic picture of human behaviour is a sheer myth.

Another argument for determinism about actions is that all physical states and events are causally determined, including states of the brain, that brain states are correlated with mental states in such a way that, given a certain brain state, just such a mental state must occur, and that actions are causally determined by mental states. This third premiss is equivalent to one used in the previous argument; it is fairly plausible but by no means established. The first premiss is somewhat undermined by the fact that the currently dominant fundamental physical theory, quantum mechanics, is indeterministic. We should need further proof that the indeterminacies are practically certain to be ironed out statistically in any structures large enough to constitute brain states, and that triggering effects which would carry the small scale indeterminacies into larger scale processes, such as are certainly theoretically possible, do not occur. The second premiss, asserting a strong correlation between brain states and mental states, is not yet established but it is intrinsically plausible, and the evidence in its favour seems to grow steadily. This argument, then, is far from watertight, but it does provide the basis of a good case for determinism about actions.

One of the main arguments against such determinism appeals to a feeling or direct experience of freedom; whenever we choose to do one thing rather than another we are, in the experience of choosing, immediately aware that we could have done otherwise. But what sort of 'could have' is this? And is it an experience or just an assumption? We may dismiss the suggestion sometimes made by determinists that 'I can ...' in such contexts *means* 'I will ... if I choose.' A sounder thesis is that 'can' and 'could have' are used to deny obstacles and limitations of various sorts, and that it is not obvious what obstacles or limitations are being denied here; 'could have' need not be meant to exclude the sort of limitation that would be entailed by the action's being (sufficiently) caused by a desire and that desire by further sufficient antecedent causes. It might well be used rather to deny obstacles and limitations external to the agent's will at the time of the action. But such disputes about meaning are not very fruitful. It is more important that if this 'could have' is contra-causal, what it expresses will be at most an assumption, not an experience or observation, whereas if it merely denies contemporaneous external obstacles, their absence may well be observed. One can be fairly directly aware of the constraints and compulsions and defects that destroy or reduce the voluntariness of actions as analysed in Section 1; but what could be a feeling of contra-causal freedom? No doubt we can observe singular causal sequences in action contexts as well as in others, though not infallibly: we can tell when an action results from and is guided by a desire. By contrast, one could be aware of an action which seemed not to be initiated or guided by any desire, but this would surely be the experience of doing something automatically, non-voluntarily, and it is not this that indeterminists mean by a feeling of freedom. Again, one can have the experience of desires arising as it were from nowhere, from no known causes; but this is not a positive experience of their being uncaused. In fact, what we

218

would most naturally take as a feeling of freedom is the consciousness of the effective operation of our thoughts and decisions; this is evidence of what we have identified as voluntariness, but not of contra-causal freedom.

Indeterminists like Kant and C.A. Campbell, therefore, who rely on this argument, have to base it not on ordinary choices motivated by desires, but specifically on the experience of moral choice motivated not by any desire but by the rational will of a noumenal self, which could not have the rational and moral character it claims to have if it were subject to causation. So developed, the argument is less one from immediate experience than from an alleged necessary presupposition of moral thought. However, it is not moral thought as a whole that has this presupposition but at most one particular interpretation of moral thought, and one which has been criticized in earlier chapters. But in any case, unless we had some other assurance of the valid applicability of the relevant moral theory, this would be no argument against determinism. The facts have to be determined by empirical evidence, and our thinking has then to conform to the facts, not the facts to our thinking.

An ingenious argument against determinism, based on Gödel's theorem about the necessary incompleteness of a certain kind of mathematical system, has been developed and defended especially by J.R. Lucas. I shall not attempt either to expound or to criticize it here, but shall bluntly state my opinion that what it shows is not that human minds are not deterministic structures, but at most that some human minds are not closed deterministic structures, that certain sorts of provocative input can change the way they work; but we knew that already.

Another argument is that determinism would undermine rational judgement, and hence that we could not both seriously adopt a belief and see our adoption of it as causally determined. But the premiss is false: it is not being causally determined in general that undermines a belief and deprives it of authority, but only being causally determined in an inappropiate way. There would be no difficulty in seeing (some of) our beliefs as arising causally but in appropriate ways, ways likely to keep

219

them in accord with reality, and continuing to hold them seriously. And (as Norman Malcolm has argued) even if the premiss were true what it would show is that determinism could not be rationally accepted, but might none the less be true.

Since the fundamental physical theory now in favour is indeterministic, it is also possible to argue from this to indeterminism about actions by way of the premiss that mental states are correlated with a physiological basis. Whereas Epicurus postulated a random tendency for atoms occasionally to swerve from their paths, not on any adequate physical grounds but mainly to leave room for human freedom, we now have strong physical evidence for an indeterminism which may carry over into actions. But only may; as we saw above the crucial but so far unanswered question is whether there are processes by which random sub-atomic occurrences trigger larger scale neural processes and so introduce some randomness into them. There could be a forceful case for indeterminism about actions along these lines. But what it would give us instead of causal regularity is literally randomness, and this is not the kind of contra-causal freedom for which the moralists who dislike determinism are looking.

4. Hard and soft determinism

The arguments for and against determinism about human actions, then, are inconclusive, so we must turn to the hypothetical question whether, *if* such determinism holds, it significantly undermines our moral ideas, so that if we accepted determinism we should, for consistency, have to make radical changes in our notions of choice, responsibility, credit and blame, resentment and gratitude, and perhaps in even more central moral notions like those of goodness, justice, and obligation. The clear-cut answers to this hypothetical question are incompatibilism – the view that determinism is incompatible with essential moral notions – and compatibilism – the view that we could accept determinism and make little or no change in our moral thinking. Being answers to the hypothetical question, these do not commit their adherents to the view that determinism holds or to the view that it does not. Hard determinism is the view which combines determinism with incompatibilism, and concludes that our judgements about responsibility and the like must be radically revised; soft determinism is the union of determinism with compatibilism. Those who reject determinism usually are, though they need not be, incompatibilists; this combination constitutes voluntarism or the doctrine of free will.

A powerful argument for compatibilism has been given, by implication, in Sections 1 and 2. For the distinctions drawn there between intentional and non-intentional actions, the explanation suggested for the straight rule of responsibility, and the considerations that might justify real or apparent divergences from this straight rule, were all developed without even raising the question of contra-causal freedom. Even if determinism holds, these distinctions can still be drawn and the moral principles related to them will still have the point that they were there shown to have.

There are several other arguments on both sides. Compatibilists accuse their opponents of mixing up determinism with fatalism and causation with compulsion, and hence with thinking wrongly that if determinism holds, human actions and their outcomes will be fixed from the outside, irrespective of what the agent wants or tries to do. Of course this would be a mistake, as it would also be to suppose that determinism would commit us to a crude mechanical account of how actions are brought about; determinists can admit that the envisaging of alternatives, the weighing of advantages and disadvantages, means-end calculation, and moral evaluation all enter into this causal process. Incompatibilists accuse soft determinists of being only half-hearted or short-sighted determinists, seeing actions as caused by desires, but ignoring the remoter sufficient causes which, in a thoroughgoing determinism, would be recognized as lying behind the desires. But compatibilism does not require such a short-sightedness, and most soft determinists are not guilty of it. They in turn complain that when hard determinists think of actions as being determined by character, they tend to assume that a person's character is laid down once and for all, whereas one can gradually remould one's character; but hard determinists reply, justifiably, that such remoulding must itself be causally determined by some pre-existing elements of the agent's character.

Such charges and counter-charges merely clarify the question, forcing us to realize that the determinism whose moral implications are at issue is a causal determinism, which allows for the sophisticated processes that obviously are at work in our practical thinking, which sees actions as determined by and through desires, deliberations, and choices, but which is still a thoroughgoing determinism, asserting that there are antecedent sufficient causes for all the items involved. But the real disagreement survives this clarification.

One thing that worries the incompatibilist is that, given determinism, though choices may be free from various sorts of obstacles and limitations, they are not really open in an absolute sense. They are fixed in advance because they are predictable in principle. Indeed only in principle. No reasonable determinist thinks it at all likely that it will in fact become possible to predict human choices and actions reliably in any detail. And it is misleading to define determinism in terms of predictability, for then we think of predictions being actually made and perhaps fed into the causal interactions with which they are concerned, so generating paradoxes of self-fulfilment and self-defeat. Still, choices would be predictable in principle. The perfect predictor would be a relevantly exact replica of the agent and his environment; since determinism accepts the 'same cause, same effect' principle, it implies that whatever choice the replica makes, the agent will also make. I think this does go against our intuitive view of choice; we tend to assume, however unwarrantably, that decisions are not fixed in advance even in this minimal way. On the other hand I do not see why this should matter. It is worth noting that while the free will doctrine is today often associated with religious beliefs, many

DETERMINISM, RESPONSIBILITY, AND CHOICE

theologians from St Augustine onwards have been compatibilists, arguing that though choices are in this sense fixed in advance (which is entailed by divine foreknowledge no less than by causal determinism) this does not relevantly undermine their reality as choices or their moral significance.

'If determinism holds, only one course is really open to me; I cannot do otherwise than I do.' But in one way I can: nothing outside me at the time restricts me to a single option. True, something inside me does so; but how does that impair my freedom? 'I do not really control my own actions; my character and my desires determine them; I can't help it, I just am like that.' But this is obscure. Is it the false statement that one's character is unalterable? Or the incoherent demand that the 'I' should be able to make that same 'I', itself at that moment, different from what it is? The most plausible interpretation is that it presupposes a distinction and contrast between my character, desires, and so on, all my contingent empirical features, and my real self – in Kantian terms, between an empirical self and a noumenal or metaphysical self. The complaint is that if determinism holds, the empirical self is no doubt operative and effective, a cause as well as an effect, but the metaphysical self is an idle spectator of a causal order in which it cannot intervene.

But here there is an important difference among incompatibilists between hard determinists and voluntarists. The latter can consistently suppose that there is such a metaphysical self, since they give it work to do. Allowing that it sometimes in fact initiates action, they can say that *if* determinism held, it *would be* idle. But hard determinists have to say that this metaphysical self always *is* idle; it is then unclear what reason they can have for postulating its existence. The view that goes naturally with determinism equates the self, the person, with some system of contingent empirical features: 'I just am my character, my desires, and the like.' And of course this view goes along with the denial of an absolute identity of persons through time.

There is a different sense in which hard determinists sometimes maintain that I do not really control my own actions.

<label>223</label>

Using Freudian ideas, but going far beyond what Freud himself claimed, they suggest that our behaviour is wholly determined by the unconscious parts of our minds, so that now the conscious self is an idle spectator, just as the supposed metaphysical self would be if actions were determined by the conscious empirical self. But there is no reason to suppose that this extension of psychoanalytic theory is even an approximation to the truth, and determinism in general is not committed to it.

Even the free will variant of the doctrine of the metaphysical self involves great difficulties. Is the self supposed to act for reasons? If so, how does its having these reasons avoid being causally related to the decisions it makes? How do its acts and decisions belong to it, how do they manage to be something other than isolated random occurrences, if they are not linked causally to contingent persisting features of this self? This doctrine seems to require an analogue of the relations we ordinarily find in actions that result from and are guided by desires and beliefs, and yet to deny the causality in terms of which we have to interpret those relations.

This doctrine of the metaphysical self, with all its difficulties, nevertheless goes naturally with the Kantian notion of a moral 'ought' which is objectively and categorically prescriptive, which demands an obedience unmotivated by anything but respect for the categorically imperative form itself. No empirical self could be expected to comprehend or respond to such an 'ought'. But I have argued in earlier chapters against this kind of moral theory. The metaphysical self and the contra-causal free will that it is supposed to display are presuppositions only of this particular kind of moral theory, which we have other reasons for rejecting; their difficulties would be additional reasons for rejecting it.

Incompatibilists have one more argument. Our judgements of responsibility, and the retributive emotions that go with them, include an element that requires an uncaused cause for its object. It is not merely that we respond differently to similar injuries we receive from a person and from an inanimate object; that difference can be explained by the greater complexity of human as contrasted with inanimate behaviour, and by the fact that we have moral concepts associated with the former precisely because moral pressures bearing upon intentions are an established and fairly effective check upon it. The point is rather that we respond differently, among similar injuries all of which we receive from persons, to those for which we have found earlier sufficient causes outside the agent even if they operate only through the agent's voluntary acts – that is, prior causes that have made him the sort of voluntary agent that he is. In other words, there is a kind of retributive feeling which shifts from even a voluntary agent to earlier causes. We have a notion of what we may call ultimate responsibility, which is transferred backwards along causal chains, and which would therefore escape to infinity if we accepted a strict causal determinism.

This might be explained as a confused development of the reasonable restriction of ordinary moral responsibility to intentional actions. But it is more plausible and more illuminating to see it as a corollary of the claim to objective prescriptivity which, I have argued in Chapter 1, is a real element in our ordinary moral thinking, and which Kantian ethics works up into a philosophical system. (What the universe required would have to be open, even from the point of view of the universe.) I believe that this claim is mistaken, but there is no reason to deny that it is commonly made; nor can we deny that we tend to employ the associated notion of ultimate responsibility.

To this extent, then, the incompatibilists are right. There are elements in our ordinary thinking about choices and actions and their moral consequences which would conflict with strict determinism, namely this notion of ultimate responsibility and the assumption that some choices are absolutely open, not fixed by antecedent conditions in accordance with causal regularities – nor, presumably, by divine foreknowledge. But these elements with which determinism is incompatible are closely linked with the claim to objective prescriptivity which we have found other reasons for rejecting. Determinism would be compatible with the kind of revised moral theory which can be developed when

225

this claim and what goes naturally with it are rejected. In particular the distinction between intentional and non-intentional action, and all that gives moral significance to this distinction, could still stand if determinism were true.

Besides, if strict determinism is not true, the most likely alternative is a partial determinism mitigated by a certain amount of randomness – an Epicurean physics. But this would be equally incompatible with the notion of ultimate responsibility. Such responsibility would evaporate if we tried to attach it to purely random occurrences just as clearly as it would disappear to infinity along causal chains. It requires for its resting point a contra-causally free and yet determinate and active self, the concept of which it is so hard to render coherent. Equally, the notion of an absolutely open *choice* is as incompatible with an Epicurean physics as with strict determinism: the metaphysical self would be left idle and imprisoned by chance no less than by law.

Chapter 10 Religion, Law, and Politics

1. The theological frontier of ethics

'If God is dead, everything is permitted.' Those who have begun by identifying morality with a body of divine commands naturally conclude that if there were no God, there could be no moral rules or principles. But the arguments of the preceding chapters, especially Chapters 5 and 8, show how there can be a secular morality, not indeed as a system of objective values or prescriptions, but rather as something to be made and maintained, and which there is some real point in making. However, it may still be argued that religion is needed to complete morality, to make it more secure or more satisfactory than it could be on a secular basis alone.

One problem is 'the dualism of practical reason'. On the one hand it is rational to act morally; on the other hand it is rational to pursue one's own long-term interests. Our earlier arguments show that these will largely coincide, but not perfectly. The two kinds of reason will sometimes give us opposite instructions. Even Butler, the most optimistic of moral philosophers, was prepared to say only that 'Duty and interest are perfectly coincident; for the most part in this world, but entirely and in every instance if we take in the future ...' He needed the next world to reconcile them completely. Many others have agreed. Paley, perhaps, offered the neatest package, defining virtue as 'the doing good to mankind, in obedience to the will of God, and for the sake of everlasting happiness', which definition, as he says, makes the good of mankind the subject, the will of God the rule, and everlasting happiness the motive of human virtue. But even if we do not put it in so crudely mercenary a way, it is clear that belief in an omnipotent and benevolent God, who

227

both makes moral demands on men and is concerned for their welfare, would entail that there is no practical discrepancy between what is morally good and what conduces to the most genuine happiness.

Let us grant that the dualism of practical reason could be resolved completely in this but in no other way; what then follows? Kant, having argued that there can be no sound speculative proof of the existence of God, thought that there is a cogent moral argument for this conclusion, that since God is needed to ensure the ultimate union of virtue and happiness, his existence can be established as a necessary presupposition of moral thought. But any such argument is back to front. What it is reasonable or rational to do may depend upon the facts, but the facts cannot depend upon what it is reasonable or rational to do. Equally, in our basic order of inference we must derive conclusions about what it is reasonable to do from what we believe the facts to be, and not the other way round. (Admittedly, if we had an authoritative ruling about what it was rational to do, we might infer from this what the facts must be, as seen by the giver of this ruling. But in the present context such a ruling would have to be a divine revelation, and it would be circular to rely on a supposed revelation in what is meant to be a proof of God's existence.) If the assertion of the existence of God is a factual claim, it cannot be given its sole or basic warrant by the desire to reconcile the two primary judgements that we are inclined to make in the sphere of practical reason.

In any case, the dualism would be acute only if the two principles, that it is rational to act morally and that it is rational to try to maximize one's own total happiness, were taken as objectively prescriptive truths, as commanding, categorically and authoritatively, what are sometimes incompatible courses of action. But I have argued that nothing has this status. Our previous discussions show in what senses each of these is rational. The rationality of morality (in the narrow sense) consists in the fact, brought out variously by Protagoras and Hobbes and Hume and Warnock, that men need moral rules and principles and dispositions if they are to live together and flourish in communities, and that evolution and social tradition have given them a fairly strong tendency to think in the required ways. The rationality of prudence consists in the fact that a man is more likely to flourish if he has, at any one time, some concern for the welfare of later phases of this same human being, and that evolution, social tradition, and individual experience and training have encouraged and 'reinforced' this egoistic prudential concern. Both these contrast with the more basic rationality of the hypothetical imperative, rationality in the sense in which it is rational to do whatever will satisfy one's own present desires; but all three cooperate in some measure. Once we understand these three sorts of rationality we can tolerate their partial discrepancies; we can see how they arise – what makes each of the three patterns rational – in the actual world, and we have no need to postulate another world to make the first two coincide more completely.

Another problem is thrown up by our discussion of absolutism in Chapter 7. On our view of morality we can defend only nearly absolute principles. But a theist can believe that strictly absolute variants of these are commanded by God, and that we both must and can safely obey them even when from the point of view of human reason the case against doing so seems overwhelming: we can rely on God to avert or somehow put right the disastrous consequences of a 'moral' choice. But though a theist can believe this, it would gratuitous for him to do so without a reliable and explicit revelation of such absolute commands. If he had to work by inference from general assumptions, he could not reasonably ascribe to God any more complete an absolutism than a secular moralist could construct using the same empirical data. And unless it can be shown independently that there is some merit in an unqualified absolutism, it is no advantage for theism that it makes it barely possible to hold such a view.

The possible relations between morality and religion are brought sharply into focus by a dilemma first presented in Plato's dialogue *Euthyphro*. Does God love what is good, or command what is right, because it is good or right, or is it good or right because he loves or commands it? That is, do human actions, dispositions, and so on have whatever moral qualities they do have independently of any divine command or approbation, so that when God commands or approves of them he is himself responding to the qualities he finds in them; or are there no moral distinctions independent of and antecedent to God's will, so that his will constitutes whatever moral qualities there are, and to be good or right is simply to be approved of or commanded by God?

The second alternative would have the consequence that the description of God himself as good would reduce to the rather trivial statement that God loves himself, or likes himself the way he is. It would also seem to entail that obedience to moral rules is merely prudent but slavish conformity to the arbitrary demands of a capricious tyrant. Realizing this, many religious thinkers have opted for the first alternative. But this seems to have the almost equally surprising consequence that moral distinctions do not depend on God any more than, say, arithmetical ones, hence that ethics is autonomous and can be studied and discussed without reference to religious beliefs, that we can simply close the theological frontier of ethics.

But the dilemma has these stark alternative consequences only if we assume that moral qualities come in one piece, as unanalysable atomic units, which must simply be assigned to one place or another, as being either wholly independent of or wholly constituted by the will of God. In fact we can take them apart. It might be that there is one kind of life which is, in a purely descriptive sense, most appropriate for human beings as they are – that is, that it alone will fully develop rather than stunt their natural capacities and that in it, and only in it, can they find the fullest and deepest satisfaction. It might then follow that certain rules of conduct and certain dispositions were appropriate (still purely descriptively) in that they were needed to maintain this way of life. All these would then be facts as hard as any in arithmetic or chemistry, and so logically independent of any command or prescriptive will of God, though they might be products of the creative will of God which, in making men as they are, will have made them such that this life, these rules, and these dispositions are appropriate for them. But, further, God might require men to live in this appropriate way, and might enjoin obedience to the related rules. This would add an objectively prescriptive element to what otherwise were hard, descriptive, truths, but in a quite non-mysterious way: these would be literally commands issued by an identifiable authority. Finally, it might be that though it is a hard fact that this life, these rules, and these dispositions are appropriate for men, this fact is not completely accessible to direct human investigation; men cannot by observation and experiment discover exactly what life is ultimately most satisfying for them; but given that God knows this, desires that they should so live, and has somehow revealed corresponding explicit instructions to them, men can reasonably resort to such revelations to infer this indirectly, so as to complete their determination of this required and ultimately satisfying life.

This theory is at least coherent; and in the face of it the dilemma falls apart. The descriptive component of moral distinctions is logically independent of God's will: God approves of this way of life because it is, in a purely descriptive sense, appropriate for men. But the prescriptive component of those distinctions is constituted by God's will. The picture of God as an arbitrary tyrant is replaced by the belief that he demands of his creatures only that they should live in what will be, for them, the most satisfying way. We can then say that God is good meaning, descriptively, just this; any prescriptive or evaluative component in 'good' *as applied to God* will be subjective, it will express *our* approval of the sort of thing God does; the God-based objectively prescriptive element in moral terms as applied to human actions can have no non-trivial application to God.

The fact that we can thus employ the descriptive/prescriptive distinction to clarify what is, I believe, a fairly orthodox view and resolve what would otherwise be an embarrassing dilemma should make theists more tolerant than many of them are of the use of this distinction in ethics. But what

231

concerns us more is that if this theistic position were not only coherent but also correct it could make a significant difference to moral philosophy. Morality could still have very largely the functions we have assigned to it, and much the same content, but the good for man might be more determinate, more unitary, than we have allowed in Chapter 8, and our task might be less that of making or remaking morality than of finding out, with the help of some reliable revelations, what God's creative will has made appropriate for man and what his prescriptive will requires of us. It therefore matters a lot for moral philosophy whether any such theistic view is correct: the theological frontier of ethics remains open.

However, this question cannot be adequately considered here. I can only state my convictions that there is no cogent positive argument for the existence of a God, that the problem of evil constitutes an insuperable difficulty for any orthodox theism, that the advance of scientific knowledge renders a theistic view of the sort sketched above superfluous as an explanatory hypothesis and utterly implausible, and that no specific revelation – such as would be needed to make the proposed view morally significant – has reliable credentials. The coherent view outlined is therefore no more than a bare theoretical possibility, and we shall in the end have to fall back on a purely secular morality.

2. Contacts and overlaps between morality and law

The view of the status of ethics for which I have argued in the first part of this book is well illustrated by the analogy of law. Most people would agree that laws are *made*, whether explicitly by legislators, or surreptitiously by judges, or informally by tradition and custom. Law is, as I have maintained that morality also is, a human product; and one of the functions it serves is closely related to that which, in Chapter 5, I have assigned to morality in the narrow sense.

This amounts to saying that all law is positive law: it is law wholly in and by being 'posited' by some society or institution, though not necessarily by a legislature or 'sovereign'. But there is a contrary view, that behind positive law there is natural law, that some legal principles are valid in themselves without having to be made, and are therefore valid at all times and in all communities, that they can be discovered by reason, and moreover that they control and limit positive law: what purports to be the law of the land is really so only if it is made in ways that agree with principles of natural law, and it can be determined not to be the law after all, no matter what the legislature or anyone else has said, if it is shown to violate natural justice.

The doctrine of natural law is clearly an analogue of objectivism in ethics. Indeed natural law would be simply that part of an objectively prescriptive ethics which was specially concerned with the topics with which law commonly deals, with the administration of law, and with the making of positive law, taken as including the rule that only what accords with it – either directly expressing it or having been posited in ways that it authorizes – is to be recognized and enforced as law. Natural law itself has sometimes been seen as being intrinsically objectively prescriptive, at other times as deriving its prescriptive component from divine command.

The argument of this book therefore has, as a corollary, the rejection of the doctrine of natural law as a philosophical theory. Whether it is, none the less, a useful fiction is a further question, and one to which no general answer can be given. Where the doctrine is adopted, judges will treat enactments with somewhat less respect, and will attend also to their 'conscience' or their 'reason'. What effects this will have depends upon the current state of these judicial organs, and on the character of the legislatures on which they impose a check. The doctrine may provide a barrier against excesses of governmental policy; it may equally set up obstacles to much-needed reforms; and of course the same operations may be described in both these ways from opposite points of view. The doctrine of natural law is a channel through which some of the contents of some morality may be fed into the law, a device by which the positing of the law may be influenced by already-posited elements of morality. But it is not the only device that does this: explicit legislation may use terms (such as 'reasonable', 'harmful', and 'corrupt') whose vaguenesses are likely to be resolved in practice in morally determined ways, and traditional methods of legal interpretation can have the same effect.

A question often discussed is whether the law should enforce morality. Taken literally, this question has an absurdly simple answer: great parts of what both the criminal and the civil law enforce, at all times and in all states, are also requirements of morality – not killing or assaulting other people, honesty, respect for property and for other rights, the keeping of agreements, and contributing in various ways to a community's organized joint purposes. In all such matters some restraints on individual inclination are needed if men are to live tolerably together. Moral principles, rules, feelings, and dispositions are the first line of defence, the formulation and authoritative statement of laws are the second, and the enforcement of law is the third. It is obvious that all three are sometimes necessary, but also that the second and third cannot work unless they are in fairly close agreement with the first. But when this question is discussed, it is with respect not to this central core of morality but to its peripheral parts, especially sexual behaviour and such related topics as obscenity and pornography. These concern morality in the broad sense rather than the narrow one, and the issue is controversial precisely because there are divergent moralities within the same society, different preferred ways of life, and also because there is often a discrepancy between the morality to which people pay lip service and that which they seriously prescribe to themselves. The real question, therefore, is whether the morality of one part of a society should be legally reinforced in its attempt to extend itself to other parts, or whether a morality which enjoys widespread lip service should be supported by the law against one by which people live but which they are ashamed to avow.

There is little in favour of the first of these proposals. What

234

has been said in Chapter 4 about the third stage of universalization, in Chapter 7 about the rationale of this, and in Chapter 8 about the general form of the good for man suggests that it
would be better, where there are in fact divergent moralities in
the broad sense, if law confined itself to the task which it shares
with morality in the narrow sense of enabling rival factions as
well as competing individuals to live together by reciprocal
limitations of their conflicting claims. Mutual toleration might
be easier to achieve if groups could realize that the ideals which
determine their moralities in the broad sense are just that, the
ideals of those who adhere to them, not objective values which
impose requirements on all alike.

At first sight there seems to be more in favour of the second
proposal, that where people hypocritically profess support for
certain rules of behaviour, their bluff should be called by
having those rules enforced by law. But in practice this would
either force resistance to the imposed morality into the open,
and so transform the second situation into the first, from which
point the argument would go on as before, or, more probably,
spread the hypocrisy further so that it infected the machinery of
law enforcement as well. Experience has shown that such corruption is the usual result of an attempt to enforce a morality
that enjoys almost universal support on the surface of which
some considerable part is insincere.

3. Political applications and extensions of morality

If politics is the general theory of how human communities
function and can flourish, then (as Aristotle saw) ethics is a part
of politics. Equally, if ethics is the general theory of right and
wrong in choices and actions, and of what is good or bad in
dispositions and interpersonal relations and ways of living, then
political activities and aims and decisions come within its scope.
In any case, the two cannot be kept apart. It would make no
sense to confine moral thinking to private life and to set up

some quite independent principles to determine political values and decisions.

In fact many of the most controversial first order moral issues, and the ones about which it is hardest for anyone both to think clearly and honestly and to take a firm stand, are political ones – questions about changing or preserving economic and social structures, and about conflicts of interest between organized groups within a state or between states or races; and even when one has chosen what seem to be laudable goals, questions about the methods one may use to pursue them, how to defend legitimate but threatened interests, to vindicate rights that have been violated. Similar problems come up in somewhat different forms for private citizens, for those working in and through political movements or influential organizations, and for statesmen who act on behalf of nations or, perhaps, of supra-national institutions. The argument of this book yields, in itself, no answers to such questions. It cannot, since its main thesis is that there is an inescapable subjective ingredient, an element of choice or preference, in the reasoning that supports any policy decision. What it does offer is only a framework of ideas within which such reasoning can go on.

Some general opinions, however, seem to me at least to be overwhelmingly plausible, but they are not so universally acknowledged as to be not worth repeating. The choice of political goals belongs to morality in the broad sense: it goes with views about the good life for man. But since there will always be divergent conceptions of the good, different preferred kinds of life, a good form of society must somehow be a liberal one, it must leave open ways in which different preferences can be realized. Also, as I said in Chapter 8, competition and conflict, as well as cooperation, are inevitable, and are to be welcomed rather than suppressed or denied; a good form of society must be able to accommodate and regulate them, and will neither try nor pretend to eliminate them. But political and economic problems are genuinely complicated: there is no single change or small number of changes, however radical or catastrophic, which would put everything right. It is simply an error, though no doubt an attractive and inspiring one, to suppose that there is some one evil – capitalism, say, or colonialism – the destruction of which would make everything in the garden lovely. No doubt there are extreme forms of injustice and exploitation which, if they persist, will give rise to disastrous civil, inter-national, and inter-racial wars. But there is more than one kind of exploitation, and the very means used to remove one can themselves turn into another.

Conflicts of interest are real, inevitable, and ineradicable. There is no question of doing away with them, but it is increas-ingly important that they should be limited and contained. It is in the long-term interests, not perhaps of every individual but of every group of individuals with their descendants, and cer-tainly of all nations and races, that conflicts should be contained and adjusted in a relatively peaceful way; but this fact, and even the widespread realization of this fact, does not in itself provide any means of achieving this result. We have a situation somewhat like the Prisoners' Dilemma, and rather more like the variant of it which Hobbes envisaged. As we saw in Chapter 5, devices need to be invented to enable the participants in such a situation to achieve even ends which they all prefer, if their interests also conflict in other ways. There is clearly scope and need for political and especially international applications and extensions of something like morality in the narrow sense. But more specific techniques of negotiation and coercion have to be developed and strengthened, and gradually increasing reliance on them is one factor that may make them more reliable.

One important aid – we can hardly call it a device, for surely no-one needed to devise it – in the containment and adjustment of conflicts is that those who are active in affairs, and also those who control or influence them, should understand what is going on and think clearly and reasonably about it. It is risky if, instead, they are content with a view which may, indeed, in-clude partial truths but which is made substantially false by oversimplification. (Unfortunately the latter sort of view is often rhetorically more effective and may help its possessor to acquire and exercise authority.) In particular, serious negotiation is easier if the opposing parties not only understand each other's claims but appreciate the motives and the moral basis on which they rest.

Notoriously, the same people and the same activities look very different from opposing points of view. What one party sees as terrorist gunmen, another sees as fearless freedom fighters. And there are many such pairs of alternatives. Traitors or patriots? Defenders of law and order or fascist thugs? Incorruptible idealists or ruthless fanatics? Resolute and far-sighted realists or bloodthirsty lovers of power? Guardians of freedom or imperialist exploiters? Negotiation and discussion between parties who see the issues only in such polarized terms are not likely to be fruitful. A first step is made when both sides see that there are points of view from which each of the rival descriptions makes some sense. A second, harder, but necessary step is made if they can each see some force in the opposing point of view, that is, give some weight to the values and ideals that underlie the aims of their opponents – in other words, introduce into their thinking a bit of what we called in Chapter 4 the third stage of universalization.

Conflicts can be of two kinds: those that have an independent source in a prior clash of interests, and those that are self-sustaining, where each party's fear and distrust of the other is itself the motive for the behaviour that gives the other party good reason to fear and distrust it. The second kind, though in a sense artificial, is no less real than the first. In practice we find few pure examples of the second kind; but many in which this second pattern overlies and reinforces the first. Of its own accord this second pattern can generate steadily increasing tension. What is needed, but harder to find, is a supplementary mechanism that will put the process into reverse and gradually reduce the artificial tension, leaving only the independent, prior clash of substantive interests to be adjusted. A further difficulty is that, as we noted in Chapter 5, though complete intransigence in either party to a vital negotiation is disastrous for both, incomplete relative intransigence is differentially advantageous to its possessor.

Even the briefest analytic survey shows why – as we know in any case from experience – political and especially international problems are so hard to resolve. But they are in part analogous to problems which arose first in relations among individuals and small groups, and (if Protagoras and Hobbes and the rest are right) morality in the narrow sense exists just in order to cope with these. Admittedly what political problems require is not merely applications but also extensions of these long established devices, and it is not clear what the appropriate extensions are; but in seeking them we may be aided by a clearer understanding of the character and working of existing morality.

Indeed, there may be a significant disanalogy here. In so far as the objectification of moral values and obligations is not only a natural but also a useful fiction, it might be thought dangerous, and in any case unnecessary, to expose it as a fiction. This is disputable. But what is not disputable is that for the changes and political extensions that are now necessary we cannot rely on the past achievements of evolution and social tradition, nor have we time to let them grow by a future process of natural selection. Here at least there are practical as well as scientific motives for understanding what we already have and for thinking explicitly about its possible development. For in the end we are all in the same position as Locke's outlaws and thieves: with no innate principles to guide us – nor even, as Locke himself thought, laws of nature discoverable by reason – we have to find principles of equity and ways of making and keeping agreements without which we cannot hold together.

Notes and References

CHAPTER 1

My views on the subject of this chapter were first put forward in 'A Refutation of Morals', published in the *Australasian Journal of Psychology and Philosophy* 24 (1946), but substantially written in 1941. Discussions current at about that time which helped to determine the main outlines of my position are recorded in, for example, Charles L. Stevenson's *Ethics and Language* (New Haven, 1941) and A.J. Ayer's *Language, Truth, and Logic* (London, 1936). An unjustly neglected work which anticipates my stress on objectification is E. Westermarck's *Ethical Relativity* (London, 1932). But the best illustration and support for the arguments of this chapter, and for much else in the book, are provided by the works of such earlier writers as Hobbes, Locke, Samuel Clarke, Hutcheson, Butler, Balguy, Hume, and Richard Price, of which substantial selections are edited by D.D. Raphael in *British Moralists 1650–1800* (Oxford, 1969): for example, Balguy brings out very clearly what I call the 'claim to objectivity'.

There is a full survey of recent controversy between critics and defenders of naturalism in 'Recent Work on Ethical Naturalism' by R.L. Franklin in *Studies in Ethics, American Philosophical Quarterly Monograph No. 7* (1973). Concentration on questions of meaning is criticized by P. Singer in 'The Triviality of the Debate over "Is-ought" and the Definition of "Moral"' in the *American Philosophical Quarterly* 10 (1973).

The quotations from R.M. Hare are from 'Nothing Matters', in his *Applications of Moral Philosophy* (London, 1972). This article was written in 1957. Hare's present view is given in 'Some Confusions about Subjectivity' in *Freedom and Morality*, edited by J. Bricke (University of Kansas Lindley Lectures – forthcoming). References to Sidgwick throughout this book are to *Methods of Ethics* (London, 1874), and those to Kant are to *Groundwork of the Metaphysic of Morals*, translated (for example) by H.J. Paton in *The Moral Law* (London, 1948). The quotation from Russell is from

NOTES AND REFERENCES

his 'Reply to Criticisms' in *The Philosophy of Bertrand Russell*, edited by P.A. Schilpp (Evanston, 1944). G.E.M. Anscombe's view is quoted from 'Modern Moral Philosophy', in *Philosophy* 33 (1958), reprinted in *The Definition of Morality*, edited by G. Wallace and A.D.M. Walker (London, 1970). The argument of Section 11 owes much to private discussion with J.M. Finnis.

CHAPTER 2

G.E. Moore's view is quoted from Chapter 1 of *Principia Ethica* (Cambridge, 1903). Those of P.T. Geach and R.M. Hare come from 'Good and Evil' and 'Geach: Good and Evil', in *Analysis* 17 (1956) and 18 (1957), both reprinted in *Theories of Ethics*, edited by Philippa Foot (Oxford, 1967). Hare's view was stated earlier in *The Language of Morals* (Oxford, 1952). My account is also influenced by that of F.E. Sparshott in Chapter 6 of *An Enquiry into Goodness* (Chicago, 1958).

CHAPTER 3

The famous remarks of Hume occur, apparently as an afterthought, at the end of Book III, Part I, Section 1 of *A Treatise of Human Nature*. J.R. Searle's 'How to Derive "Ought" from "Is" ' appeared in the *Philosophical Review* 73 (1964) and is reprinted, with a reply by Hare, in *Theories of Ethics*, edited by Philippa Foot. Searle further discusses this argument in Chapter 8 of *Speech Acts* (Cambridge, 1969). Arguments essentially similar to his had been given by E.F. Carritt and, long ago, by Thomas Reid and perhaps even by Hobbes; these are reported and criticized by A.N. Prior in Chapter 5 of *Logic and the Basis of Ethics* (Oxford, 1949); Prior paraphrases and develops an argument of Hume's against the possibility of creating an obligation by resolving to do so.

CHAPTER 4

Universalizability is of central importance in R.M. Hare's moral philosophy; he discusses it especially in *Freedom and Reason* (Oxford, 1963) but also in many other writings. He is the chief exponent of the view that there are only formal, but no material, constraints on what can be moral. Universalizability plays a large part in Kant's *Groundwork*, and also provides the main theme of M. Singer's *Generalization in Ethics* (New York, 1961). John Rawls's view is most fully stated in *A Theory of Justice* (Oxford, 1972). Different kinds of universalization are discussed in Chapters

13 to 16 of D.H. Monro's *Empiricism and Ethics* (Cambridge, 1967). The quotation from Bernard Shaw is from 'Maxims for Revolutionists' in *Man and Superman.*

CHAPTER 5

The title of this chapter is taken from G.J. Warnock's *The Object of Morality* (London, 1971). Hobbes's view is developed especially in Chapters 13 to 17 of *Leviathan*, and Hume's in *Treatise* Book III Part II; the essentials of both are in *British Moralists 1650–1800*. A classic of game theory is T. Schelling's *The Strategy of Conflict* (Cambridge, Mass., 1960). The Prisoners' Dilemma is discussed in Chapter 5 of R.D. Luce and H. Raiffa, *Games and Decisions* (New York, 1957). The quotation from Anscombe is from the article mentioned in Chapter 1.

CHAPTER 6

Act and rule utilitarianism are discussed fully by David Lyons in *Forms and Limits of Utilitarianism* (Oxford, 1965). Act utilitarianism is strongly advocated by J.J.C. Smart in his contributon to *Utilitarianism: For and Against* (Cambridge, 1973); his co-author, Bernard Williams, supplies a contrary case.

D.D. Raphael, in 'The Standard of Morals', in *Proceedings of the Aristotelian Society* 75 (1974–5) follows Edward Ullendorff in pointing out that whereas 'Thou shalt love thy neighbour as thyself' represents the Greek of the Septuagint (Leviticus 19: 18) and of the New Testament, the Hebrew from which the former is derived means rather 'You shall treat your neighbour lovingly, for he is like yourself.' References to J.S. Mill are to *Utilitarianism* and to Book VI Chapter 12 of *A System of Logic*, while that to J. Austin is to Lecture 2 of *The Province of Jurisprudence Determined*, edited by H.L.A. Hart (London, 1954), which I take as the classic formulation of rule utilitarianism. Warnock's objections to act utilitarianism are in *The Object of Morality*, and echo those of D.H. Hodgson in *Consequences of Utilitarianism* (Oxford, 1967). But these are criticized in P. Singer's 'Is Act-utilitarianism Self-defeating?' in the *Philosophical Review* 81 (1972) and in my 'The Disutility of Act Utilitarianism' in the *Philosophical Quarterly* 23 (1973). The passage quoted from Sidgwick is in Book IV Chapter 2 of *Methods of Ethics*. The earlier remark that utilitarianism can swallow up its common-sense or intuitionist rival sums up, but of course simplifies, Sidgwick's argument throughout this work. His position in Chapters

4 and 5 of Book IV is close to that which I adopt at the end of this chapter. Joseph Butler's account of self-love and the particular passions is in the Preface and Sermons 1 to 3 of his *Fifteen Sermons*, extracts from which are in *British Moralists 1650–1800*.

CHAPTER 7

The issues raised in this chapter are discussed by G.E.M. Anscombe both in the article referred to in Chapter 1 and in 'War and Murder' in *Nuclear Weapons: A Catholic Response*, edited by W. Stein (New York, 1961) – published also in the U.K. as *Nuclear Weapons and Christian Conscience* – which is reprinted in *War and Morality*, edited by R.A. Wasserstrom (Belmont, California, 1970); also by J. Bennett in 'Whatever the Consequences' in *Analysis* (1965–6) and by R.M. Hare in 'Principles' in *Proceedings of the Aristotelian Society* 73 (1972–3). Applications of the principle of double effect are examined in Chapters 6 to 8 of Glanville Williams's *The Sanctity of Life and the Criminal Law* (London, 1958); Aquinas's statement of this principle is in *Summa Theologica* II – II Question 64 Article 7. Bentham's distinction between direct and oblique intention is in *Principles of Morals and Legislation* Chapter 8 Paragraph 6. Machiavelli's doctrine that the end justifies the means is stated in Chapters 15 and 18 of *The Prince* and in *Discourses on Livy*, Book 1 Chapter 9. I owe to George Cawkwell the ironical remark about a man of principle who has a new principle for every case.

CHAPTER 8

J.F. Stephen's views are quoted from *Liberty, Equality, Fraternity* (London, 1873; reprinted Cambridge, 1967). On the analysis of rights, see for example Chapter 9 of R.W.M. Dias's *Jurisprudence* (London, 1964). Locke's views are to be found in the *Second Treatise of Civil Government*, and R. Nozick's in *Anarchy, State, and Utopia* (Oxford, 1974). The way in which the labour of indefinitely many workers contributes to the value of goods produced in a modern economy is, of course, a central theme of Karl Marx's *Capital*. Quotations from Mill in Section 3 are from *On Liberty*, that from Machiavelli is from Chapter 18 of *The Prince*, and those from Hume are from *Treatise*, Book III Part II Section 11. Aristotle's account of moral virtue is in the *Nicomachean Ethics*, Books II to V; Spinoza's account of how the intellect can have power over the emotions and so make men free is in Part V of his *Ethics*.

CHAPTER 9

The classic treatment of voluntary action and responsibility is in Aristotle's *Nicomachean Ethics*, Book III; modern discussions include H.L.A. Hart's *Punishment and Responsibility* (Oxford, 1968) and J. Glover's *Responsibility* (London, 1970). Free will, determinism, and their implications constitute a topic that has, throughout the history of philosophy, been more discussed than any other. A classic defence of compatibilism is in Section 8 of Hume's *Enquiry Concerning Human Understanding*; the free will position is represented by Section 3 of Kant's *Groundwork*, by Lecture IX of C.A. Campbell's *On Selfhood and Godhood* (London, 1957) and by J.R. Lucas's *The Freedom of the Will* (Oxford, 1970). Collections of articles which present all sides of the question are *Determinism and Freedom in the Age of Modern Science*, edited by S. Hook (New York, 1958) and *Essays on Freedom of Action*, edited by Ted Honderich (London, 1973). On 'the denial of an absolute identity of persons through time', compare Chapter 3 of this book and Chapter 6 of my *Problems from Locke* (Oxford, 1976).

CHAPTER 10

The title of Section 1, and also that of Part III as a whole comes from W.G. Maclagan's *The Theological Frontier of Ethics* (London, 1961). The quotations from Butler and Paley can be found in *British Moralists 1650–1800*, as can statements by Cudworth and Samuel Clarke which accept the first horn of the *Euthyphro* dilemma. The orthodox solution which I sketch is much influenced by H. Meynell's 'The Euthyphro Dilemma' in *Aristotelian Society Supplementary Volume* 46 (1972).

Additional Note (1981)

In *Hume's Moral Theory* (1980) I have examined the arguments of some of the British Moralists of the seventeenth and eighteenth centuries, showing how they illustrate and support the views stated in this book, as claimed in the Note to Chapter 1. In *The Miracle of Theism* (forthcoming) I defend in detail the conclusions summarized on page 232.

Index

247

Discover more about our forthcoming books through Penguin's FREE newspaper...

Penguin Quarterly

It's packed with:

- exciting features
- author interviews
- previews & reviews
- books from your favourite films & TV series
- exclusive competitions & much, much more...

Write off for your free copy today to:
Dept JC
Penguin Books Ltd
FREEPOST
West Drayton
Middlesex
UB7 0BR
NO STAMP REQUIRED

READ MORE IN PENGUIN

In every corner of the world, on every subject under the sun, Penguin represents quality and variety – the very best in publishing today.

For complete information about books available from Penguin – including Puffins, Penguin Classics and Arkana – and how to order them, write to us at the appropriate address below. Please note that for copyright reasons the selection of books varies from country to country.

In the United Kingdom: Please write to *Dept. EP, Penguin Books Ltd, Bath Road, Harmondsworth, West Drayton, Middlesex UB7 ODA*

In the United States: Please write to *Consumer Sales, Penguin USA, P.O. Box 999, Dept. 17109, Bergenfield, New Jersey 07621-0120.* VISA and MasterCard holders call 1-800-253-6476 to order Penguin titles

In Canada: Please write to *Penguin Books Canada Ltd, 10 Alcorn Avenue, Suite 300, Toronto, Ontario M4V 3B2*

In Australia: Please write to *Penguin Books Australia Ltd, P.O. Box 257, Ringwood, Victoria 3134*

In New Zealand: Please write to *Penguin Books (NZ) Ltd, Private Bag 102902, North Shore Mail Centre, Auckland 10*

In India: Please write to *Penguin Books India Pvt Ltd, 706 Eros Apartments, 56 Nehru Place, New Delhi 110 019*

In the Netherlands: Please write to *Penguin Books Netherlands bv, Postbus 3507, NL-1001 AH Amsterdam*

In Germany: Please write to *Penguin Books Deutschland GmbH, Metzlerstrasse 26, 60594 Frankfurt am Main*

In Spain: Please write to *Penguin Books S. A., Bravo Murillo 19, 1° B, 28015 Madrid*

In Italy: Please write to *Penguin Italia s.r.l., Via Felice Casati 20, I–20124 Milano*

In France: Please write to *Penguin France S. A., 17 rue Lejeune, F–31000 Toulouse*

In Japan: Please write to *Penguin Books Japan, Ishikiribashi Building, 2–5–4, Suido, Bunkyo-ku, Tokyo 112*

In Greece: Please write to *Penguin Hellas Ltd, Dimocritou 3, GR–106 71 Athens*

In South Africa: Please write to *Longman Penguin Southern Africa (Pty) Ltd, Private Bag X08, Bertsham 2013*

READ MORE IN PENGUIN

PHILOSOPHY

What Philosophy Is   Anthony O'Hear

'Argument after argument is represented, including most of the favourites
... its tidy and competent construction, as well as its straightforward style,
mean that it will serve well anyone with a serious interest in philosophy'
– *The Journal of Applied Philosophy*

Montaigne and Melancholy   M. A. Screech

'A sensitive probe into how Montaigne resolved for himself the age-old
ambiguities of melancholia and, in doing so, spoke of what he called the
"human condition"' – Roy Porter in the *London Review of Books*

Labyrinths of Reason   William Poundstone

'The world and what is in it, even what people say to you, will not seem
the same after plunging into *Labyrinths of Reason* ... Poundstone's book
merits the description of *tour de force*. He holds up the deepest
philosophical questions for scrutiny and examines their relation to reality
in a way that irresistibly sweeps readers on' – *New Scientist*

I: The Philosophy and Psychology of Personal Identity
Jonathan Glover

From cases of split brains and multiple personalities to the importance of
memory and recognition by others, the author of *Causing Death and
Saving Lives* tackles the vexed questions of personal identity.

Ethics Inventing Right and Wrong   J. L. Mackie

Widely used as a text, Mackie's complete and clear treatise on moral
theory deals with the status and content of ethics, sketches a practical
moral system, and examines the frontiers at which ethics touches psychology, theology, law and politics.

The Central Questions of Philosophy   A. J. Ayer

'He writes lucidly and has a teacher's instinct for the helpful pause and
reiteration ... an admirable introduction to the ways in which philosophic
issues are experienced and analysed in current Anglo-American academic
milieux' – *Sunday Times*

READ MORE IN PENGUIN

POLITICS AND SOCIAL SCIENCES

National Identity Anthony D. Smith

In this stimulating new book, Anthony D. Smith asks why the first modern nation states developed in the West. He considers how ethnic origins, religion, language and shared symbols can provide a sense of nation and illuminates his argument with a wealth of detailed examples.

The Feminine Mystique Betty Friedan

'A brilliantly researched, passionately argued book – a time-bomb flung into the Mom-and-Apple-Pie image ... Out of the debris of that shattered ideal, the Women's Liberation Movement was born' – Ann Leslie

Peacemaking Among Primates Frans de Waal

'A vitally fresh analysis of the biology of aggression which deserves the serious attention of all those concerned with the nature of conflict, whether in humans or non-human animals ... De Waal delivers forcibly and clearly his interpretation of the significance of his findings ... Lucidly written' – *The Times Higher Educational Supplement*

Political Ideas David Thomson (ed.)

From Machiavelli to Marx – a stimulating and informative introduction to the last 500 years of European political thinkers and political thought.

The Raw and the Cooked Claude Lévi-Strauss

Deliberately, brilliantly and inimitably challenging, Lévi-Strauss's seminal work of structural anthropology cuts wide and deep into the mind of mankind, as he finds in the myths of the South American Indians a comprehensible psychological pattern.

The Social Construction of Reality
Peter Berger and Thomas Luckmann

The Social Construction of Reality is concerned with the sociology of 'everything that passes for knowledge in society', and particularly with that 'common-sense knowledge' that constitutes the reality of everyday life for the ordinary member of society.

READ MORE IN PENGUIN

POLITICS AND SOCIAL SCIENCES

Conservatism Ted Honderich

'It offers a powerful critique of the major beliefs of modern conservatism, and shows how much a rigorous philosopher can contribute to understanding the fashionable but deeply ruinous absurdities of his times' – *New Statesman & Society*

Karl Marx: Selected Writings in Sociology and Social Philosophy Bottomore and Rubel (eds.)

'It makes available, in coherent form and lucid English, some of Marx's most important ideas. As an introduction to Marx's thought, it has very few rivals indeed' – *British Journal of Sociology*

Post-War Britain A Political History Alan Sked and Chris Cook

Major political figures from Attlee to Thatcher, the aims and achievements of governments and the changing fortunes of Britain in the period since 1945 are thoroughly scrutinized in this stimulating history.

Inside the Third World Paul Harrison

This comprehensive book brings home a wealth of facts and analysis on the often tragic realities of life for the poor people and communities of Asia, Africa and Latin America.

Medicine, Patients and the Law Margaret Brazier

'An absorbing book which, in addition to being accessible to the general reader, should prove illuminating for practitioners – both medical and legal – and an ideal accompaniment to student courses on law and medicine' – *New Law Journal*

Bread and Circuses Paul Veyne

'Warming oneself at the fire of M. Veyne's intelligence is such a joy that any irritation at one's prejudice and ignorance being revealed and exposed vanishes with his winning ways … *Bread and Circuses* is M. Veyne's way of explaining the philosophy of the Roman Empire, which was the most successful form of government known to mankind' – *Literary Review*